THE AUTHOR Dr Mentzel is currently Associate Professor of European and Near Eastern History at Utah State University. He has travelled extensively throughout the former Venetian Empire in the Adriatic and eastern Mediterranean. His research interests have focused on the social and economic history of that area and he has contributed many papers to academic journals.

SERIES EDITOR Professor Denis Judd is a graduate of Oxford, a Fellow of the Royal Historical Society and Professor of History at the London Metropolitan University. He has published over 20 books including the biographies of Joseph Chamberlain, historical and military subjects, stories for children and two novels. His most recent books are the highly praised *Empire* and (with Keith Surridge) *The Boer War*.

THE TRAVELLER'S HISTORY SERIES

'Ideal before-you-go reading' *The Daily Telegraph*

'An excellent series of brief histories' *New York Times*

'I want to compliment you. . . on the brilliantly concise contents of your books.' *Shirley Conran*

Reviews of Individual Titles

A Traveller's History of France

'Undoubtedly the best way to prepare for a trip to France is to bone up on some history. The Traveller's History of France by Robert Cole is concise and gives the essential facts in a very readable form.' *The Independent*

A Traveller's History of China

'The author manages to get 2 million years into 300 pages. An excellent addition to a series which is already invaluable, whether you're travelling or not.' *The Guardian*

A Traveller's History of India

'For anyone. . . planning a trip to India, the latest in the excellent Traveller's History series. . . provides a useful grounding for those whose curiosity exceeds the time available for research.' *The London Evening Standard*

A Traveller's History of Japan

'It succeeds admirably in its goal of making the present country comprehensible through a narrative of its past, with asides on everything from bonsai to zazen, in a brisk, highly readable style ... you could easily read it on the flight over, if you skip the movie.' *The Washington Post*

A Traveller's History of Ireland

For independent, inquisitive travellers traversing the green roads of Ireland, there is no better guide than *A Traveller's History of Ireland.'* *Small Press*

A Traveller's History of Venice

A Traveller's History of Venice

PETER MENTZEL

Series Editor   DENIS JUDD
Line Drawings   *PETER GEISSLER*

Interlink Books

An imprint of Interlink Publishing Group, Inc.
Northampton, Massachusetts

First published in 2006 by

INTERLINK BOOKS
An imprint of Interlink Publishing Group, Inc
46 Crosby Street, Northampton, Massachusetts 01060
www.interlinkbooks.com

Library of Congress Cataloging-in-Publication Data

Mentzel, Peter.
 A traveller's history of Venice / by Peter Mentzel.-- 1st American ed.
     p. cm. -- (A traveller's history)
 Includes bibliographical references and index.
 ISBN 1-56656-611-8 (pbk.)
 1. Venice (Italy)-History. 2. Historic sites-Italy-Venice. I. Title.
II. Series.
 DG676.M46 2005
 945'.31--dc22

                                        2005006471

Printed and bound in Canada by Webcom

To order or request our complete catalog
Please call us at 1–800–238–LINK or write to:
INTERLINK PUBLISHING
46 Crosby Street, Northampton, MA 01060–1804
email: info@interlinkbooks.com
www.interlinkbooks.com

Table of Contents

Preface

Venice holds a special place in the world's imagination. At its most basic, it is a miracle of environmental survival – a sort of ecological bucking of the trend and a shining example of the human capacity to resist the encroachment of natural forces. To put a softer gloss on that robust reality is the perception of Venice as one of the most romantic and sensual cities in the world, the sort of place where love may be just around the corner and where new passions may be lit and old ones rekindled.

Above all, as Peter Mentzel point out in this immensely readable and scholarly book, Venice's intimate relationship to the water that surrounds it is the key to understanding and appreciating the city. From the outset the lagoon provided local people with much of their food – seafood and wild fowl - as well as salt, their first significant trading commodity. Crucially, however, the waters of the lagoon also made the city easier to defend from sea borne attack.

Venice's proximity to the sea had another, infinitely positive, impact. It put its people easily in touch with the wider world through maritime trade and activity. Making full use of this opportunity, Venice had achieved the control of the Adriatic Sea by the end of the eleventh century and a little over a hundred years later was the major sea power in the eastern Mediterranean, with its bustling Levantine trade bringing the spices and luxuries of the east to Europe's doorstep. Just to guarantee its power, the city had also extended its control over a considerable portion of northern Italy by the early 1400s.

These commercial, military and political achievements gave Venice its unique character. It was a city that simultaneously looked both east and west. It was a great sea power, but also a substantial land power.

Venetians were adventurous, cosmopolitan, ambitious, searching and shrewd. The Lion of the Sea preferred to trade peacefully, but it could also assert its interests through naval and military force if need be, as the many, often elegant, Venetian fortifications scattered throughout the Mediterranean bear witness.

It is worth noting that so significant was Venice in the imagination of post-Renaissance Europe that Shakespeare entitled one of his plays *The Merchant of Venice*, and made Othello, 'the Moor of Venice', the central character in another. Equally, the earlier exploits of Marco Polo, consisting of a barely credible, but extraordinarily successful, overland journey to the sumptuous court of Kublai Khan in China, had provided a benchmark for Venetian daring and diplomatic skills.

Like all empires, that of Venice could not last. Once the Portuguese and the Spanish, soon followed by the English and the Dutch, had broken the Levant's stranglehold on the spice trade by rounding the Cape of Good Hope, as well as opening up a 'New World' across the Atlantic, Venice's days of Mediterranean based prosperity and glory were finished.

Venice did not, however, wither away. Like a once ravishingly lovely Grande Dame, the city managed to hang on to enough of its good looks, high spirits and charm to remain an alluring siren figure in a more uncertain age. Better still, the accumulated wealth of the city, expressed through the magnificent architecture and art that adorned it, was to provide a magnet for generations of visitors.

Today Venice is one of the most popular tourist destinations in the world. Best seen, perhaps, on a bright Spring morning, it provides cultural, sightseeing and culinary delights in equal measure. Simply to approach it from the sea is to experience one of the most unforgettable visual thrills any traveller can hope for.

Venice particularly rewards the visitor who pays attention to its history, complexity and treasures. Any traveller equipped with this excellent and fascinating book, will thus be able to benefit fully from their time in this magnificent city.

Denis Judd
London

Author's Acknowledgements

Many people helped me with the preparation of this book, but ten deserve a special mention. My friend and colleague, Bob Cole, suggested that I take on this project and was a valuable source of advice. Two other colleagues, Steve and Ona Siporin, both specialists in Venice's history, shared their expertise and skill in proofreading and commenting on a first draft of this book. My editor at Chastleton Travel, Victoria Huxley, guided me with her tactful, constructive criticisms. Aldo and Miriam Giuponi, our friends in Venice, were generous with their time and patient with our questions. My sister, Susan Eckhardt, and my parent, Joanne and Siegfried Mentzel, helped with the research for this project in many different ways. Finally, my wife, Tami Coleman, deserves special thanks for her constant support and encouragement. It is to her that I dedicate this book.

Introduction

Of the many sculptures and paintings of lions that appear all over Venice, one of the most famous hangs in the Palazzo Ducale in the Sala Grimani (named after Doge Marino Grimani, r. 1595-1606). Vittore Carpaccio painted this famous feline in 1516 for the offices of the treasury (near the Rialto Bridge). This lion of St Mark the Evangelist has features common to most other lion portraits one encounters in Venice: the wings, a peculiar grin, the open book with the famous lines 'Peace to you Mark, my evangelist'. But the striking thing about this particular lion, as noted by Gary Wills, is that it seems to be amphibious. While its front paws are set firmly on land (the better to keep the book dry, perhaps), its rear legs are in the waters of the lagoon.

Perhaps no other allegorical painting of Mark's lion so neatly sums up one of the most striking features of the history of Venice. In many ways, Venice occupied through most of its history a position on the borders of numerous categories. It is this 'in-betweenness' that makes Venice such a magical and fascinating place.

An Amphibious Empire

One of the most obvious, and striking, aspects of this position is, of course, the very geographical setting of the city itself. From its origins Venice was a unique and improbable place. Its daring relationship with the lagoon was symbolic of a wide range of phenomena. From the dawn of their history, the people of the lagoon had an intense and close relationship to its waters. It provided most of their food, in the form of seafood and waterfowl, and also salt, their main product for trade. Perhaps most importantly of all in the long run was the excep-

1

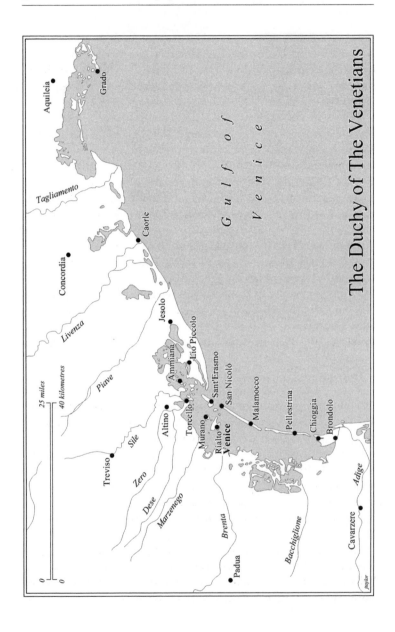

The Duchy of The Venetians

Gulf of Venice

Aquileia

Grado

Tagliamento

Caorle

Concordia

Jesolo

Livenza

Lio Piccolo

Piave

Ammiana

Sant'Erasmo

25 miles

40 kilometres

Torcello

San Nicolò

Malamocco

Altino

Murano

Pellestrina

Sile

Rialto

Venice

Chioggia

Treviso

Zero

Brondolo

Dese

Marzenego

Adige

Brenta

Bacchiglione

Cavarzere

0

0

Padua

tional defensive position provided by the lagoon. Even invaders who possessed a good knowledge of naval warfare (and few of Venice's early barbarian enemies did) were stymied by the innumerable sandbars, shallows, and strange currents, which the Venetians themselves knew intimately.

This close relationship with the water meant that Venice very early became a maritime power. As George Wills has argued persuasively, Venice resembles in many ways ancient Athens in that it conceived of its fortunes as being tied to the sea. Venice achieved mastery of the Adriatic by the end of the eleventh century, and by the early thirteenth was the major naval power in the entire eastern Mediterranean, which was dotted with numerous Venetian outposts, forts, and colonies.

On the other hand, Venice began to build a land empire on the northern Italian mainland as early as the fourteenth century. By the early 1400s, the Venetian Empire, like Carpaccio's amphibious lion, occupied the sea and the land, and was an admired (or feared) power on both. Even though Venice's land empire in northern Italy became more important to its political and economic future after approximately 1500, Venice never lost its aquatic nature. Indeed, given its geography, how could it?

OF ITALY AND THE ORIENT

One of the first things to strike a newcomer to Venice, besides its magical setting, is its 'Eastern' appearance. At every turn, one is confronted by art and architecture indelibly stamped with the mark of the Orient. At the same time, the visitor is constantly reminded that this is a great Christian, Italian city. But the striking thing is the way in which even the familiar lines and motifs of Gothic or Renaissance architecture are combined, sometimes in the same building, with designs or elements that would be more at home in Istanbul, or even Damascus.

This startling, and delightful, expression of eastern forms and designs is not an accident, nor is it a carefully contrived artificial trope, like the 'follies' or *Chinoiserie* of eighteenth and early nineteenth-century European tastes. Rather, Venice bears an unmistakable eastern stamp because, for most of its history as an independent republic, it was as much a Levantine as an Italian state. Indeed, perhaps even more so. For while the *Serenissima* was geographically and linguistically linked to the other republics and principalities of northern Italy, its political and economic fortunes, at least until the middle of the fifteenth century, were really determined by events in the Aegean and eastern Mediterranean littorals. Similarly, while it was always aware of the politics and warfare of north-eastern Italy, and while it amassed a considerable land empire in the area during the fifteenth century, much of the Venetian aristocracy seemed to have regarded these involvements (initially at least) as unfortunate but necessary obligations to ensure that none of its Italian neighbours became strong enough to choke off the Republic's overland trade routes to the north, or to strangle its supply of grain from *terra firma*. Until around 1500, the overwhelming majority of Venice's military and political capital was invested in the East. A look at the history of the Republic's expansion makes it abundantly clear that the main focus for most of its history was the Levant. The manipulation of the crusading movement, culminating in the ignominious, but for the Venetians highly successful, Fourth Crusade is but the most spectacular example of this eastern Mediterranean focus. The ferocious yet futile defence of Cyprus from the Ottomans and the economically ruinous forty-year fight with the same foe over Crete both demonstrate the resolve of the Venetian oligarchy that its empire in the Levant was crucial to its survival. Less confrontationally, one can note the concerted, and usually successful, efforts of Venetian merchants and diplomats to maintain cordial, even friendly, relations with the 'infidel' powers in Egypt, Palestine, and Asia Minor, especially the Fatimids and Mamluks.

Some historians have argued that Venice's history in fact manifested its 'Eastern' and 'Western' roots at different times. From the development of the communes of the lagoon until around 1300, it is argued, Venice was firmly rooted in the East. After the Greek reconquest of Constantinople in 1261, however, and faced with increasingly avaricious neighbours in its own *terra firma* backyard, Venetian government policies and cultural models shifted increasingly towards the West (especially Renaissance Italy). This increasing engagement with its northern Italian neighbours coincided with events such as the so-called Chioggia War against Genoa, which ended in 1380. Some historians have used this date as a convenient marker for the beginning of Venice as a mainly Italian, rather than 'Levantine' power. On a cultural level it is certainly true that Venetian society began to gravitate increasingly toward 'Western' models after around 1400. Nevertheless, the Republic was a relative latecomer to the Renaissance, although one might argue that it more than made up for this late arrival.

Monarchy, Oligarchy, and Republic

Venice's mind-boggling political system is yet another example of its unique, 'in-between' nature. The office of Duke (or 'Doge' as he is known in Venetian dialect), originated as an appointee of the Byzantine Emperor. By the ninth century, however, the Doges had come to resemble independent princes, several of whom set up short-lived dynasties. While the nobility, wealthy citizens (eventually called *cittadini*) and commoners held various vaguely defined political powers, the Doges ruled increasingly like monarchs. This situation began to change by the early eleventh century and by 1172, following the assassination of the ill-fated Doge Vitale Michiel, the nobility established the Great Council. By 1300, the noble families of the Great Council had succeeded in concentrating political power in the Venetian Republic in their own hands, at the expense of the commoners and the Doge. For the rest of Venice's independent existence, it was ruled by an oligarchy of Venetian nobility. In this, it was not terribly different from many other northern Italian states of the time. What makes the Venetian political experiment unique, however, is the extent to which the patricians were aware of the horrible possibility of strife in such a system (which bedevilled the politics of Renaissance Italy) and went out of their way to try to prevent it in Venice. Venice was therefore spared both the depredations of ambitious *condotierri* and local dynastically minded despots. Despite several attempts by both, the clique of wealthy merchant families that controlled the Republic carefully guarded against the political ambitions of any mercenary captain and at the same time made sure, through a devilishly complex electoral system, and an equally involved hierarchy of overlapping institutional organs, that none of their number might establish himself as absolute or hereditary ruler.

POPE AND PATRIARCH

Even in matters of religion, Venice occupied a unique, even strange, position in Christendom. Venice's close historical connections with Byzantium meant that much of its early religious art and architecture was closely modelled on that of the Christian East. Yet, Venice sided with the Pope after the Great Schism of 1095 and so subsequently developed within the fold of Western, Catholic Christianity instead of Eastern Orthodoxy. Nevertheless, the actual organization of the Church in the Venetian Empire was peculiar. As travel writer Jonathan Buckley described it, the Venetians ran a 'franchise' of the Roman Catholic Church. This curious situation was illustrated by the existence in Venice (until 1451) of a Patriarch, the only one in the Catholic Church, as well as a Bishop. The communities of the lagoon were part of the jurisdiction of the nearby Patriarch of Grado, while the island of Olivolo (in the *sestiere* of Castello) was also the See of the Bishop of Venice. In 1451, Pope Nicholas V united the two offices in the new Patriarchate of Venice based in the church of San Pietro di Castello, which was the Cathedral of Venice until 1807. While the Church in Venice was undeniably Catholic, its unique organization was mirrored by an unusual relationship between the Doge and the Church hierarchy. As in the case of the Orthodox churches, but unusual in the history of Western Christendom, the Doge was almost always able to exercise close control over the Venetian clergy. During the several episodes in which the Pope placed Venice under the dreaded interdict (the last time as late as 1605), the vast majority of the clergy followed the Doge's instructions and continued to perform their functions in blatant disregard of the Pope's wishes. The 'basilica' of St Mark itself provides an example of the curious place of the Church in the history of the *Serenissima*. While the Cathedral of Venice, St Peter's, was on the outskirts of the city centre (and on its own island), the Doge's chapel, St Mark's Basilica, was in the political centre of the Republic, next door to the Ducal Palace itself. On the other hand, the Church occupied a tremendously important place in the spiritual, social, and artistic life of the Republic.

Venetian Patriotism or Italian Nationalism?

In modern history, the Venetians again occupied a strange place. While some were interested in the ideas of the Enlightenment and subsequent American and French Revolutions, the old oligarchy was overthrown, not by a popular uprising but by the invading armies of Napoleonic France. Similarly, in the rise of Italian nationalism and the struggle and ultimate triumph of the *Risorgimento*, the Venetians played a part that was generally supportive, though not very involved. The heroic, but ultimately futile, uprising led by Daniele Manin against Austrian domination in 1848 was as much an expression of Venetian patriotism as Italian nationalism. While Manin and his associates had close connections with the Italian nationalists who looked for liberation to the House of Savoy, they also had a clearly developed identification with Venice itself. Even after the incorporation of Venice into the Kingdom of Italy in 1866, Venice occupied a somewhat unique position in the subsequent history of Italy. During the whole tragic episode of Fascism, world war, and German occupation, for instance, Venice had an ambivalent position. Although it played host to various Fascist and proto-Fascist agitators and literati (the most famous of whom was Gabrielle D'Annunzio) the Venetians themselves were not generally enthusiastic supporters of the Duce.

The City of Bridges

Venice is thus a city of bridges, literally and figuratively. It was certainly Catholic, but had its own patriarch. It was linguistically and perhaps geographically Italian, but had as much to do with the Greek, Slavic, and even Muslim, worlds as the Western one for most of its history. The Venetians themselves seemed to recognize this exceptionalism; the way in which they were a special, even a 'chosen' people. Thus, perhaps, the unprecedented visibility of Mosaic and Israelite stories as the themes for Venetian paintings, as well as the unusually large number of churches dedicated to Old Testament figures.

It is this historic role as a commercial, artistic, and political bridge between the East and West that has contributed much to give Venice

The Lion of St Mark, the ever-present symbol of Venice

its unique place in the history of Italy, and indeed of Europe. At different periods, Venetian political, military, and artistic sensibilities tilted toward one pole or the other. Yet, until the end of its independent existence in 1797 (and arguably until today), Venice always occupied an intriguing and exciting space that was both Eastern and Western, both Byzantine and Roman, and (like Carpaccio's wonderfully amphibious lion) both maritime and terrestrial. In the rest of this short book, we will explore this fascinating legacy.

CHAPTER ONE

Barbarians and Refugees
450-828

The most obvious fact about Venice, bound to strike even the most casual visitor, is the utter improbability of the place. The sight of a great and beautiful city rising out of a shallow lagoon has stimulated the imaginations of visitors and residents alike through most of Venice's history and produced numerous stories to explain its origins.

Like all myths, the legends about the origins of Venice are constructed around a kernel of truth. Perhaps the most resounding and long-lived of all of the origin myths is that Venice was the first and only settlement in the history of the lagoon, and that it was founded as, and has always remained, a free community. One of these tales, for example, told how Antenor of Troy, fleeing the destruction of his home town, found refuge in the lagoon and constructed a castle on one of the islands (known to this day as Castello).

As delightful as many of these myths are, we must straight away dispense with some of their most common themes. First of all, there had certainly been people living in the lagoon, off and on, for a very long time before a permanent community first appeared in the sixth century. Secondly, Venice was most certainly not 'free' in any sense of the word before the ninth century, at the earliest, and instead was subject to whatever power happened to have political control of the mainland. In fact, the various communities of the lagoon long remained part of the (Eastern) Roman Empire, and their emergence as the single, autonomous Duchy of Venice was a long and tortuous process.

The final point about the origins of Venice, which is at least implied by most of the origin myths, is that the original inhabitants of the territory that would eventually become the Most Serene Republic were, in fact, terrified men and women fleeing the destruction and chaos that accompanied the disintegration of the Western Roman Empire. It is with these dramatic events that we shall begin to unravel the history of the origins of Venice.

THE FIRST SETTLERS

The islands and sandbars of the Venetian lagoon were inhabited by scattered groups of hunters and fishermen since the dawn of the Christian era, if not earlier. The Roman historian Livy (himself a native of Padua), for example, tells the story of an expedition by King Cleomenes of Sparta to the lagoon during the fourth century BCE in which the plucky proto-Venetians managed to defend themselves against the invaders. While this encounter has the strong whiff of legend about it, there is considerable archaeological evidence that there were indeed scattered semi-permanent settlements in and around the lagoon as early as Neolithic times. There are also indications that there were even more substantial habitations by the first century AD when people from the mainland (probably Altino) established a short-lived settlement on Torcello.

The human population of the lagoon increased dramatically, however, with the beginning of the barbarian invasions of Italy during the fifth century. The first of these invaders were Alaric's Visigoths who, on the way to their famous (or infamous) sack of Rome in 410, took the time to plunder the rich city of Aquileia in 402. The passage of the Visigoths through the Veneto sent a wave of refugees into the relative safety of the lagoon. Most of these people returned to their homes on the mainland, or what was left of them, after the danger had passed. Unbeknownst to these refugees, however, Alaric's people were only the first of what was to turn out to be several waves of invaders sweeping down into Italy. They also had no way of knowing that the Visigothic invaders were themselves fleeing an even more terrible enemy: the Huns. By 452, these central Asian horsemen, led by their famous Khan Attila, invaded northern Italy. Aquileia was once again sacked and a new wave of refugees fled from the mainland to the lagoon. Again, after the Huns departed, many of these mainlanders returned to the remains of their old towns and villages.

During these troubled times, there is evidence that the populations of the lagoon's scattered settlements increased as some of these refugees decided to stay after most of their fellows had returned to their increasingly precarious existence on the mainland. These lagoon dwellers, though increasing in numbers, hardly constituted a united community, much less an embryonic city. However, one of the most famous of Venetian origin myths tells the story of three consuls from the Roman city of Padua founding Venice on the wonderfully exact stroke of noon on 25 March 421. According to the legend, they marked the event with the construction of the little church of San Giacomo di Rialto, which to this day claims to be the oldest church in Venice. This story seems to have emerged in the fifteenth century at what was perhaps the height of Venetian power, in an obvious effort to provide a pedigree for the city from the time of Imperial Rome, which at the same time stressed its free origins. It is worth noting, by the way, that the legend emerged shortly after the 1420 fire in Padua which conveniently destroyed most of that city's archives.

While we can pretty safely relegate the charming story of the visit of the Paduan consuls to the realm of legend, it is nevertheless fairly clear that some sort of rudimentary administration was emerging in the lagoon by the middle of the fifth century. In 466, representatives of the small communities scattered throughout the northern Adriatic lagoons met at Grado and agreed to elect twelve 'tribunes' from among the people of the lagoon each year. While hardly a sophisticated or fully developed system of government, we might, with hindsight, recognize this 'congress' at Grado as the beginning of what would eventually become the Republic of Venice.

In the meantime, however, what was left of Roman Italy was in an advanced state of disintegration and the fall of the last Emperor, the young Romulus Augustulus in 476, merely formalized the end of the Roman Empire in the West. Its place was soon taken, in Italy at any rate, by the Ostrogothic Kingdom of Theodoric, based in the city of Ravenna. The communities of the lagoon maintained correct, if not cordial, relations with the new masters of Italy and were certainly politically and economically connected to the mainland. Yet, given their strange geographical conditions and their embryonic self-government, they seem even at this early stage of their history to have occupied a political space that was somewhat different from that of their mainland neighbours. The nature of the relationship between the lagoon settlements and the Ostrogothic rulers at Ravenna is hinted at in a vivid letter written in 523 by Cassiodorus, a minister in the court of Theodoric. The letter is addressed to the tribunes of the lagoon communities and is basically a request for assistance in the transportation of supplies of wine and oil from Istria to Ravenna. In it, however, Cassiodorus goes out of his way to praise the lagoon dwellers and their lifestyle. In part he writes (here quoted by John Julius Norwich):

> For you live like sea birds, with your homes dispersed…across the surface of the water. The solidity of the earth on which they rest is secured only by osier and wattle; yet you do not hesitate to oppose so frail a bulwark to the wildness of the sea. Your people have one great wealth; the fish which suffices for them all. Among you there is no difference between rich and poor; your food is the same, your houses are all alike. Envy, which rules the rest of the world, is unknown to you. All your energies are spent on your salt-fields; in them indeed lies your prosperity, and your power to purchase those things which you have not. For though there may be men who have little need of gold, yet none live who desire not salt. Be diligent, therefore, to repair your boats – which, like horses, you keep tied up at the doors of your dwellings – and make haste to depart.

As scholars such as Frederic Lane have commented, this remarkable document reads like the wistful imaginings of a harried bureaucrat on a particularly bad day at the office. But, this obviously idealized picture of an aquatic arcadia nevertheless tells us a great deal about the early lagoon settlements. Perhaps most importantly, the lagoon people pictured in this letter have already carved out some sort of place for themselves in the maritime transportation network of the northern Adriatic. That is, after all, why Cassiodorus wrote this gushing letter to them in the first place. The letter also notes the importance of salt and fish. Indeed, besides their growing role as merchants transporting other people's goods, the lagoon dwellers were beginning their own production and sale of salt, which they also used to preserve the fish harvested from the waters of the lagoon. Indeed, there is evidence that by the time of Cassiodorus' letter, Venetian merchants and bargemen were already quite active along the coasts and rivers of northern Italy.

One unpleasant aspect of lagoon life not mentioned by Cassiodorus was (and remains) periodic flooding. There were apparently major floods in 527 and again in 589. The latter seem to have been particularly fierce, and people at the time reported that 'we are living neither on land nor on water' (here quoted by John Keahey).

The relationship between the developing community in the lagoon and the Ostrogoth Kingdom was cut short, however, by the Byzantine reconquest of Italy. By 539 the Byzantine general Belisarius had conquered Ravenna and restored imperial rule to most of the Italian peninsula. The settlements in the Venetian lagoon duly became part of the Roman province of Venetia, and were ruled, like the rest of Imperial Italy, from Ravenna by a Byzantine official called an Exarch, who was assisted by a military commander known as the *magister militum*. The Venetians seem to have maintained relations with their new mainland masters that were just as good, or probably better, than those with their erstwhile rulers the Ostrogoths. Indeed, in an expression of gratitude for Venetian help during the reconquest, the Byzantine eunuch General Narses (who succeeded Belisarius) is said to have constructed two churches on the then largely uninhabited islands of the *Riva Alto* (the 'high bank' which later becomes known as the Rialto and the centre of Venice). One of these churches was dedicated to the Saints Geminianus and Menna and probably stood in what is currently the centre of St Mark's Square. The other was dedicated to St Theodore of Amasea who became Venice's first patron saint.

No sooner had the Byzantines begun to consolidate their control of northern Italy than the area was invaded by the last of a long series of Germanic peoples, the Lombards. The Lombard invasions, beginning in 568, ultimately ended Byzantine rule of northern Italy and devastated much of the area. Once again, people from the mainland fled to the lagoon. But this time, they were not individual men and women but entire communities, led by their Bishops and carrying their sacred relics. The people who arrived in the lagoon in the face of the Lombard invasion came not as temporary exiles or refugees seeking a short-term safe haven, as had the earlier arrivals, but as immigrants.

The number and organization of these newcomers rapidly transformed the scattered settlements on the islands, mudflats, and sandbars

The square at Torcello with the cathedral of Santa Maria Assunta
and the church of Santa Fosca

of the lagoon as different areas were settled by different communities
from the mainland. Each group of islands in the lagoon was eventually settled primarily by people from a particular part of the Veneto.
Thus, Malamocco and Chioggia were settled mainly by refugees from
Padua while people from Altino (near the present-day Marco Polo
Airport) went primarily to Burano, Murano, and Torcello, the latter
settlement becoming, from a very early date, the dominant commercial area of the lagoon. The beautiful church of Santa Maria Assunta
on Torcello was begun as early as 639.   Grado became home to
refugees from Aquileia (which had been sacked three times over the
previous 150 years) including the Metropolitan Bishop, or Patriarch,
of that town.

This new influx of refugees significantly altered the make-up of the
lagoon settlements. Whatever aspects of the primitive egalitarianism
described in Cassiodorus' letter that had actually existed evaporated
within a century of the Lombard invasions. Deeds, wills, and other
records show that a nobility, perhaps connected genealogically with
the refugees, established itself in the lagoon, and that the nobles controlled many of the best fishing spots and salt-pans, as well as farms and
estates on the mainland.

The Lombard invasions also marked a watershed in the political
evolution of Venice. Byzantine control of the northern Italian main-

land was finally ended in 639 with the Lombard conquest of Oderzo. What was left of the Byzantine administration of the area now fled to the lagoon, where the *magister militum* (answerable to the Byzantine Exarch still hanging on at Ravenna) established himself in the settlement of Cittanova (near the modern town of Cortelazzo) which was renamed Eraclea after the reigning Byzantine Emperor Heraclius. The settlements in the lagoon thus became the last stronghold of the Eastern Roman Empire in northern Italy.

THE DUCHY OF VENICE

It was during this turbulent period of Lombard invasion and Byzantine retreat that Venice underwent another important stage in its political and civic evolution. The turmoil of the eighth century led to the transformation of the scattered settlements of the lagoon from a Roman province into a Duchy, subordinate to the Eastern Roman Empire. This process was neither straightforward nor inevitable and was certainly quite different from the legendary accounts describing the establishment of a free and independent Venetian Republic. It was crucial for the history of Venice nevertheless.

According to a legend going back at least to the eleventh century, the Patriarch of Grado summoned all the dignitaries of the lagoon to Eraclea in the year 697 to discuss the continued threat posed by the Lombards. According to the story, the assembly decided to replace their existing system of government based on the tribunes with one dominated by a single leader, a *dux* (*doge* in the Venetian dialect). A certain Paoluccio Anafesto was straight away elected the first Doge of Venice by the assembled citizens at Eraclea.

Although this story has the weight of tradition behind it, and although Paoluccio's portrait is right there in the Hall of the Great Council in the Ducal Palace as the first of the line of the Doges of Venice, the entire account is almost certainly a myth. As noted at the outset of this chapter, however, most myths, especially those involving great and momentous events, are usually grounded in a handful of historical realities. In this case, it seems that around the year 697 the Byzantine authorities indeed made the territory of the Venetian lagoon subordinate to a single military leader (*dux*) in place of the tribunes. Another intriguing twist to this legend is the possibility that the mythical Paoluccio Anafesto is based on Paul, or Paulicius, the Byzantine Exarch of Ravenna. Like the mythical Doge Paoluccio, Exarch Paulicius was indeed the ruler of the settlements of the Venetian lagoon during a time of growing threats by the Lombards. And, again like the legendary Doge, the Exarch did manage to negotiate a truce with the increasingly bold barbarians, part of which included a delineation of the borders of the Byzantine province of the Venetian lagoon. To further clinch the relationship between the Doge and Exarch, Paulicius' *magister militum* Marcellus, who would have been the local Byzantine authority in the lagoon, is sometimes named as Venice's second Doge.

The legend of the Council of Eraclea hints at another, much broader, historical development. While the Byzantines maintained a presence in Italy, based on their headquarters at Ravenna, and while the settlements of the lagoon remained an Imperial province, the entire edifice of Byzantine rule in northern Italy was crumbling in the face of the continued Lombard threat. Byzantine authority in Italy endured yet another blow in 726 as a result of a political and religious crisis, known to history as the iconoclast movement, precipitated by Emperor Leo III (the Isaurian). The Imperial provinces in Italy, encouraged by Pope Gregory II, opposed the movement and used the occasion to revolt against the Empire's rule. The uprising reached such an extent that Paulicius, the Byzantine Exarch and namesake of the mythical first Doge, was assassinated in 727 and the local communities in what was left of Byzantine Italy chose their own leaders. It was in this context that the people of the lagoon, sometime between 727 and 730, chose a certain Ursus or Orso, a native of Eraclea, to head the former Imperial administration in the lagoon. Thus, Orso is considered the first historical Doge of Venice.

The election of Doge Orso by no means severed the ties between Venice and the Byzantine Empire. In fact, the rebellion against the Empire proved short-lived and after a few years Doge Orso was even integrated into the re-established Byzantine administration and named Hypatos (Imperial Consul) of the province. Orso was so proud of this distinction that he and his descendants took the surname 'Ipato' and he, and his ducal successors, soon modelled their official garments and court ceremonial on those of the Byzantine Emperor. Likewise, subsequent Doges, well into the tenth century, took all sorts of Byzantine honorific titles for themselves.

On the other hand, if the emotional and cultural links with Constantinople were as strong as ever, the actual political ties to the Imperial centre were becoming ever weaker. In 742, Orso's son Teodato transferred the capital from the old Imperial city of Eraclea to Malamocco, on the eastern shore of the Lido. This symbolic break from the old centre of Imperial authority in the lagoon paralleled the rapidly weakening Byzantine presence in Italy. In 751, the Lombards under their King Aistulf, finally took Ravenna, thus effectively ending Byzantine control of most of Italy.

The Lombard victory proved to be ephemeral, however, for in the meantime a new military and political regional power, the Carolingians, had been growing beyond the Alps. In the same year that Aistulf took Ravenna, Pepin seized the Frankish throne from the Merovingians, and by 756, at the invitation of Pope Stephen III, invaded Italy and subdued the Lombards. While Pepin turned over most of his conquests in northern Italy to Pope Stephen (thus laying the foundation for the Papal States), the Franks henceforth constituted the main power in northern Italy.

THE RIVO ALTO AND THE BIRTH OF VENICE

As the Franks consolidated their rule over northern Italy during the next several decades, the communities of the lagoon struggled to develop institutional structures that suited their peculiar geographic, political, and even religious situation. Contrary to another long-standing Venetian myth which tells the story of the early Venetian commonwealth as having been united and free of factional feuds and quarrels, the people of the lagoon were in fact deeply divided and mistrustful, not only of their fellows on the other islands and sandbars, but of members of different families. These family feuds and local antagonisms overlapped with broader questions about the future of the area.

The problems posed by Venice's political geography eventually elicited three broad factional responses. The first two sought to bring

Venice closer to either the Franks, on the one hand, or the Byzantines, on the other. The third faction reflected a growing spirit of independence among the inhabitants of the lagoon communities, and wanted to maintain a cordial distance from both Franks and Byzantines. These three groups also had conflicting ideas about the political future of the lagoon in general, and about the nature of the office of Doge, in particular. While some saw the Dogeship as a hereditary position, others considered it an elected one. Likewise, the actual powers at the Doge's disposal, and his relationship to the Byzantine Emperor, were by no means clear.

These factional tensions rapidly led to violence. The second Doge, Teodato Ipato, was deposed and blinded. The next two Doges likewise met violent ends. In the meantime, the powerful families of the lagoon determined to elect two tribunes each year who were to guard against abuses of power by the Doge. It was in these circumstances that the fifth Doge, Maurizio Galbaio, provoked a crisis that was to have far reaching implications for the future of the communities of the lagoon. Maurizio was from an old Eraclean family and claimed descent from the Emperor Galba (hence the family name). As staunchly pro-Byzantine, his election in 764 represented a challenge to the growing feelings of particularism among the inhabitants, to say nothing of exacerbating the old and violent rivalry between the Eracleans and the Malamoccans. Doge Maurizio furthermore alarmed many of his subjects when he named his son, Giovanni, as co-ruler and successor in 796. Clearly, Maurizio was attempting to establish a dynasty. Popular resentment culminated in 804 with the overthrow and exile of the Galbaii. The next Doge, however, a former tribune named Obelario degli Antenori, who had led the revolt against the Galbaii, immediately set about establishing a dynasty of his own.

The embryonic republicanism that led to the demise of the Galbaii also threatened Obelario's plans. To further complicate matters, the old rivalries between Malamocco and Eraclea reached new heights (or depths) that culminated in open warfare resulting in the almost total destruction of the latter city. In the face of rising unrest, Obelario sought to avoid the fate of the hapless Galbaii family by hitching his dynastic ambitions to the rising star of the Carolingians. For, in 800,

Charlemagne had been crowned Emperor of a newly (re)constituted Western Empire, much to the chagrin of the Byzantines. Although the Antenori had no particular love for the Franks, they reckoned that the Carolingians might be able to protect them against their domestic enemies, and act as a counterweight to the increasingly suspicious Byzantine Empire. Accordingly, in 805, Obelario personally made the trip to Aachen to recognize Charlemagne as Emperor of the West, during which he married one of the ladies of the Carolingian court.

Obelario's pro-Frankish strategy backfired badly, infuriating his Byzantine suzerain and many of his own subjects. In desperation, he called upon Charlemagne's son Pepin, based in Ravenna, to occupy and garrison Venice with Frankish forces. Pepin eagerly agreed and attacked Venice in early 810. Much to their chagrin, however, Obelario and his two brothers found themselves abandoned by their subjects who were outraged at their traitorous behaviour. The peoples of the different islands united in the face of the Frankish threat under Agnello Participazio, an old settler from the still largely uninhabited Rialtine islands. It was to those muddy and hitherto ignored islands that many of the people of the Malamocco and the other outer island settlements now retreated. The Venetians prepared for Pepin's attack by removing the warning markers from shallow channels and by driving numerous pointed stakes into the lagoon, creating a kind of palisade. For six months the Frankish armies occupied most of the mainland settlements (e.g., Chioggia, Pellestrina, Grado, and Jesolo) but they were never able to penetrate into the heart of the lagoon. Finally, in the summer of 810, Pepin, faced with an increase of disease in his troops, a rumour of an approaching Byzantine fleet, and the offer by the Venetians of the payment of an annual tribute, raised the siege.

The Venetian victory was thus not quite as dramatic as one might surmise from the monumental paintings by Andrea Vicentino commemorating the event in the Sala dello Scrutino in the Doge's Palace. At the very least the Franks retained control of most of the mainland, to say nothing of the tribute which the Venetians were now obliged to pay. But the siege had other results which were much more important for the subsequent history of the Duchy of Venice. First of all, the entire episode represented a victory for the republican faction of

Venetian opinion. While there would be other attempts by certain Doges to establish dynasties up through the eleventh century, the failure of both the Galbaii and the Antenori represented the defeat of the dynastic idea (at least for the time being) and set a trend in which the powers of the Doge would be inexorably diminished over the following centuries. The second far reaching consequence of Pepin's attack was a shift of the political, social, and commercial life of the lagoon to the Rialtine islands, the most important of which were Rialto, Dorsoduro, Giudecca, Luprio, and Olivolo. These muddy, low-lying, flood-prone, and inaccessible islands had not been major areas of settlement until the eighth century. During the years after 810, growing numbers of people left the faction-ridden outer islands for the seclusion and relative neutrality, not to mention safety, of the Rialto. Agnello Participazio, a native Rialtine himself and the hero of the anti-Frankish resistance, became the new Doge in 811.

Ironically, perhaps, it was the ill-fated Doge Maurizio Galbaio who encouraged the settlement of the islands long before the Frankish threat emerged by instituting a new bishopric (under the ecclesiastical authority of the Patriarch of Grado) on the island of Olivolo in 775. In the process, an old church on the island dedicated to Saints Bacchus and Sergius was rebuilt as the bishop's new cathedral, consecrated to St Peter.

But perhaps the most important result of the Frankish attack was that it was instrumental in the growth of a common civic identity among the different communities of the lagoon. As the historian John Julius Norwich trenchantly observed, 'Pepin had marched against a group of bickering communities; he had been defeated by a united people.' The civic identity of Venice was bolstered in 814 with the conclusion of the so-called *Pax Nicephori*, negotiated between Charlemagne and Emperor Nicephorus. One of the terms of the agreement was that, in exchange for recognition as Emperor of the West, Charlemagne was to renounce his claims over Venetia, which he recognized as a Duchy within the Byzantine Empire. The Byzantines, on the other hand, while remaining the titular rulers of the lagoon, were rapidly losing their ability to exercise any real control over Venetian affairs. The result of this unusual combination of circumstances was that Venice ended up in the best possible situation. While gaining a *de facto* independence, it at the same time was in a position to enjoy the cultural and commercial benefits of belonging to the Byzantine Empire. As a result, Venetian history for the next two centuries was largely different from that of the rest of Italy, to say nothing of Western and Central Europe.

As Venice was asserting a growing political independence, it also was moving toward an ecclesiastical autonomy quite unique in Western Christendom. The Lombard invasions, besides shattering the remnants of Roman political power, also altered the religious landscape of the northern Adriatic. The entire area had been for centuries under the religious jurisdiction of the Metropolitan Bishop of Aquileia, who (uniquely in Western Christendom) held the title Patriarch. This unprecedented position resulted from the legendary establishment of the See of Aquileia by St Mark the Evangelist himself who, while on his way to Rome, had stopped off in Aquileia and appointed the city's first Bishop, St Hermenagorus. As already mentioned, the Patriarch of Aquileia, along with much of his flock, fled to the lagoon settlement of Grado in 568 in the face of the Lombard invasion. He took with him, among other odds and ends, the throne of St Mark and established himself in Grado in the church of St Euphemia. The Lombards, however, soon installed a new cleric in Aquileia who claimed to be the rightful Patriarch and Bishop of the entire See (and thus the inheritor of St Mark's legacy), instead of the Bishop in Grado. The dispute continued for many years. In 710, the Pope established Grado as a separate See, with jurisdiction over the lagoon, while the Patriarch of Aquileia exercised ecclesiastical control over the northern Adriatic mainland. The essential question of which Bishop was St Mark's true successor (and could claim the title Patriarch) was thus left undetermined until 827 when, at the Council of Mantua, the Pope declared that the Bishop of Aquileia (now under the control of the pro-papal Franks) was to be the sole Patriarch and the true successor of Saint Mark, infuriating the Bishop of Grado and his Venetian supporters. Coincidentally, a spectacular series of events during the following year would give the Bishop of Grado an irrefutable counter-claim to St Mark's legacy, and would also further underline Venice's emerging sense of an independent, civic identity.

The Translation of St Mark's Relic

In 828, two Venetian merchants named Buono Tribuno de Malamocco and Rustico de Torcello returned from Alexandria with a body which they claimed was that of St Mark the Evangelist. According to the story, through a series of cunning ruses (or clever arguments), they obtained the relic from the Alexandrian clerics charged with guarding it, and sneaked it past the Egyptian customs agents hidden beneath a shipment of pork, a repulsive and forbidden product for Muslims. On the return trip to Venice, moreover, the ship miraculously avoided a wreck due to the intervention of St Mark himself.

This audacious episode of body-snatching, called the 'translation', tied very neatly into the stories about St Mark's connections to the See of Aquileia, claimed, it will be remembered, by the Patriarch of Grado. The importance of the 'translation' was further bolstered by a legend (now conveniently remembered) that St Mark himself had

·CARNIB ABSCONSV̄·VVERVNT FVGIVNTQ·RETRORSV·

How the body of St Mark was stolen from Alexandria as depicted in the thirteenth century mosaic in the Basilica

actually stopped off on the islands of the Rialto while on a trip to Rome. There, on the very spot of the future basilica that would bear his name, he had received a vision in which an angel appeared and said: '*Pax tibi Marce, evangelista meus. Hic requiescet corpus tuum* '(Peace to you Mark, my evangelist. On this spot shall your body rest) words (at least those of the first sentence) which should be familiar to any perceptive visitor to Venice, since they are inscribed on the open book held in the holy paws of St Mark's ubiquitous lions.

The events connected to the 'translation' of St Mark have been exhaustively debated and analyzed by historians and have provided generations of Venetian artists with material for their works. The beautiful mosaics above the south transept in St Mark's Basilica, for example, provide perhaps the earliest artistic interpretations of these events. Centuries later, Tintoretto painted a haunting version of the 'Identification of St Mark's Body', (now in the Accademia). Incidentally, contrary to popular belief, Tintoretto's powerful 'Rescue of St Mark's Body' (also in the Accademia) does not depict the translation of the relic in 828, but a much earlier (and more obscure) event in the saint's life. Shortly after his death, the pagans of Alexandria planned to steal the body and burn it, but a miraculous storm gave the Christians the cover they needed to save and secretly bury the corpse.

While the historical accuracy of the specific events of the 'translation' of 828 are extremely doubtful, neither is the story of the transportation of St Mark's body entirely fanciful. The oldest extant written sources which tell of the 'translation' date from about 1050, but it is clear from other sources that by the late ninth century most of Christendom believed that the relic of St Mark was indeed in Venice. The story also hints at the close commercial relations between Venice and the eastern Mediterranean. Despite the fact that both the Eastern Emperor and the Pope had proclaimed a ban against trading with the Muslim Egyptians, there were, according to one version of the story, ten Venetian ships at anchor in Alexandria harbour at the time of the body-snatching. The Venetians were not, however, violating the embargo but had (according to the legend) been blown into the harbour by a storm. Whatever the case may be, the story suggests a growing commercial and political boldness on the part of the Venetians.

Indeed, the arrival of the relic of St Mark could hardly have come at a better time. While still technically a Duchy within the Byzantine Empire, the treaty of 814 had provided the Republic with wide ranging autonomy. Similarly, the move of the political and commercial centre of gravity to the Rialtine islands helped create a feeling of civic unity. The presence of so august a relic as St Mark's body fostered sentiments of pride and independence, and helped secure the Patriarch of Grado almost as much prestige as the Pope himself.

However, it was crucially important for the future political and cultural development of Venice that this powerful relic was entrusted neither to the Patriarch of Grado, nor to the Bishop of Castello, but to the Doge himself who ordered the Saint's remains honoured, not in the Bishop's cathedral on the peripheral island of Olivolo, but in a new chapel, built by the Doge. Thus, the basilica of St Mark, the ducal chapel, rather than the Bishop's cathedral, or the patriarchal church at Grado, became the true spiritual heart of Venice and St Mark became the patron saint of the Republic in the place of the Byzantine St Theodore.

At a stroke, therefore, the presence of St Mark's relics helped secure not only the political and ecclesiastical independence of the Republic, but symbolized a subordination of the spiritual authority of the Patriarch of Grado and the Bishop of Castello to the Doge and his government. This relationship, rare in Western Christendom (though normal in the Byzantine world) was to have far reaching implications for the rest of Venetian history. The cult of St Mark, and indeed his famous winged lion, were for the next thousand years the symbol of the Republic of the lagoon.

CHAPTER TWO

The Republic and St Mark
828–1095

The ninth century began well for Venice. The treaty of 814 gave the city a wide degree of autonomy within the Eastern Empire without estranging the newly emerging Holy Roman Empire in the West. The people of the lagoon likewise survived a number of serious threats to their survival and had moreover emerged from these crises with the beginnings of a common civic identity.

These political and military victories, not to mention the internment of the relics of St Mark the Evangelist in the ducal chapel, the Basilica of St Mark, were emblematic of the profound transformation the communities of the Venetian lagoon underwent during the ninth and early tenth centuries. Certainly one of the most important of these developments was the growth during this period of the settlements around the Rialto that became the city we now know as Venice. This urbanization of the lagoon settlements accompanied the evolution of the Venetian political system, and especially the curtailment of the powers of the Doge.

These developments in the geographic and political landscape closely paralleled major changes in the Venetians' economic and commercial activities. In particular, the Venetians began to extend their trading networks from the rivers of northern Italy out into the Adriatic. In the process, the Venetian merchants who had for centuries transported and sold the products of the lagoon (especially fish and salt) to the cities along the Po, the Adige, and the Brenta, now ventured out into the open sea in search of the fine products of the East, which they then transported back to their markets in Italy. They were so successful that by the end of the eleventh century Venice was the 'Queen of the Adriatic', the unofficial title it was to hold (usually with considerable

0   125 miles
0   200 kilometres

Trieste
Venice   Capodistria
Ferrara   Parenzo
Comacchio   CROATIA
    Pola
Ravenna
ROMAGNA   Rimini   Zara
Ancona   Split
MARCHES   ADRIATIC SEA   Curzola
    Ragusa
    Gargano   Scutari
    Peninsula
    APULIA   Bari   Durazzo
    Brindisi
    Otranto
TYRRHENIAN   CORFU
SEA   CEPHALONIA
    ZANTE
Messina   MOREA
Palermo   Modon
MEDITERRANEAN   SICILY   IONIAN   Coron
    SEA
    MALTA
    SEA

Venice and the Adriatic

jtaylor

justification) for the next seven hundred years. The turn to seafaring as the main economic activity of the Venetians not only involved them in direct trade with the Byzantine Empire and the Levant, but also led to a number of wars against their maritime enemies and rivals. The 'Marriage to the Sea', the most famous of all Venetian public cere-monies, had its origins in a victory celebration after one of these cam-paigns.

The Development of the Rialtine Islands

As we have seen, an unintended consequence of Pepin's ill-fated attack on Venice in 810 was the move of Venice's centres of political and commercial gravity away from the more exposed Malamocco and Eraclea (the latter had been in any case more-or-less demolished even before Pepin's invasion) to the Rialtine islands. While the sandy and swampy terrain of many of these islands made construction a chal-lenge, the protection they offered due to their sheltered position made up for these problems. Most of the buildings were originally built of wood and rested on foundations of numerous wooden pilings sunk into the muddy soil. Until the thirteenth century, most of the land-reclamation projects in the area we now call the city of Venice were pri-vate ventures carried out by important families or, more commonly, religious orders. In the southern islands, for example, the Franciscans worked on drainage projects near their church of San Toma, even as the ancient Badoer family was active in the same area. The Benedictines reclaimed large tracts of land in Dorsoduro. Draining and reclaiming an area was a slow and laborious process. First, a wall of wood and stone was dug or sunk into the area of the proposed plot and made watertight. Next, any water within the enclosure would be pumped out. The third step involved sinking numerous tightly packed pilings into the still muddy soil. Ideally, the slender, alder pilings would be of different lengths, between ten and fifteen feet long, with small-er numbers of long poles alternating with a majority of shorter, thick-er ones. The differently sized pilings thus rested on different strata of subsoil, ensuring that at least some would, in any given set of environ-mental conditions, have a sure footing. The spongy soil was further consolidated by the addition of dirt, gravel, debris from construction sites, and virtually any other solid matter that could be found. The poles, driven deep into the mud, eventually petrified in their oxygen-free atmosphere. After the pilings had been sunk a sort of raft of wooden planks and beams (mostly oak) was laid over the exposed tops of the pilings. The foundation for the building, consisting of several courses of hard, Istrian stone, was then laid on top of this raft of oak beams.

Two of the earliest and subsequently most famous buildings in Venice, St Mark's Basilica and the Doge's Palace, were begun during this period of the early ninth century. Most of the area now occupied by these buildings and the other structures of St Mark's Square (the Piazza) was at this time an island called Morso. Two old churches, St Geminianus and St Theodore (the latter, it will be remembered, the original patron saint of Venice) occupied part of this space and most of the remainder was taken up by gardens. As it happened, the new Doge Agnello Participazio owned some of this real estate and it was on his own land near the church of St Theodore that the first Ducal Palace was erected.

While the current palace occupies this same site, we have only hints and vague descriptions about what the original building looked like. Most of the available information describes the palace as one of the few stone buildings on the Rialtine islands. Its primary function was military and most historians believe that it was probably heavily fortified, with towers and battlements, and might even have had a drawbridge.

Another of the older stone buildings in the area built at about the same time as the Doge's Palace was the convent church of San Zaccaria. The original church (no trace of which now remains after centuries of remodelling) was a gift of the Byzantine Emperor Leo V (known as 'The Armenian'). The Emperor generously supplied not only the money and skilled craftsmen to construct the church, but the holy relic of Zacharias (the father of John the Baptist) as well.

But certainly the church that was to have the most sensational impact in the area was the 'Basilica' of St Mark. Begun immediately after the arrival of the holy relic from Alexandria and consecrated in 832, it was not architecturally a basilica at all, but rather had (and still has) a Greek Cross floor plan, in this case probably modelled on the church of the Holy Apostles in Constantinople. Although the original church was smaller than the third and final version (basically the one we see today, consecrated in 1094) it was still judged at the time to have been a splendid structure. As noted in the last chapter, it is crucially important for the rest of Venetian history that Doge Giustiniano Participazio chose to house the sacred relic in what amounted to his private chapel rather than the Cathedral of Venice on the island of Olivolo. The Doge thus linked the relic, with its awesome symbolic power, not to the Church, but to the Venetian state.

THE RISE OF LONG DISTANCE TRADE

For the first four centuries of its existence, the communities of the Venetian lagoon had depended on the production of two main products: salt and fish. Venetian merchants transported these materials on barges and boats up the Brenta, Po, and Adige Rivers to markets farther inland. When the merchants returned to the lagoon they brought wheat, wine, oil, and other products from the farms and industries of the mainland. From a very early date, Venice was also the main maritime base of the Byzantine Empire in the northern Adriatic. This meant that Venice was northern Italy's (and by extension, Western and Central Europe's) main depot for the fine manufactured goods (especially silk) and spices coming from the East. The volume of this trade was not great, but it is clear that the Venetian barges that carried their prosaic cargoes of salt and fish up the northern Italian rivers also transported some of the more exotic products of the Orient. The long-distance trade between Venice and the eastern Mediterranean ports (especially Constantinople) was mostly in the hands of Greek and Syrian merchants.

This situation began to change during the late eighth and, especially, early ninth, centuries. The 'translation' of St Mark's relic is only the most dramatic example of the increase in Venetian mercantile activity in the eastern Mediterranean. By the late ninth and early tenth centuries, the Byzantines, faced with mounting military challenges and invasions, increasingly lacked the ability to keep the Adriatic secure, with a resulting drop in the volume of Greek and Syrian trade coming to Venice. Venetian commercial and military shipping expanded into this vacuum.

The merchandise handled by this new generation of Venetian merchants still included the exotic goods from the East. These, however, were now traded directly by Venetians who, instead of waiting for Greeks or Syrians to bring them to the Rialto, now went themselves to the great entrepots of Constantinople, Aleppo, and Alexandria. In exchange for the spices, silks, and fine manufactured goods of the Levant, the Venetians had their old stand-bys of salt and fish, as well as certain manufactured goods, especially glassware, which by the ninth century was already becoming an important Venetian product. But these trade goods were soon overshadowed in importance, at least as far as the long-distance trade was concerned, by two very important products which the northern Adriatic supplied in abundance: timber and slaves. The lowlands and river valleys of northern Italy still had extensive forests of hardwoods, whereas the foothills of the Alps, quite convenient to Venetian merchants, had practically inexhaustible supplies of evergreens. By the tenth century, much of the Mediterranean basin, especially North Africa and what we today call the Middle East, had become largely deforested, and timber was a rare and valuable commodity. It was also, quite naturally, considered a war material and as such both the Western and Eastern Emperors and the Popes issued frequent bans and injunctions, studiously ignored by the Venetians, against selling timber to the Islamic world.

The other great cargo on which the Venetian long-distance merchants relied was slaves. The pagan peoples of the Balkans and eastern Europe provided a large and geographically convenient pool of human merchandise for Venetian slave traders. Especially sought as slaves were the Slavs, a people recently arrived in those areas. The similarity, by the way, between the words 'Slav' and 'slave' is not a coincidence. The Riva degli Schiavoni, as its name suggests, was the main Venetian marketplace for this sort of commerce. The conversion of most of the Slavic peoples to Christianity during the eleventh century theoretically put them off limits for enslavement, but the Venetian slavers usually ignored such legalistic niceties, reasoning, perhaps, that as Orthodox (rather than Catholic) Christians, most Slavs were at any rate little better than heretics and thus good candidates for enslavement.

While there was a lively demand in Italy for slaves, the greatest market, as in the case of the timber trade, was the Islamic world. Once again, the Pope and the Emperor condemned the sale of slaves to Muslims as a violation of the military embargo, since many Muslim states used slaves as soldiers. But, as in the case of its timber trade, Venice was hardly willing to forgo commerce based on such a lucrative product.

The increase in the long-distance trade during the ninth and tenth centuries by no means entirely replaced Venice's more local commerce. Venice had, in fact, for some time been consolidating its control over the coastal waters of the northern Adriatic, by force if necessary. The most dramatic example of this activity was the war with the settlement of Comacchio, south of Venice, which functioned as Ravenna's main port. Comacchio, somewhat like Venice, was built partially in a lagoon and relied not only on shipping but, importantly, on the production and sale of salt. The increasing tensions over this trade led to war in 886 during which the Venetian forces destroyed Comacchio, a blow from which it never recovered. It is interesting to reflect, as historian Frederic Lane has done, that if the war had gone the other way, it is quite possible that Comacchio would have developed into the Adriatic's superpower while Venice descended into obscurity. As it happened, Comacchio reverted to a small settlement, famous mainly for its eels, as it remains to this day.

New Invasions

The increasingly assertive, even bellicose, stance developing in Venice during this time soon involved the Venetians in a number of wars against other would-be masters of the Adriatic. In the ninth century, Venice, along with much of the rest of Europe, found itself quite unexpectedly facing a series of invasions on a scale not seen since the sixth century. The most serious of these new invaders were the Magyars and the Arabs, or Saracens, as they were known to Europeans of the time.

The Magyar invasion of Europe, beginning around 896, represented one of the last explosions of the central Asian steppe nomads into Europe until the Mongol-Tatar incursions of the thirteenth century. By 899 the Magyars had arrived in north-eastern Italy and, after devastating much of the area, they tried to attack Venice itself. They advanced from the southern lagoon, following the line of islands and sand bars from Chioggia all the way to Albiola, where Doge Pietro Tribuno (888-912) and the Venetian forces were positioned. The Magyars, who had no experience of naval warfare, were quickly overwhelmed and destroyed by the Venetians. Those who remained gradually withdrew to the Pannonian Plain and eventually converted to Christianity under their Saint-King Istvan (Stephen) who established the Kingdom of Hungary in the year 1000. The Christian Hungarians nevertheless continued to threaten Venetian territories, this time in Dalmatia, on and off, well into the thirteenth century.

In the meantime, Doge Pietro Tribuno and many of the inhabitants of Venice were deeply disturbed by how close the Magyars had actually come to the population centres of the Republic. The next enemy to attack the lagoon might have more maritime experience than the Magyar horsemen. Accordingly, Doge Pietro ordered the construction of various fortifications to protect the Rialtine islands. In particular, a wall was constructed beginning on the eastern side of the island of Olivolo continuing all the way to the church of Santa Maria del Giglio, via the Riva degli Schiavoni. Furthermore, the Venetians made an immense iron chain (modelled, perhaps, on the one which was used to close off the entrance to the Golden Horn in Constantinople) which, if stretched, could close off the Grand Canal. One end of the chain was secured near the church of San Gregorio on Dorsoduro. The opposite end was anchored to the site where the seventeenth century Palazzo Gaggia now stands. Some historians point to the construction of Doge Pietro Tribuno's wall as the event marking the transformation of the scattered settlements on the Rialtine islands into the City of Venice.

While the Magyars threatened the security of mainland territories important for Venetian commerce, a more direct threat to the security of the Republic's maritime trade was posed by the increasingly bold raids by the Muslim Saracens who, by 827, had seized Sicily and parts of southern Italy. The raids of the Saracen corsairs became more and more daring. In 846 they actually sailed up the Tiber and attacked Rome itself. Of more importance for Venice were their activities in the southern Adriatic.

While the depredations of these Muslim pirates continued, off and on, for many centuries, the actual danger that they posed to Venice, and indeed to Christendom in general, had abated by the end of the eleventh century for a variety of reasons. Relentless military pressure by the Byzantines and their Venetian allies forced the Arabs to abandon most of their possessions on the Italian mainland by 916, and in 1002 a Venetian fleet was able to force the Muslims to abandon their siege of Bari. The Venetians combined their martial activities with equally determined diplomatic efforts aimed at the Muslim states which gave the pirates their bases. As the Muslim princes of Sicily and Egypt became increasingly wealthy, their interest in maintaining safe and secure shipping (for markets for their own goods as well as supplies for the products they wanted) increased, and their willingness to protect the buccaneers who preyed on such commerce proportionately decreased. By the first decade of the eleventh century, Venetian relations with the Islamic world had actually become quite cordial, if not actually warm, and the Muslim corsairs (for the time being) came to constitute little more than a minor nuisance.

THE DALMATIAN PIRATES AND THE 'MARRIAGE TO THE SEA'

The defeat of the Magyars and the decline of the raiding and piracy by the Saracens still left one persistent threat to the security of the Adriatic, namely, the Dalmatian pirates. The pirates belonged to various embryonic states that the Slavs had been building since their arrival in the Balkans during the eighth century, and warfare between the Venetians and Dalmatians had been endemic since the ninth century. As was quite normal for the time, most of these seafarers mixed mercantile activity with piracy and their increasing boldness (and success) in both ventures forced the Venetians to take action to secure their developing control over the Adriatic.

The pirates were a difficult quarry. Their main bases were located up the Narenta (modern Neretva) River and were thus practically inaccessible to an enemy naval attack. The mouth of the Narenta was in any case guarded by two islands, Curzola and Langosta (Korchula and Lastovo), both of which were also havens for the Dalmatian pirates. Doge Pietro Candiano I became the first Doge to die in battle (after a reign of only five months) on 18 September 887 while fighting the pirates. The raids of these Dalmatian buccaneers continued during the Venetian wars against the Magyars and Saracens. But by the year 1000, those erstwhile enemies had been either defeated or placated, and Doge Pietro Orseolo II (991-1008) was determined to end the power of the pirates once and for all. On Ascension Day, 9 May 1000, Doge Pietro celebrated Mass at the Cathedral of San Pietro di Castello and the Venetian fleet set sail for Dalmatia. It flew a banner blessed by the Bishop that, probably for the first time, was emblazoned with the winged lion of St Mark.

The Doge had prepared the fleet's way diplomatically by carefully working to divide the different Slavic princes of Dalmatia. Thus, the Venetians faced little opposition on their way down the coast toward the Narenta River. Rather than try to attack the pirates in their riverside strongholds, Doge Pietro instead concentrated on taking control of the offshore islands in the vicinity, all the while blockading the Dalmatians' main fleet in the Narenta. Using this strategy he was able to pick off the Dalmatian bases one by one. Soon the Dalmatian pirates were beaten and Doge Pietro sailed back to the lagoon a hero, taking the title 'Duke of Dalmatia'. While this title had little legal meaning (the Doge acknowledged the titular rule of Dalmatia by the Byzantine Emperors) it reflected what was, in fact, the beginning of a Venetian economic and political sphere of influence over the eastern coast of the Adriatic. In recognition of this status, the different Istrian and Dalmatian cities were obliged to pay various annual tributes to Venice. Veglia (modern Krk), for example, was obliged to pay fifteen marten skins and twenty fox skins, while Pola (modern Pula) was to supply 2,000 pounds of oil for lighting St Mark's Basilica. The real advantages of the domination of Dalmatia, however, was the increased security these new territories provided to Venice. Indeed, Dalmatian supplies of raw materials, especially food, became crucial elements in subsequent Venetian Imperial strategies.

While the Dalmatian pirates no longer constituted any serious threat to Venetian shipping, the various cities of the Dalmatian coast, especially the largely Italian city of Zara (modern Zadar), were not terribly happy with their new status as subjects of the Venetian Doge and were a constant source of unrest. Nevertheless, the success against the Dalmatians meant that by the end of the year 1000, Venice was the unquestioned master of the Adriatic.

One of the most enduring legacies of the Dalmatian campaign had nothing to do with economics or military security. This was the so-called 'Marriage to the Sea'. In commemoration of the victories over the Dalmatians, every Ascension Day the Doge, the Bishop of Castello, and the nobles and citizens sailed out past the Lido into the open sea. There, accompanied by the singing of the choir, the Doge uttered a brief prayer (here quoted by Norwich) in which he asked the Almighty that '...for us and for all who sail thereon, the sea may ever be calm and quiet'. As we will see in Chapter Six, by the sixteenth century this ceremony had become a good deal more elaborate and included the now familiar ritual of tossing a gold ring into the waves.

Venice between Two Empires

The military victories of Doge Pietro Orseolo II (991-1009) were paralleled by the astounding success of his diplomatic strategies. While the depredations of Magyars, Saracens, or Dalmatian pirates might threaten Venice's wealth and security, the hostility of either the Holy Roman or the Byzantine Emperor could potentially end Venice's very existence as an independent entity. In the tenth and early eleventh centuries, such threats could by no means be ruled out. Thus, Venetian diplomacy, at least until the mid-twelfth century, was based on the need of staying on good terms with both Empires while at the same time making sure that neither was in a position to threaten Venice's growing independence.

As we saw in the previous chapter, the Pact of Nicephorus in 814 (following Pepin's ill-fated attack on Venice) between the Western and Eastern Emperors put Venice firmly within Byzantium's sphere. About thirty years later, in 840, Doge Pietro Tradonico (836-864) and the

Pietro *Orseolo II*
XXVI *Doge* *di Venezia*

The successful Doge Pietro Orseolo II (991–1009)

Holy Roman Emperor Lothair concluded the Pact of Lothair (*Pactum Lotharii*). Besides confirming that the Holy Roman Empire had no claims on Venice, this agreement also recognized the Venetian Doge's freedom to conclude alliances and otherwise freely interact with the Byzantine Empire on his own terms.

The delicate diplomatic balancing act between the two superpowers of the day was carried out with marvellous aplomb by Doge Pietro Orseolo II. The Doge strengthened the already cordial relations between Venice and the Western Empire by arranging the marriage of a son to the sister-in-law of the Holy Roman Emperor. But the crowning event of Doge Pietro's 'Western' diplomacy was the visit to Venice of the Holy Roman Emperor Otto III himself, in 1001 (an event commemorated, considerably after the fact, in a painting in the Church of San Zaccaria by the early eighteenth-century artist G. A. Fumiani).

The reasons for the young Emperor's visit, conducted moreover in conspiratorial secrecy, are still not clearly understood. Emperor Otto, who was known to have been an admirer of Venice, was famous for a strong mystical religiosity. He might have wanted to go to Venice partially to cement the Empire's alliance with the Republic as part of his ongoing attempts to subjugate Italy (he had been forced to flee Rome in February 1001 after an uprising there), or he might simply have wanted to see the city's many famous shrines and churches, including the nearly completed Basilica of St Mark. Whatever the case, Otto's visit was indeed conducted in secret, and we have no record of what sorts of discussions he and Doge Pietro might have had. Nevertheless, Otto was apparently deeply impressed by what he saw and released Venice from its annual tribute obligations (a robe of state and fifty pounds of silver) which had been in force since the days of Emperor Otto the Great (936-973). Although Otto III died of some illness (probably smallpox) while trying to retake Rome in January 1002, his successor, Henry the Holy, turned out to be equally well disposed towards Venice. Besides confirming all of Venice's commercial privileges in the Western Empire, he also confirmed Doge Pietro as 'Duke of Venice and Dalmatia'. Thus, Venetian relations with the Holy Roman Empire not only remained quite friendly, but Venetian merchants gained valuable rights and privileges in Imperial territory, all the better to market the increasing volume of spices, silk, and other valuables acquired in the Levant.

While working to secure Venice's position relative to the Holy Roman Empire, Doge Pietro was also scrupulously careful to portray himself as a loyal ally of the Byzantine Empire. After his victories in Dalmatia, for example, he went out of his way to acknowledge that the territory was the legal possession of the Emperor Basil II (known as the 'the Bulgar Slayer' for his victories over the Bulgarians). Doge Pietro even arranged for his son Giovanni to marry the Emperor's niece, Princess Maria Argyra. Although some Venetians were disgusted by the princess's decadent habits (such as eating with a fork and regular bathing in rainwater), the marriage, coming right after the diplomatic triumphs with the Western Empire and the military victories over the Dalmatians and Saracens, brought Doge Pietro to the peak of his career. He seemed so confident and proud that some Venetians began to fear that he might try, like the Galbaii or Antenori had done before him, to establish a dynasty.

Their fears turned out to be unfounded. In the autumn of 1005, a comet appeared in the night sky signalling, as everyone knows, coming misfortunes. A famine followed, which affected not only the Veneto, but also Venice's Dalmatian breadbasket. The famine had scarcely ended when some sort of plague killed hundreds of Venetians, including Giovanni, his Byzantine wife, and their infant son. Doge Pietro, though still a relatively young man (he was in his late forties), seems to have lost the will to live. He designated his third son, Otto (named after the late Emperor), acting Doge, and shut himself up in a wing of the palace. He was dead within two years.

THE RISE AND FALL OF THE DYNASTIC DOGES

The fears that some Venetians had entertained about the dynastic ambitions of Pietro Orseolo II were certainly not without foundation. Since the time of the first Doges the emerging Venetian political order had exhibited a number of serious tensions. None was perhaps so fierce, and of such longevity, as the question of the actual nature of the Doges' rule. From the time of the very first Doges they had ruled in concert with the Tribunes and other important members of the community. The Tribunes held their own places by virtue of heredity, but the Doge was originally regarded as an elected officer. Almost immediately, however, the Doges tried to convert their office into a hereditary one. The fate of the dynastically minded Galbaii had certainly not ended the desire among many of the Venetian nobility to establish themselves as hereditary Dukes of the lagoon.

After the fall of the Galbaii, the next major attempt at establishing something like hereditary rule in Venice began in 932 with the election of Pietro Candiano whose family was to dominate Venice (with only short interruptions) for the next forty-four years. The Candiani were a powerful, charismatic, and ambitious family. The four Candiani Doges, all of them named Pietro, had distinguished careers as soldiers, and diplomats (and, of course, merchants) before being elected Doges. By far the most enigmatic, and ultimately destructive, of them all was the fourth and last Pietro Candiano.

His father had made him joint ruler in 942, thus ensuring that he would be elected the next Doge. But the younger Candiano, while probably as shrewd and ambitious as his father, also showed himself to be a far less subtle politician. He began to amass increasing power for himself, and eventually his gangs of supporters battled in the streets with rivals, even with those of his own father. The situation became so chaotic that the community's leaders decided to send the younger Pietro into exile.

For the next several years Pietro lived as a soldier of fortune in Italy, gaining a reputation as a cunning and audacious adventurer. He eventually even became a pirate preying upon Venice's ships. He never forgot, however, what he considered his hereditary right to the office of Doge. In 959 when his father died, the electors met and, quite unexpectedly, invited Pietro to return to Venice as the next Doge! Perhaps they reasoned that Pietro would be less of a threat to their security if they elected him Doge, thus making him subject to the increasing web of restrictions that the councils were weaving around the Doges, than if they left him to his increasingly daring piratical exploits.

If this was the reasoning of the leading figures of Venetian society, they turned out to be gravely mistaken. Pietro Candiano IV had no intention of governing under any restrictions at all. He quickly moved to consolidate his own hold on power by appointing his son Patriarch of Grado (second only to the Doge himself in economic and political, to say nothing of ecclesiastical, power). He also found himself, as a result of a controversial marriage, ruler of a considerable territory on the mainland. Rather than turn these lands over to Venice itself, as was expected, he kept them instead as his personal fiefs, from which he even raised a private army.

His increasingly high-handed and dictatorial attitude had already created a deep feeling of foreboding among many Venetians when, in the summer of 976, he overplayed his hand. In response to a threat to his mainland fiefs, he tried to get the Republic to mount a defence of them at public expense. For the already exasperated Venetians, such audacity was too much to bear. A riot in front of the Palace quickly turned into a fully fledged revolt. Doge Pietro defended himself in the Palace as best he could, but the besiegers eventually set fire to it, starting an inferno that ended up destroying most of the building, St

Mark's Basilica, and much of the surrounding neighbourhood. In the meantime, Doge Pietro, along with his wife and infant son, attempted to escape through the smoke and flames but they were caught in the atrium of the basilica. His wife somehow managed to escape, but Pietro and his son were killed by the mob.

The dramatic end of the last of the Candiani Doges was followed by a reaction. The people of Venice had had enough of the brilliant and charismatic, but also ambitious and outrageous, Candiani. As their next Doge they elected a dour and ascetic, but also wealthy, merchant named Pietro Orseolo (976-978). During his two-year reign he tried to rebuild the ravaged city and heal the rifts caused by the Candiani. To help pay for the massive restoration projects he instituted the first of many tithes, while also spending huge sums out of his personal fortune. As part of the rebuilding of St Mark's Basilica (reconsecrated in 978) he ordered an altar screen, the famous *pala d'oro*, from Constantinople.

But in a very short time Doge Pietro Orseolo I seems to have become disenchanted with his role as Doge. This was hardly any wonder, since as public resentment mounted against the tithe, rumours began to circulate that he had personally engineered the end of the Candiani for his own benefit. In September 978, his son-in-law, Giovanni Morosini, helped him to leave Venice in disguise (in the process abandoning his wife and child), and he made his way to the monastery of a friend located in the far-off French Pyrenees, where he lived for the rest of his life. Centuries later, in 1731, Doge Pietro Orseolo I became the first republican head of state to be canonized.

Despite, or perhaps because of, Pietro Orseolo's career, the Venetians seemed to want another calm, competent Doge. In 979 they elected just such a man, Tribuno Memmo (also known as Menio). He was known for his peaceful and gentle nature, as well as for his accomplishments as a horticulturalist. Although a son-in-law of the murdered Pietro Candiano IV, he declared a general amnesty for all those associated with that Doge's assassination. He was also, incidentally, related by marriage to the Morosini family. When Giovanni Morosini returned to Venice from the Pyrenees in 982, he asked Doge Memmo for land on which to establish a monastery. The Doge offered the

Island of Cypresses, across from the Ducal Palace, which subsequently became the island of San Giorgio Maggiore.

Although it seems that Doge Memmo tried his best to quell the endemic quarrelling and in-fighting in Venetian high-society, he was eventually hounded out of office and retired to live out his days in the monastery of San Zaccaria. Memmo was succeeded by Pietro Orseolo II, whose brilliant (if ultimately tragic) career we have already encountered. As noted above, Doge Pietro designated his son Otto as his successor, and when Pietro died in 1008, Otto (sometimes known as Ottone) became, at sixteen, the youngest Doge in Venice's history. Otto turned out to be much like the other members of his illustrious family, especially in his love of pomp and power, and he further advanced his dynastic ambitions by marrying the daughter of the Hungarian King Istvan. Doge Otto Orseolo wasted little time in his efforts to secure his family's position. Between 1017 and 1026 he engaged in a number of highly questionable activities, including the appointments of his brothers Orso and Vitale as Patriarch of Grado and Bishop of Torcello, respectively. These shenanigans worried the patricians of Venice who engineered a *coup d'état* in 1026 that sent Otto off into exile in Constantinople.

The new Doge, Pietro Centranico, immediately faced a number of domestic and international crises. Otto's brothers Orso and Vitale, who between them controlled most of the Venetian clergy, plotted to retrieve their brother from his exile in Constantinople. Internationally, the situation was even more dangerous. Otto's Hungarian in-laws were furious and invaded Venetian-dominated Dalmatia with the aid of Otto's son Peter, who lived in Hungary (and, by the way, eventually succeeded King Istvan to the Hungarian throne). Otto's excellent relationship with the Byzantine Emperor also paid off as the Empire abrogated a number of commercial treaties previously negotiated with Otto's father.

Doge Pietro Centranico, overwhelmed by these challenges, abdicated in 1032. Although Orso and Vitale began preparations for their brother's restoration, news soon reached them that Otto, who had been ill for some time, had died. In the resulting confusion, another member of the family, Domenico Orseolo, mounted a coup and held power for about twenty-four hours before being overthrown. Patriarch Orso, by the way, who had ruled as Doge for several months after Centranico's abdication, dutifully left the Ducal Palace and returned to his ecclesiastical duties as soon as he found out his brother Otto had died. He turned out to be the last Patriarch to reign from Grado. After his death in 1045 the patriarchal office was moved to Venice where it occupied several sites before finally being combined (as we have already noted), in 1451, with the Bishopric of Castello, thus creating the Patriarchate of Venice.

In the meantime, the patricians and citizens of Venice had finally had enough of dynastically minded Doges. The pyrotechnic end of the Candiani followed by Domenico Orseolo's outrageous coup attempt apparently deeply shocked the Venetians. They elected as the next Doge a wealthy silk merchant, known for his anti-dynastic views, named Domenico Flabanico. Historians of Venetian history regard his election as a milestone marking the end of hereditary rule by various ducal families (such as the Candiani and Orseoli) and the beginning of the development of the quasi-democratic oligarchy that was to rule the Republic for the next seven centuries.

The reigns of Flabanico and his successor, Domenico Contarini (1043-1071) were, in general, peaceful and prosperous. Under the latter, St Mark's Basilica began its third (and final) major reconstruction (finally completed in 1094). But before the century had ended, the Venetians were faced with one of their most serious challenges, and ended up achieving one of their greatest triumphs.

The Norman Menace and the Golden Bull

By the late eleventh century Norman princes captured Sicily from the Muslims. While this event struck a blow at the piratical activities of the Saracen corsairs, the Normans turned out to be a far greater threat to the growing power of Venice than the Muslims had ever been. The ruler of Norman Sicily, Robert Guiscard ('the Crafty'), soon embarked on an ambitious plan of conquest in southern Italy, Dalmatia, and Albania. While he clearly wished to build an empire in this region, he might well have been contemplating the ultimate seizure of the Byzantine Empire itself. By 1081, Robert, aided by his son Bohemond, had captured Bari, Amalfi, Salerno, and was in the process of attacking Durazzo (modern Durres), the Adriatic terminus of an ancient Roman highway that led to Constantinople. Robert had also stirred up Dalmatia (only, it will be remembered, just barely pacified by the Venetians), and, in fact, had many Dalmatian sailors in his fleet.

The new Byzantine Emperor Alexius I Comnenos (1081-1118), confronted by the Normans in the west and a Turkish invasion in the east, appealed to the Venetians for help against the former. The Venetians, their own interests in serious jeopardy, responded vigorously and sent a large fleet under the personal command of Doge Domenico Selvo (1071-1084) to relieve the Norman siege of Durazzo, in co-ordination with a Byzantine army advancing overland.

The Venetians encountered the Norman fleet at Durazzo and won a decisive victory, in which Bohemond himself was nearly killed. The Venetians employed all sorts of ingenious tactics in the battle. For example, they hoisted small rowing boats (filled with archers who were able to fire down onto the Norman decks), high up in the spars and masts of their large ships. They also constructed a variety of heavy missile weapons made of huge blocks of wood studded with nails with which they were able to smash holes in some of the Norman ships.

Although the Norman fleet was beaten, their army managed to defeat the Byzantine relief force and to take Durazzo anyway. The Venetians would not let the Normans rest, however, and fought several more, admittedly indecisive, naval engagements with them off the coast of Corfu. In 1085, however, Robert the Crafty died (at age seventy) and his followers, exhausted from the years of inconclusive warfare, abandoned their quest for an Adriatic empire.

In the meantime, Emperor Alexius was so impressed by the Venetian support against the Normans that he issued the famous Golden Bull (or *Chrysobull)* of 1082. By its provisions, Venetian merchants were given the right to trade, free from tariffs or tolls, throughout the entire Byzantine Empire. The Venetian colony in Constantinople received further concessions, including anchorages on the Golden Horn, and the right to operate a bakery and to maintain warehouses. Thus, by the dawn of the twelfth century, the Venetians not only secured their mastery of the Adriatic, but also gained commercial privileges in the Byzantine Empire which, in fact, put them in a better position than the Emperor's own subjects. Building on these two strengths, the Venetians went on to establish themselves as the foremost naval and commercial power in the eastern Mediterranean. They were aided tremendously in these endeavours by the eruption of the Crusades.

CHAPTER THREE

The Crusades
1095–1261

By the end of the eleventh century Venice had become a major commercial power in the eastern Mediterranean. The victories against pirates, Normans, and Arabs had secured its maritime routes and had also increased its independence from its nominal suzerain, the Byzantine Emperor. The twelfth century would witness the birth of the Venetian Empire and its rise to the status of the dominant commercial, political, and military power of the entire Levant.

The First Crusade

Even as Venice was aiding its master the Byzantine Emperor against the Normans in the Adriatic and western Balkans, a far greater threat to the Byzantines was taking shape in eastern Asia Minor. In 1071 a Byzantine army was utterly defeated by the Seljuk Turkish Sultan Alp Arslan. With this victory, Muslim Turkish colonization of Asia Minor, a process that changed the eastern Mediterranean forever, began. The panicked Byzantines appealed for help to the Western Empire. Through a long series of complex events that had as much to do with the politics of the Popes and Western temporal rulers as anything going on in the East, the Byzantine Emperor's appeal for help ultimately culminated with Pope Urban II's preaching of the First Crusade in 1095.

Although crusading fever quickly swept through most of western Christendom, the people of Venice found themselves in a rather difficult situation. War was not, in general, good for trade and the Venetians had always used their gifts for diplomacy in an effort to stay on good terms with their neighbours, and their Muslim neighbours most of all.

The Venetian government was reluctant to get involved in the crusading movement at all, and eventually became a participant, not out of any zeal for the Cross, or hatred of Muslims, but because its two main mercantile rivals, Pisa and Genoa, saw in the Crusades an excellent opportunity to seize from Venice a lucrative share in the treasures of the East. Similarly, the Venetians eventually decided that they needed to get involved in the wars of the crusaders because of their peculiar relationship with the Byzantine Empire. While the Venetians felt no particular love for the Greeks (and vice versa), the Venetian government generally pursued a policy of 'protecting' the Byzantine Empire against the depredations of other powers, Christian and Muslim alike. While the Venetians certainly did not hesitate to fight the Byzantines when they felt it necessary, they much preferred to maintain the Byzantine Empire intact so that they could extract as many concessions as possible from it through their various monopolistic trading privileges.

THE BATTLE OF RHODES AND THE BODY OF ST NICK

The first several years of the Crusades gave a good indication of the attitude of the Venetians toward the crusaders' enterprise. The new Doge, Vitale Michiel I (1096-1102), waited until after the Franks had taken Jerusalem in 1099, massacring the Muslim and Jewish population in the process, to launch an expedition of 200 ships commanded by his son Giovanni. The Bishop of Venice, Enrico Contarini (son of the former Doge Domenico Contarini) accompanied the expedition.

The decision to dispatch a fleet was probably due less to Venice's hostility to Muslims (of which there seems to have been relatively little) than to her growing suspicions toward her commercial rivals the Pisans and Genoese. The former, especially, had wasted no time in sending a flotilla to the Levant. It was, of course, supposed to be part of Christendom's vanguard against the Muslim occupiers of the Holy Land, but in fact it spent most of its time engaging in piracy against the Byzantines. As early as 1098 the Pisans had, for example, seized the strategically located Byzantine island of Corfu.

The Venetians soon found an opportunity to take care of these rivals. While wintering at the island of Rhodes in 1099, Giovanni

Michiel's fleet encountered the Pisans, on their way to the Levant from Corfu. The Venetians reckoned that eliminating these upstarts would be more profitable than attacking Muslims. In the ensuing battle, the Venetians won a great victory, capturing twenty Pisan ships and about 4,000 prisoners. More importantly, they made the Pisans promise to quit the waters of the eastern Mediterranean once and for all.

Flushed with victory, the Venetians decided to add yet another triumph to their crusading adventure. They were, however, still in no hurry to do battle with the Muslims. Instead, the Venetian crusaders decided that this would be an excellent opportunity to add to the growing collection of holy relics in their home city.

Bishop Enrico, accompanying the Venetian expedition, dearly wished to get the body of St Nicholas of Myra (the very 'St Nicholas' of Father Christmas or Santa Claus fame) for the church on the Lido used by many of Venice's sailors. The relic of St Nicholas, as the patron of both sailors and merchants, would obviously be a valuable addition to the other relics already piling up in the churches of Venice. And in fact, the ensuing 'translation' of the body of St Nicholas is clearly parallel to the story of St Mark's arrival in Venice over two centuries earlier.

Conveniently for Bishop Enrico and the Venetians, Myra was a coastal city (not far from the modern Turkish city of Kas). When the Venetians arrived they made their way to St Nicholas' church. The resident clerics, however, had some bad news for these eager relic-hunters. It turned out that they were too late: the saint's body had already been stolen by a group of sailors from Bari (one of Venice's maritime rivals). Bishop Enrico did not believe this tale for a moment, however, and prayed fervently that the body might be discovered. Naturally, his prayers were answered immediately and he found a secret tomb in the church occupied by the body of St Nicholas, as fresh as the day it was buried. The party straight away packed up the corpse (rounding out their collection with the body of St Theodore, which also happened to be in the church) and returned to their ship. Unfortunately for the Venetians, however, it later turned out that a party from Bari really had beaten Bishop Enrico to St Nicholas' body in Myra, and had in the meantime entombed it in a church in their own city. This did not seem to trouble the Venetians overmuch, however. Bishop Enrico and the rest of the Venetian clerical establishment confidently proclaimed that they, and not the people of Bari, had the genuine relic, and so the body of St Nicholas (or whosoever's body it actually was) was duly ensconced in the church of San Nicolò di Lido. The church and the relic of St Nicholas quickly became a centre of devotion second only to the Basilica of St Mark. As Gary Wills observed, with both Saints Mark *and* Nicholas as their protectors, Venice's merchants and sailors felt that they had nothing to fear. Incidentally, the relic of St Theodore (who, it will be remembered, was the patron saint of Venice before Mark's relic arrived in 828), was eventually placed in the church of San Salvador and became an important place of devotion in its own right.

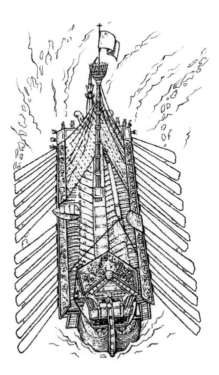

In the meantime, the Venetians were at last on their way to wrest the Holy Land from the infidels. They arrived just in time to help the crusaders seize the city of Haifa, although they do not seem to have taken part in the wholesale massacre of the city's Muslims and Jewish population that followed. Their Christian duty accomplished, their Pisan rivals chastened, and their ships full of treasure, the Venetian fleet returned to Venice in time for St Nicholas' Day, 1100.

Over the next century the Venetian navy was engaged, off and on, in the crusading struggle against the Muslims of the Levant. In the course of these adventures, the Republic acquired its Empire. For example, in gratitude for Venetian help in taking the city of Sidon in 1110, King Baldwin of Jerusalem granted Venice control over part of the port city of Acre, as well as extensive trading privileges throughout the Kingdom of Jerusalem. In 1123, the Venetians destroyed the Egyptian navy in the Battle of Ascalon, thus eliminating Muslim maritime power in the eastern Mediterranean (for the time being), and the next year assisted the crusaders in their conquest of Tyre, of which the Venetians were granted a third.

Besides the actions against the Muslims, the Venetians also found themselves engaged in a series of inconclusive battles with the Hungarians over the control of Dalmatia. While Doge Ordelafo Falier died in 1118 fighting the Hungarians for control of Zara (modern Zadar), Doge Domenico Michiel (1118-1130) added to his many other triumphs by capturing Spalato (Split) while on his way home from the Levant in 1124. The Venetians also became involved for the first time in serious political and military activities on the Italian mainland. In 1141 the little city of Fano, beset by hostile neighbours, more-or-less willingly put itself under the 'protection' of the Lion of St Mark and became a tributary of the Republic. A short while later, in 1143, the Venetians fought a brief war with Padua when that city refused to give up its attempts to redirect the course of the Brenta River, which flows into the Venetian lagoon. This conflict was the first completely land-based war in Venetian history. Significantly for the conduct of future land warfare, the Venetians relied exclusively on mercenaries. These events also signalled the first, tentative forays of the growing Venetian Empire into the complex and dangerous world of northern

Italian politics. By 1167, the Venetians had allied themselves with the Lombard League against the ambitious Holy Roman Emperor, Frederick Barbarossa.

But for the time being, these events were overshadowed by the intensifying hostilities between the Venetians and their supposed allies, the Byzantines. While sometimes allying themselves with the Empire (when the Normans, Genoese or some other power seemed about to take control of Byzantine territory) the Venetians themselves increasingly plundered Byzantine coastal towns and ships. For example, as Doge Domenico Michiel (the victor at Ascalon), led his fleet back to Venice in 1124, his men freely looted several Greek islands. Upon their return to the lagoon, their fleet actually had more booty from the lands of their Byzantine 'ally' than from those of the Muslim 'enemy'. Among the spoils were yet more relics, perhaps the most prized treasures of all, including the body of St Donatus (subsequently laid to rest in his church on Murano).

THE END OF THE 'ROYAL DOGES'

As relations with the Byzantines continued to deteriorate, in March 1171, the Byzantine Emperor Manuel Comnenus arrested all of the Venetians in his Empire that could be found and confiscated their property. In Constantinople alone, ten thousand Venetians were arrested. Doge Vitale Michiel II (1156-1172) immediately organized an expedition against the Byzantines. To help pay for this venture, the city was organized into six districts (the *sestieri* which exist to this day) each of which was obliged to come up with a particular sum of money. With remarkable speed, the Venetians were able to dispatch a fleet of 120 ships under the command of the Doge in September 1171. The strategy was to ravage the Byzantine coast until the Emperor came to his senses and agreed to compensate the Venetians for their losses. Doge Vitale, however, was too concerned about the fate of the thousands of imprisoned Venetians (who were, after all, hostages) to do too much damage to Byzantine property. Instead, he tried to negotiate some sort of solution to the crisis. All through the winter of 1171 his lieutenants (including the future Doge Enrico Dandolo) engaged in interminable discussions in Constantinople with the Byzantine officials while Doge Vitale and his fleet spent the winter on the island of Chios. In the meantime, however, some sort of epidemic broke out in his fleet and by springtime thousands were dead or dying. To make matters even worse, Dandolo and the other ambassadors finally returned from Constantinople to report that they had gained nothing and that the 'negotiations' had in fact been a complete sham. Doge Vitale, it turns out, had fallen into the Byzantine Emperor's trap. With what was left of his crew on the verge of mutiny, he had no choice but to return, humiliated, to Venice.

When he arrived in Venice in May 1172, 'bringing pest instead of plunder' (in the words of historian Frederic Lane), patricians and commoners alike were infuriated. As the tempers of the nobility listening to his story inside the Ducal Palace grew more heated, Doge Vitale apparently decided to risk the wrath of the mob outside and fled. He slipped out of the Palace and tried to reach the safety of the convent of San Zaccaria by way of the Ponte della Paglia. He almost made it to the sanctuary of the convent, but was stabbed by someone in the mob while running through the Calle delle Rasse. Despite the anger of the patricians toward Doge Vitale, such a crime could not go unpunished. The murderer was executed and his house destroyed. For good measure, the government decreed that no stone building should ever be built on the spot where the criminal's house had stood. This order was honoured until 1948 when the new annexe of the Danieli Royal Excelsior Hotel was built on the site. Up to that time, modest old houses of wood, brick, and plaster had nestled for centuries in amongst the grand stone buildings of the neighbourhood.

To be fair, it should perhaps here be noted that besides the epidemic and the terrible news about his mission, Doge Vitale did, in fact, bring back some loot and other assorted trophies, among the most famous of which were three classical columns. With his seemingly endless supply of bad luck, the Doge dropped one of these into the baccino, where it lies buried in the muck to this day. The other two were raised on the Molo and were eventually topped with the statues of St Theodore and the Lion of St Mark. These statues are quite interesting in their own rights. The statue of St Theodore now on display is a copy (the original is in a courtyard in the nearby Palazzo). The original statue, erected in 1329, is a hodgepodge of bits and pieces of ancient and fourteenth-century statuary. The origins of the lion statue, which is about 4.5 metres (fifteen feet) long, are equally obscure. It was in Venice at least as early as 1293 (at which time some restoration work was performed on it) but the statue itself is certainly much older. Its origins are mysterious, though most scholars now believe that its original home was Cilicia (in southern Turkey) where it was cast around 300 BCE. The wings and open gospel on which it rests its paws were added some time after it arrived in Venice.

With the reign of Doge Vitale Michiel II, the era of the 'Royal Doges' came to an end. The powers of the Doges were more and more circumscribed as the patricians took increasing control of the government. In particular, the powers of the *aregno*, the ancient assembly theoretically made up of all the adult males of Venice, were severely curtailed. Most of its powers were handed over to a new body of 480 important Venetians, called the *Maggior Consiglio*, or Great Council. The nobles also increased the number of the Doge's inner council of advisors from two to six, the better to monitor the Doge's activities. These six advisors and the Doge himself together formed a kind of cabinet, called the *Signoria*. The nobles furthermore increased the power of another council, called the *Pregadi* or Senate, which came to function as a kind of ministry of foreign affairs. These changes established the constitutional foundations for the oligarchical government that eventually came to rule the Republic.

The Rebuilding of Venice and the Growth of the Guilds

Already a major commercial power, Venice had become by the early twelfth century, an imperial power as well. Changes in the city itself, especially during the reigns of Doges Ordelafo Falier (1102-1118), Domenico Michiel (1118-1130), and Sebastiani Ziani (1172-1178) reflected this transformation.

One of the most important of these changes, the use of brick and stone in architecture instead of wood, occurred (at least in part) as the result of the natural catastrophes of the year 1106. In January of that year Venice experienced, for not the first time in its history, a horrible flood. It was so severe that it obliterated the ancient town of Malamocco on the Lido, along with many of its inhabitants. The survivors eventually returned to the Lido and built the present village of Malamocco on the western, more protected, shore.

No sooner had the Venetians recovered from the floods, however, than they were faced with a catastrophic fire which destroyed much of the city. The fire was so fierce in spots that there are reports that the flames actually leapt across the Grand Canal. In the aftermath of this holocaust, the Venetian government embarked on an ambitious rebuilding programme in which red bricks and Istrian white stone were used instead of the previously ubiquitous wood. These subsequently became the favoured construction materials in Venice.

As the rebuilding projects continued, Doge Domenico Michiel issued a decree that resulted in Europe's first street lighting system, providing Venetians a degree of nocturnal comfort and security unknown elsewhere. By the early twelfth century, more and more of the popular little shrines (*ancone*) at street intersections or by gondola piers dedicated to the Virgin Mary or a local patron saint, were being erected. Doge Domenico decreed in 1128 that every evening all of the *ancone* in the city were to be lit by lamps at government expense. Venice thus became perhaps the first city in Europe to provide a kind of public street lighting.

Near the end of the century, Doge Ziani undertook a major reconstruction of the area around St Mark's Basilica. The area now covered by the Piazza San Marco was, when Ziani became Doge, bisected by a canal (the Rio Batario) which ran right in front of the basilica. There was also an orchard there owned by the convent of San Zaccaria. Ziani ordered that the canal be filled in, the orchard cut down, and the entire area paved, thus creating the Piazza. Ziani also oversaw an expansion of the Ducal Palace (although the exact nature of this work is not known) as well as a redevelopment of the Piazzetta which included the destruction of the ancient sea wall built by Pietro Tribuno in the early tenth century.

It was as a part of this century of urban reconstruction, as well as a reflection of Venice's newly awakened imperial ambitions, that con-

struction on the Arsenal began in 1104 under the direction of Doge
Ordelafo Falier. Doge Ordelafo (whose strange name, by the way,
seems to be a palindrome of one version of his family name: Faledro)
picked a marshy, underdeveloped area in the eastern end of the city as
the site for a vast complex to be called the Arsenal (derived from the
Arabic *Dar al-Sin`a*, 'Place of Industry', or 'House of Construction').
The Arsenal was, until the late thirteenth century, used mainly as a sort
of naval warehouse to store oars, rigging, and weapons, and as a repair
shop for galleys. Most shipbuilding was carried out, under strict governmental regulations and supervision, at private shipyards scattered
throughout the lagoon. Since ancient times, Mediterranean ship
builders had constructed their crafts from the keel upwards of carefully notched and fitted boards. The Venetian shipwrights pioneered a
new method of ship construction, introducing rib-and-plank construction in which a frame or skeleton was constructed first and then
covered with planks. This method, which subsequently became the
most common means of building wooden ships, was not only much
faster than the old process, but also made standardization of design
much easier.

The surge in construction and other sorts of economic activity led
to several important developments in the organization of the work-
place in Venice. Since early times, certain craftsmen such as glass makers, jewellers, and weavers, were grouped in loose organizations bound
together by a set of rules important to the functioning of their craft.
In 1173, Doge Ziani set up three government officials, called the
Justices (*Giustizieri*) with the responsibility of regulating and supervis-
ing the growing numbers of craftsmen and shopkeepers. In particular,
the Justices were supposed to supervise the standardization of weights
and measures. During the same period, many of the (increasingly well-
off) tradesmen banded together in religious fraternities called *scuole*.
These were mainly self-help organizations and mutual aid societies.
The members usually also worshipped together at a particular chapel,
or at an altar in a larger church. For example, the charming little
church of San Giovanni Elemosinario near the Rialto market has several altars dedicated to different craftsmen and merchants who operated in the area (among them, the *gallineri* [dealers in poultry], and the

biavaroli [fodder merchants]). Although the present church, and its contents, all date from after 1530, a church dedicated to San Giovanni Elemosinario has stood on the same spot since at least 1071, if not earlier, and there is every reason to believe that it was long a place of devotion and worship for the workers and craftsmen in the nearby Rialto market.

By the end of the twelfth century, some of the *scuole* had come to attract members from one particular trade or craft. These evolved into guilds. They maintained their earlier functions as charities and mutual-aid societies, but also established rules regulating working conditions and the quality of the products or services provided by the members of the guild. Some of the earliest recorded guilds were those of the tailors, goldsmiths, dyers, coopers, cordage makers, and barbers (which included also surgeons and physicians). By the middle of the thirteenth century, there were more than one hundred different guilds. Significantly, however, the functioning of the guilds, including all of their various rules and regulations, were carefully supervised by the three Justices, who could (and did) intervene in the internal workings or regulations of a guild if they determined that its economic or political activities were detrimental to public order or prosperity. It is worth noting that, as in so many other aspects of Venetian society, most of the craftsmen and shopkeepers who made up the *scuole* and guilds did not seem to resent their subordination to the Venetian state. On the contrary, they seemed to embrace, in the words of Frederic Lane, their 'honourable but subordinate position in Venetian society'.

A DIPLOMATIC TRIUMPH

In the midst of these developments, Venice scored a major diplomatic triumph. For over a decade the Holy Roman Emperor Frederick Barbarossa had tried to subdue Italy, defended by the northern Lombard League and the Papacy. Four costly campaigns, culminating in his disastrous defeat in 1176 at Legnano, convinced him that his plans to conquer Italy had to be abandoned and that he needed to reach some sort of understanding with Pope Alexander III. The two agreed to meet in Venice in the Spring of 1177. In the meantime, however, the Pope had already fled with his entourage to Venice where, the story goes, upon his hasty arrival he spent the night in the covered entrance to the Sottoportego della Madonna near the church of Saint Apollinare (or Sant'Aponal in the Venetian dialect). A plaque there marks the spot, and informs the reader that an Our Father and Hail Mary, recited there, will grant a plenary indulgence to the supplicant.

Venice, under Doge Sebastiani Ziani, played (as usual) a very delicate, nuanced, game between the forces of the Papacy and the Italian communes on the one hand, and the Holy Roman Empire on the other. The Empire and the Papacy were potential Venetian allies, balancing Venice's relationship with the Byzantines (and vice versa). In other words, Venetian diplomacy at this (and other times), focused on keeping several potentially hostile powers in a state of benign neutrality toward the Republic. But in this case, Venetian diplomacy surely outdid itself.

On 24 July 1177, Venice hosted the historic meeting (what today might be called a summit) between Pope Alexander and Frederick I Barbarossa. It was attended by most of the political and religious dignitaries of the Italian peninsula. Venetian mediation assured that the Pope and the cities of northern Italy (including Venice itself) were to be free of Imperial control. A moment of high drama occurred when the Emperor knelt before Pope Alexander as a sign of submission. The spot is marked by a white lozenge set into the floor inside the narthex of St Mark's Basilica. Paintings imagining the event (executed much later) can be seen in the chambers of the Council of Ten in the Ducal Palace.

But perhaps the most lasting legacy of the meeting between Pope and Emperor was the story that the Pope presented Doge Ziani with a golden ring with which Venice could 'marry the sea' on Ascension Day. The ceremony itself, as noted in Chapter Two, was certainly very old by the time of the Pope's visit. The Ascension Day trip, made by the Doge and his entourage with much pomp and circumstance, out to the Lido and then into the open sea, dates from at least the year 1000. The original ceremony (which, as Gary Wills points out, is similar to many pagan fertility rituals), in which the Doge cast the ring into the sea, was probably seen as a kind of offering, or a request for protection and aid. But by the late twelfth century, the ceremony, with its obvious nuptial overtones, had taken on the character of a marriage in which Venice dominated the sea as a husband dominated his wife.

Unfortunately, there is absolutely no evidence that the Pope presented a ring to Doge Ziani, thereby changing the character of the ceremony. However, the development of this ceremony into a quasi-matrimonial rite might well have been finalized around the late twelfth century, right around the time of Pope Alexander's visit. The legend, therefore, might have been invented to explain the sacramental underpinnings of these nautical nuptials.

The Fourth Crusade

By the end of the twelfth century, therefore, Venice had became a major political power in Western Christendom. Many Venetian merchants, however, still felt themselves thwarted by their rivals the Pisans and Genoese. Perhaps more importantly, relations with the Byzantine Empire had gone from bad to worse. The Venetian oligarchy perceived, quite correctly, that the Byzantine Emperor was trying to counter Venice's growing influence by granting privileges to her Italian mercantile rivals. As already noted, Venetian-Byzantine relations reached a new low in 1171, and it was not until 1189 that they were patched up. Even so, feelings between the two parties remained quite hostile. This growing conflict resolved itself in a way that characterized the increasingly audacious and opportunistic spirit of the Venetian Republic. The Venetians would 'resolve' their troubled relationship with their supposed suzerain by conquering the Byzantine Empire itself.

In 1199, Count Tibald of Champagne decided to launch a fourth Crusade to retake Jerusalem. He and his (mainly French) knights decided to enlist the services of the Venetians to provide transport to the Holy Land. Arriving in Venice in the summer of 1202 to negotiate the terms, and completely bedazzled by the city's surreal grandeur, the crusaders allowed themselves to be bamboozled by the Republic's officials into contracting for a number of ships far in excess of what they could pay. To make matters even more interesting, the stalwart crusaders found, when they were finally about to embark, that they had rather inconveniently spent all of their money enjoying Venice's many attractions (an uncomfortable situation familiar to many modern tourists as well). The Venetian government was very sympathetic and agreed to speed the crusaders on their holy way free of charge, provided, of course, that the knights were willing to exchange this good turn by helping the Venetians tie up some territorial loose ends. The Venetian fleet with its cargo of crusaders finally set sail on 8 October 1202. It was an immense flotilla of 480 ships. Doge Enrico Dandolo, eighty-years old and almost blind (completely blind according to some accounts), sailed with the fleet while Boniface of Montferrat commanded the crusaders in the wake of Count Tibald's untimely death. On its way to Palestine, the Venetian fleet stopped at several contested locations, among them Zara, Durazzo, and Corfu, each seized in turn by the crusaders on behalf of their Venetian allies. Paintings imagining the conquest of Zara by Andrea Vicentino and Domenico Tintoretto (the son of Jacopo) can be seen in the Hall of the Great Council in the Ducal Palace.

The conquest of these chunks of real estate had gone so well that Dandolo decided that this would be the perfect opportunity to settle matters with the Byzantines once and for all. Instead of sailing to Palestine, the Venetian fleet made for Constantinople. Doge Dandolo had made sure not only to have an army, but also to have something of a justification for his obviously bellicose arrival in the city. The Venetians had with them a pretender to the Byzantine throne, Prince Alexius Angelus, as well as the Prince's brother-in-law, Philip of Swabia. They were both in favour of diverting the fleet to Constantinople and it seems hardly coincidental that they had been part of the fleet from the very beginning of the Crusade. Indeed, their presence is a strong indication that Dandolo and at least some of his lieutenants had planned on attacking Constantinople all along.

On 26 June 1203, the fleet arrived at Constantinople. When Alexius' efforts at gaining the throne through discussion with the Byzantines failed, a general attack on the city commenced, led by Doge Enrico and Boniface. The city walls thwarted all attempts by the attackers to take the city until the Venetians hit upon the stratagem of beaching their galleys hard upon the walls along the Golden Horn, and then using their ships' masts and spars as bridges to attack the walls. Aided by a general uprising in the city, the Venetians were victorious and Alexius became the new Emperor. The crusaders and Venetians withdrew to quarters north of the Golden Horn and anxiously awaited their promised reward from Alexius.

The situation quickly deteriorated, however, as Alexius and his advisors grew nervous as to the intentions of his erstwhile supporters, especially as the demands of the Venetians and the crusaders for compensation for their assistance grew increasingly vociferous. By January 1204, Alexius was overthrown by a palace faction and soon murdered. The new Emperor, Alexius V Ducas, had no interest at all in dealing with the crusaders or Venetians, and immediately set to work strengthening the city's defences against them. In the face of these developments, Dandolo, who had by now become the *de facto* leader of the Crusade, urged an immediate attack. On 9 April 1204, the Venetians and crusaders again attacked the city, which fell after four days of fierce fighting. Paintings by Domenico Tintoretto and Jacopo Palma il Giovane in the Hall of the Great Council in the Ducal Palace give very dramatic renditions of these events.

This time, Dandolo decided to do without the pretence of a puppet Byzantine Emperor and proclaimed the Byzantine Empire finished. Its place was to be occupied by a 'Latin Empire'. Baldwin of Flanders was elected Latin Emperor of the East by an assortment of crusaders and Venetian noblemen on 10 May 1204. Significantly, Boniface, because of his Genoese sympathies, had been vetoed by the Venetians for this position.

In the meantime, the city was thoroughly sacked as the crusaders and Venetians grabbed virtually everything that was not nailed down (and, indeed, much that was). Even in an age when captured cities were routinely subjected to rape and pillage, the three days following the capture of Constantinople shocked eyewitnesses. One (quoted here by John Julius Norwich) described the looting of the church of St Sophia, one of the grandest in Christendom, carried out by the soldiers of Christ:

They destroyed the high altar, a work of art admired by the entire world, and shared out pieces among themselves...And they brought horses and mules into the Church, the better to carry off the holy vessels and the engraved silver and gold that they had torn from the throne, and the pulpit, and the doors, and the furniture wherever it was to be found...A common harlot was enthroned in the Patriarch's chair, to hurl insults at Jesus Christ; and she sang bawdy songs, and danced immodestly in the holy place...nor was there any mercy shown to virtuous matrons, innocent maids or even virgins consecrated to God...In the streets, houses and churches there could be heard only cries and lamentations.

After three days Boniface (still the titular leader of the Crusade) ordered the loot collected to be divided among the crusaders and Venetians. The resulting sum was valued at a staggering 400,000 silver marks. By way of comparison, the annual income of the King of France at the time was about 43,000 marks. While the crusaders simply destroyed many of the artworks they encountered in order to get

The bronze horses in the Piazza San Marco were brought to Venice in 1204 from Constantinople during the Fourth Crusade. They are of Greek origin, third century BCE

at the precious metals and gems with which they were encrusted, the Venetians at least recognized the incredible craftsmanship and beauty of what they found and tried to steal as much as they could intact. Bits and pieces of the loot can be found all over Venice, sometimes in unlikely places. For example, the beautiful green column in the right transept of the Church of San Giacomo dell'Orto (that so fascinated the nationalist poet Gabriele d'Annunzio many centuries later) was one of the more cumbersome treasures snatched by the opportunistic Venetians. Most of the loot, however, ended up in St Mark's Basilica, either as part of the building's decoration or in its treasury. In addition to the famous horses carted off from the Hippodrome, the Venetians also helped themselves to numerous sacred relics. Among those to be seen to this day in the Basilica's treasury are the arm of St George, a piece of John the Baptist's head, part of the True Cross, and even some of the blood of Jesus Christ.

But the physical looting of much of the wealth of Byzantium was less important than the awesome power Venice gained by this conquest. By the terms of the new treaties between the Latin Empire and the Venetians, the Doge became 'Ruler of a Quarter and a half Quarter of all the Empire of the Romans'. This audacious move translated into Venetian ownership of most of the strategic islands and stretches of mainland in the Aegean Sea, including much of the Peloponnesus. Among the most important territories gained by the Venetians were the ports of Coron and Modon (the 'Eyes of the Republic') on the southern coast of the Peloponnesus, as well as the large islands of Negroponte (modern Euboea) and Crete. Venice even gained territorial rights to three-eighths of the city of Constantinople itself, including the church of St Sophia. As a result of these territorial and political gains, Venice also succeeded in completely ousting its chief opponents, the Pisans and Genoese from any real power in the eastern Mediterranean.

The events of 1204 marked a major turning point in Venetian history. Venetians began to see themselves not merely as another seafaring Italian city state, like their rivals Pisa and Genoa, but as an imperial power. In fact, with the conquest of Byzantium, some Venetians began to think of Venice as a kind of 'Third Rome', and superior both

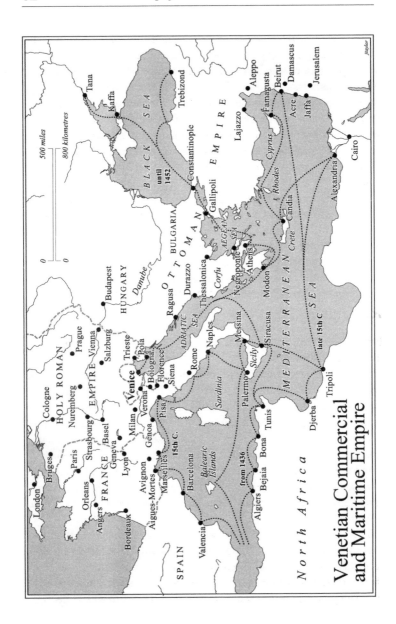

Venetian Commercial and Maritime Empire

to pagan Rome and the decadent, schismatic Byzantium. There is even a legend that the Venetian government considered moving the capital of their Empire to Constantinople. While almost certainly a later fabrication, the story does underline the tremendous psychological importance that was attached to the conquest of the Byzantine Empire. It also hints at the importance of Venice's new territorial possessions in the eastern Mediterranean, many of which were ruled by Venetian noblemen. Among the most famous were the Sanudo family, which ruled the so-called Duchy of Naxos and the Barozzis, who dominated Santorini. Crete was divided among aristocrats and adventurers from Venice who were granted fiefs in return for promises of maintaining security and order on that strategic island. While some feelings of local identity or particularism tied to these territories seem to have developed among the colonists, they nevertheless maintained strong feelings of attachment to the City of Venice.

The First Genoese War and the Byzantine Reconquest

By the middle of the thirteenth century, the Venetians' successes during the Crusades had led to increasing tension with their long-time rivals, the Genoese. In 1257, the first of what were to be several wars between the two maritime powers broke out. The immediate cause for hostilities seems to have been a fight between a Genoese and a Venetian merchant in Acre. In response, Doge Renier Zeno (1253–1268) decided to include a sizeable number of war galleys with the full 'caravan' of ships setting off for the Levant in 1257. The Venetian commander (and future Doge), Lorenzo Tiepolo, outmanoeuvred and outfought the Genoese forces and expelled their colony from Acre. In triumph, Tiepolo brought back two square columns from the Genoese fort in Acre, which now stand beside the Basilica of St Mark.

The Venetians and Genoese adopted different strategies in the ensuing war. The Venetians decided to concentrate on maintaining the security of their merchant shipping routes. Thus, they devoted most of their energy to organizing convoys made up of merchant ships and war galleys. While this system was generally successful, it also tied up most of Venice's warships and thus prevented the Venetians from very actively engaging Genoese fleets or raiding the enemy's well protected colonies. The convoys were also potentially vulnerable if the protecting galleys could be somehow diverted or lured away.

The Genoese strategy was to try just such manoeuvres. Their naval commanders, on occasion, were indeed able to lure the war galleys away from the merchant convoys using various ruses, after which the Venetian ships could be easily plundered. The Genoese also raided Venetian colonies. After several years of such warfare, however, it was plain that neither side could expect to score a major victory over the other. While the Venetian convoys were generally well guarded and usually made it to their destinations, the costs of transporting goods in convoys severely cut into the profits from these ventures.   The Genoese, on the other hand, scored some successes in their raids on Venetian fleets and settlements, but their cut-and-run attacks did not really give them the kind of command of the sea that they would have needed to cripple their Venetian enemies.

In the meantime, the Greek nobility, which had been effectively barred from the exploitation of what was left of the Byzantine Empire in 1204, had largely absconded to territories in western Asia Minor. There, in the city of Nicaea, a nobleman named Lascaris eventually proclaimed himself Emperor and ruled a sort of shadow Byzantine Empire known to historians as the 'Empire of Nicaea'. By the 1260s the Lascarid dynasty was overthrown by another Greek nobleman named Paleologos. Under the direction of this 'Emperor', and with considerable help from the Genoese, the Nicaean forces conquered Constantinople for Greek Orthodoxy in July 1261. The Venetians in Constantinople were declared pirates. About fifty were captured, blinded, and had their noses cut off.

The results of the reconquest were very serious for the Venetians, at least in the short run. The new Paleologian Emperor rather naturally regarded the Venetians as dangerous enemies and revoked all of their trading privileges in what remained of the Byzantine Empire and instead favoured the Genoese. To them was awarded a territory, eventually known as Galata, on the north shore of the Golden Horn, wherein they were allowed to establish an autonomous enclave.

Visitors to modern Istanbul can still visit their most enduring monument, the Galata Tower.

In the long run, however, the Greek reconquest of Constantinople was not as big a disaster as the Venetians initially had feared. The new Byzantine Emperor, Michael VIII Paleologos, soon had second thoughts about the close relationship he had cultivated with the Genoese and gradually invited the Venetians back into his territory as a counter-weight to the Genoese influence. Although they lacked the monopolistic advantages they had earlier enjoyed, Venetian merchants were soon trading throughout the Empire's territories once again. Moreover, the Venetians managed to hang onto most of their territorial holdings in the eastern Mediterranean and Aegean, including the important islands of Negroponte and Crete. The conflict with Genoa which had begun in 1257 was now aggravated further by the re-establishment of Greek rule in Constantinople. The war continued to drag on, with neither side able to win a decisive victory over the other, until 1270. It ended only because King Louis IX of France wanted peace between the two maritime powers in preparation for his Crusade against Egypt. Indeed, he threatened the Genoese with the confiscation of their properties in France unless they agreed to make peace with the Venetians. Thus, the peace treaty between the two maritime powers solved nothing and amounted to little more than a twenty-four-year truce between Venice and Genoa before war broke out again.

CHAPTER FOUR

The Struggle for the Empire
1261–1400

A symbol of Venice's growing power and self-confidence in this period is the famous merchant and adventurer Marco Polo (1254-1324). Between 1271 and 1295, Polo, in the company of his father and uncle, travelled and traded in Central and East Asia. By the time he returned to Venice, Marco Polo had become fabulously wealthy. He was subsequently captured in the war against Genoa, and his captivity gave him the leisure to prepare his now famous memoirs.

While Polo's life does not exactly coincide with the dates covered by this chapter, his experiences nevertheless are symbolic of this period in Venetian history. Historians have argued that after the Greek reconquest of Constantinople in 1261, Venetian interests and especially cultural models, increasingly focused on the other cities of northern Italy. Similarly, Venetian elites began to pay more attention to the Italian *terra firma* during this period. This was also the period in which myths connecting various Venetian patrician families, or even the city itself, with ancient Rome were concocted. On the other hand, the bulk of the Republic's trade and military orientation was still directed overwhelmingly eastward.

Hence, the career of Marco Polo is especially instructive. He was a member of a family involved for many years with long-distance trade in Central Asia and spent a good deal of his life in travels in the area. Upon his return to Venice, he immediately became an important member of society again. Likewise, it is worth noting that he dictated his famous travelogue to a fellow POW in a Genoese prison.

Thus, the period from around 1261 to 1400 was a time of cultural and political flux in Venetian history. Culturally and politically, the Republic was being drawn further into the orbit of the northern

Italian city-states. This was also the period in which the Venetian 'constitution' was reaching its final articulation. The membership in the *Maggior Consiglio* was restricted in 1297 only to those families who had already participated in government. Venice was being transformed from a kind of elected monarchy to an oligarchy of around two hundred leading families.

MONGOLS, MAMLUKS, AND MARCO POLO

Marco Polo's trip to China occurred at a time of flux and confusion, not only for the *Serenissima*, but for most of Eurasia as well. In 1258, the Mongol army of Hulegu Khan, a grandson of Jenghiz Khan, sacked Baghdad and destroyed the Arab Abbasid Caliphate. Most of the Muslim world was subsequently conquered by the pagan Mongols. Their advance into North Africa was halted near the modern Israeli-Egyptian border at Ayn Jalut ('The Spring of Goliath') by a caste of Muslim slave soldiers, called the Mamluks, who had recently established a kind of military dictatorship in Egypt. The Mamluks succeeded in maintaining Muslim control of Syria, Egypt, and western Arabia, including the trade routes across the Red Sea. The Mongol rulers established two rival commercial arteries. One centred on the Persian Gulf, from where the precious cargo of the East Indies was sent overland to Tabriz and then on to Trebizond, on the Black Sea, or to a Mediterranean port called Lajazzo. The other route was an overland caravan route that connected the Sino-Mongol capital of Peking (Beijing) to the Black Sea ports of the Crimea.

During this turbulent period, Nicolo Polo and his brother Matteo had established themselves as merchants based in Constantinople and were exploring the possibilities of the Crimean trade. In 1260, they departed for the Crimea with a cargo of precious stones and other items. As the reader might recall, this was indeed an auspicious time for Venetians to be absent from Constantinople, since the Greeks and their Genoese allies were ill disposed to any Venetians who happened to be present at the Byzantine reconquest of the city in the summer of 1261. The Polo brothers were thus more or less marooned on the Black Sea coast. They knew of the trade routes that linked the Black Sea ports to Tabriz, and then to the Mediterranean, but found them rather inconveniently blocked by warring Mongol Khans. They subsequently decided to head east, with the apparent hope of finding some other way to double back to the Mediterranean. Instead, they ended up spending three years in the Central Asian city of Bukhara. Eventually they met a Mongol official who invited them to return with him to the Mongol court in Peking. The Polo brothers accepted, and after a three-thousand-mile trip across Central Asia, they arrived at the court of Kublai Khan (becoming, in the process, the first Mediterranean Christians to see the Great Wall of China).

The Polo brothers were apparently a big hit in the Mongol court. Kublai Khan was curious about Catholicism and so asked the Polos to return to the West as his ambassadors and return with some missionaries who could explain this religion. On their return trip, the Polos found the route for which they had earlier searched and thus ended up on the Mediterranean at Lajazzo. They dutifully fulfilled their embassy and embarked on a return trip to China in 1271, accompanied by two missionaries and Nicolo's twenty-one-year-old son Marco. The missionaries lost their nerve shortly after setting out and turned back, but the Polos continued to China and, in fact, spent the next twenty years in various adventures there. When they eventually set off on their return to Venice, they took the sea route through the South China Sea and the Indian Ocean to the Persian Gulf. From there they travelled overland to Trebizond, on the Black Sea, by way of the Mongol city of Tabriz. By choosing a Black Sea port for their return to Venice, the Polos were once again either lucky or well informed (or both). In 1291, the last crusader stronghold of Acre had fallen to the Mamluks and travel through Syria to the Mediterranean became very dangerous, at least for the time being. Similarly, the Byzantines, fearful lest the Genoese became too powerful, had relaxed some of their restrictions against Venetian commerce in the Black Sea.

When the Polos returned to their home in Venice in 1295, the legend recounts that their household and neighbours neither recognized them nor believed their fantastic stories until they slit open the seams of their cloaks, out of which spilled a trove of gems. The story, though impossible to prove, does have at least the ring of truth. As long-distance traders, precious stones would have been a logical cargo since gems were small and could easily be concealed.

Marco Polo quickly became famous with his tales of 'Cathay', even though by the 1290s other Venetians had made the long trip. He is said to have regaled friends and acquaintances (and possibly anyone who would hold still) with his stories to such an extent that he got the nickname 'Sir Marco the Millionaire' (*Ser Marco il Milion*) due to his wealth as well as to his frequent use of numerical superlatives in his tales. He did not, however, write any of his marvellous history until after he was captured by the Genoese at the Battle of Curzola in 1298. Making the best of a bad situation, he dictated his travelogue to a fellow prisoner, Rustichello of Pisa, who retold Marco's stories in the fashion of the day and an instant bestseller was born. Back home by 1300, Marco Polo died in 1324. He was buried in the church of San Lorenzo, but his sarcophagus was somehow lost when the church was remodelled in 1592.

Incidentally, no one knows exactly where the Polo home was located. Popular and scholarly opinion both agree that it was somewhere near the modern day Malibran Theatre. Two nearby courtyards, behind the church of San Giovanni Crisostomo, are even named '*del Milion*' after Marco's nickname. Some Veneto-Byzantine decorative plaques and masonry incorporated into the buildings there are sometimes alleged to have been part of the Polos' house.

THE GENOESE WARS

Polo was captured in what is known to history as the Second Genoese War. As increasingly bitter rivals, Venice and Genoa fought two long and very expensive wars during the second half of the thirteenth century. The first of these, ending in 1270, we have already encountered. The Second Genoese War broke out in 1294, largely over control of the Black Sea trade, which became more important than ever after the fall of Acre in 1291. In any event, the truce of 1270 solved very little, and the Venetians and Genoese continued to skirmish with one another.

The Second Genoese War was different from the first. This time, neither the Venetians nor the Genoese tried to protect their convoys of merchant fleets, but instead used their galleys to seek out and fight the enemy's warships and to raid and plunder their colonies. In 1295, the Genoese led a raid on Crete in which they sacked Hanea. The Venetians countered with a daring raid on Galata (the Genoese colony at Constantinople), led by Rogerio Morosini, who bore the evocative *nom de guerre* of *Malabranca* ('the Evil Claw').

Over the next few years both sides continued to ravage the other's Mediterranean colonies until in 1298 they met near the island of Curzola (modern Korcula). In the ensuing battle, the outnumbered Genoese won a staggering victory. The Venetians lost sixty-five of their ninety-five ships and nine thousand men. The victorious Genoese took another five thousand prisoner. While Ser Marco il Milion arrived safely in Genoa and spent the next year dictating his memoirs in prison, it is said that the captured Venetian admiral committed suicide during the trip by smashing his own head against a mast.

Despite their victory, the Genoese had sustained heavy losses, and their brilliant admiral, Lamba Doria, decided he was unable to strike at other Venetian targets in the Adriatic. Thus, Venice was spared a serious attack and was able to rebuild its war fleet. In the meantime, Venetian morale was boosted by reports that one of their naval commanders, a privateer named Schiavo, had conducted an audacious raid into Genoa's harbour. By the following year, however, both sides were exhausted. While the Genoese had won some spectacular victories, and Venetian prestige in the Mediterranean was at an all time low, Genoese commerce actually suffered almost as much as that of the Venetians. The Genoese were also well aware that their enemies had greater wealth and reserves on which to rebuild. Besides these factors, the Genoese had to reckon with a dangerous new Venetian ally on their very doorstep. In 1297, the Grimaldi family had been expelled from Genoa following a failed rebellion. Leaving Genoa, the family captured Monaco, after which it concluded an alliance with Venice.

In the peace treaty brokered by Matteo Visconti of Milan in May 1299, Genoa and Venice returned almost completely to the old *status quo*. The lingering questions of commerce in the Black Sea and the Levant were left unresolved, while (due to the absence of an Imperial delegation at the peace conference) the Venetians felt free to continue their raids on Genoa's Byzantine ally. The peace treaty thus provided a breathing space for the two antagonists and a time to prepare for their third, and final, war.

Besides the rigours of the conflict with Genoa, the Venetians also had to recover from a major flood in 1268. Reports of that incident include the first mention of casualties due to a flood. As quoted by John Keahey, a report noted that 'the water rose from eight o'clock until mid-day. Many were drowned inside their houses or simply died of the cold'.

The War of Ferrara and the Interdict

In the midst of the Second Genoese War, the patricians elected one of the most controversial Doges in the history of the Republic, Pietro Gradenigo (1289-1311). He had been unpopular from the moment of his election, the common people preferring another nobleman, Jacopo Tiepolo, and the lukewarm and inconclusive peace treaty that ended the war with the Genoese did nothing to help his reputation. Gradenigo soon embroiled the Republic in yet another war, which was to have a number of grave consequences.

The Venetians had taken Ferrara in 1240 during a war there between rival factions. Subsequently, members of the Este family (who sided with the Guelfs in northern Italian politics) ruled Ferrara as *de jure* independent princes, although they were economically dependent on Venice. As part of a dispute over the succession of the Este family, Venetian forces occupied the city, and a member of the family ceded Ferrara to Venice. For many of the north-eastern Italian cities, the Venetian seizure of Ferrara confirmed their fear that Venice was determined to dominate all of northern Italy. The move also angered Pope Clement V (at Avignon) who revived an old papal claim to the city. The Venetians refused to yield to the Pope's demands for withdrawal and were, in turn, threatened with excommunication and interdict. Jacopo Tiepolo led the faction of old aristocratic families who argued for abandoning Ferrara, while Doge Gradenigo, at the head of the 'new' patrician families, countered that Venice must hold onto the city. After much discussion and argument, the Doge's supporters won the votes necessary to defy the Pope, who duly declared the interdict on

27 March 1309.

Besides the horrible threat of damnation implied by excommunication, the Pope's action against Venice had serious political and economic consequences. Interdiction meant that Christians were released from their treaty obligations or personal oaths with Venetians and that Venetian property and persons could be seized without fear of legal or spiritual penalties. Indeed, throughout northern Italy and the eastern Mediterranean, Venice's enemies took the opportunity to plunder Venetian goods and assets. Ironically, the only trading partners with whom the Venetian merchants could now work were the Muslim Mamluk rulers of Egypt, with whom Venice had concluded an amicable commercial treaty, against the Pope's express wishes, in 1297.

Accompanying the interdict, the Pope proclaimed a Crusade against Venice, which was duly answered by the Republic's main rivals in northern and eastern Italy, among them Ancona, Florence, and Lucca. The Venetian garrison at Ferrara fell, after a horrible siege, on 28 August 1309, but the *Serenissima* refused to surrender and the war continued. Despite its setbacks, Venice's position was not as weak as it might have seemed. The Republic's ships managed to maintain control of the Adriatic, from which the city could supply itself with food and other goods, and trade with the Egyptians continued, unencumbered by the terms of the interdict as they were. Since much of Ferrara's grain came up the Po from the Adriatic, the Venetians were able to block this vital source of supply. To make matters worse (for the papal forces) Venice was able to conclude an alliance with Verona and discussed cutting a canal, above Ferrara, which would link the Po and Adige Rivers. Such a project would have destroyed Ferrara's economy. This awful possibility, in addition to the growing weariness of the crusaders, persuaded the Pope to lift the interdict in 1313, thus effectively ending the war.

By the terms of the treaty, Venice had to surrender Ferrara and pay the Pope a large indemnity, besides abandoning the Po–Adige canal project. These humiliations, coupled with the significant losses of lives and treasure, made the War of Ferrara one of Venice's worst defeats in centuries. Venice, however, emerged from the war with its Adriatic and eastern Mediterranean trade intact. Ferrara, no matter who ruled it, still had to rely on Venice for its food and merchandise.

THE *SERRATA* OF THE GRAND COUNCIL

In the midst of the Genoese War and the War of Ferrara, Venice under-went a number of major reforms that resulted in the establishment of the Venetian 'constitution' in more or less the form it would hold until the extinction of the Republic in 1797. The first, and probably most important of these reforms involved the make-up of the Grand Council, the main legislative and judicial body in Venice. Traditionally, membership in the council belonged to people whose ancestors had held it, or those who had held some office in the government. A hap-hazard system of elections to the council were held once a year, dur-ing which the nominating committee named one hundred new mem-bers. By the late thirteenth century, however, this situation was becoming unsatisfactory, at least in the view of many of the patricians. Some members of the council, and the ranks of the *cittadini* (or 'citi-zens'), were concerned that the numbers of people who merited inclusion in the council each year exceeded the one hundred possible new nominations. On the other hand, some patricians worried that too many new people were being admitted as it was.

The other worry presented by the Venetian political system as it stood was the continued importance of the *Aregno* or General Assembly. This ancient body was theoretically made up of all adult male citizens of the Republic, and although its powers had been in decline since the late twelfth century, it still, theoretically, held a num-ber of powers, in particular relating to the election of members of the Great Council and even the Doge himself.

This situation was of particular concern to the unpopular Doge Pietro Gradenigo. Northern Italian politics, into which Venice was slowly but surely being drawn provided some troubling illustrations of what Gradenigo might have to expect. In other northern Italian cities, including Venice, family rivalries and feuds were on the increase and discontented noblemen were able to call on others, as well as the sup-port of the general assemblies, to overthrow the existing ruler and seize power for themselves.

It is therefore likely that the reforms on which Doge Gradenigo embarked in 1297 (and which were finally completed in 1323) were meant to forestall the growth in Venice of the sort of interminable, internecine warfare between the families of the nobility that plagued most of contemporary northern Italy.

The thrust of Gradenigo's reforms was to expand the size and power of the Great Council by accepting both old and new patrician families, while at the same time effectively closing it to any subsequent new members through a complex and carefully crafted new nomination procedure. The reforms were clearly aimed at solving the problem of the ongoing strife (of the kind that was about to become endemic in most of northern Italy) between noble families by simply enclosing all of them in an exclusive council.

The reform of 1297 is known as the 'locking' or 'closing' (*serrata*) of the Great Council. From this time until the end of the Republic, with few exceptions, no new members were admitted to the council. The two hundred families who were members of the council after the *serrata* were henceforth considered the Venetian nobility and their names were recorded in an official registry, the *Libro d'Oro*.

THE QUERINI-TIEPOLO CONSPIRACY

Naturally, there were many people who did not like this new arrangement. Somewhat surprisingly, opposition from the *cittadini* and lower classes was muted. We know of one case, perhaps because it was exceptional, of a wealthy, social-climbing citizen named Marino Boccono who hatched a plot in 1300 to assassinate Doge Gradenigo. His plot was discovered, and he and ten of his co-conspirators were arrested and hanged, as usual, between the two columns on the Molo (although the fact that they seem to have been hanged upside down was probably rather unusual). That the reforms inspired little organized unrest by the non-patricians might seem odd, unless we remember that the same reforms had, in fact, ennobled a great many *cittadini*. Those who were not elected to the council nevertheless could console themselves with the powers they held in the *scuole* and elsewhere in the Venetian administration (see below). Far more serious for the political stability of Venice was the reaction to the reforms by many of the nobility. Especially peeved were some members of the old aristocratic families who feared being swamped by 'upstarts'. Others viewed the reforms, rightly, as an effort by Doge Gradenigo to overwhelm the politically adventurous members of the nobility within a much expanded, and therefore much less easily manipulated, Great Council. These tensions finally boiled over in 1310. Opposition to the Doge centred around the Tiepolo family, and a conspiracy led by Bajamonte Tiepolo and his father-in-law Marco Querini.

The motives of the conspirators, and their attempted coup, are complex and subject to a number of interpretations. The Querinis and Tiepolos, as *case vecchie*, ('Old Houses,' i.e., members of the older patrician families) opposed the reforms because they proportionally diluted the families' power. The conspirators had some sympathy from other old noble families, and even some from the lower classes. The non-noble classes of Venice, it may be recalled, had wanted Jacopo Tieoplo as Doge instead of Gradenigo all along, and the popularity of the Tiepolo family persisted. Bajamonte, Jacopo's son, was able to maintain this popularity, although he has come down in history as a questionable character indeed. While portrayed by some nineteenth-century historians as a hero of the people against a tyrannical Doge, he probably had it in mind to establish himself as Lord of Venice, on the model of the emerging despotic rulers in other northern Italian city-states. Venice was, in any case, in a terrible situation and Gradenigo's popularity was not helped by the Papal interdict and the disastrous, on-going war against Ferrara, coming as it did on the heels of the inconclusive and horribly expensive Second Genoese War. Furthermore, there is some speculation that Querini, who (like the Tiepolo family) sided with the Pope, may have hoped that the coup would bring Venice more in line with the other, Guelfish, northern Italian states.

In any case, by June 1310, the Querini-Tiepolo conspirators were ready to act and appointed Bajamonte as leader. His father, Jacopo, it should be mentioned, though a life-long political rival of Pietro Gradenigo, was very much against the idea of a coup. By June, however, Jacopo was conveniently out of the city on a government mission to Constantinople. The conspirators fixed 15 June, St Vitus Day, for their coup. According to the plan, the Querinis and Tiepolos were each to lead their henchmen separately, along different routes, to converge on the Piazza. Another noble involved in the conspiracy, Badoero Badoer (a member, by the way, of another old family) was to land a group of men from the *bacino* at the same time, thus overwhelming the Doge's forces from the rear.

Whatever the conspiracy's chances to begin with might have been, the plot was, in any case, revealed to the authorities several days before 15 June. Significantly (given the occasional portrayal of Bajamonte Tiepolo as a hero of the common man) the informer, one Marco Donato, was in fact a citizen, not a patrician. The Doge, forewarned, gathered as many supporters as he could find, including the workers from the Arsenal. If this were not bad enough for the conspirators, a storm on the fifteenth prevented Badoer's amphibious assault, unbeknownst to his allies.

When the revolutionary forces arrived at the Piazza they found themselves surprised and overwhelmed by the Doge's supporters. Jacopo and Marco Querini, father and son, were both killed in the fighting. Their remaining forces tried to regroup in the Campo San Luca but were defeated by members of the Scuola della Carità and the Painters' Guild. Tiepolo's forces fared no better. Advancing on the piazza by way of the Merceria, they paused by the Sottoportego del Cappello, perhaps somehow sensing the fate of the Querinis. An old woman in the neighbourhood named Giustina Rossi leaned out of her upstairs window and dropped a flower-pot or piece of mortar (the stories are mixed) onto the crowd of rebels below. As it happened, the falling object narrowly missed Bajamonte himself, but struck his standard bearer squarely on the head, killing him. The Tiepolo banner dropped into the muddy street, and Bajamonte's forces fled in confusion back across the canal to the Tiepolo palace in San Agostino (or, in the Venetian dialect, San Stin) destroying the Rialto Bridge after their retreat. Rather than execute Bajamonte, thus making him a martyr, Gradenigo persuaded him to go into exile, but the family palace was completely demolished. Badoer, however, was captured and executed.

Those who had aided in the defeat of the conspirators were, of course, all rewarded. At least two of these cases are worth noting in some detail. Signora Giustina Rossi's airborne assault on Bajamonte's forces was duly noted and commended. When asked what she wanted in return for her service to the Republic, she answered that she wanted the privilege of flying the banner of San Marco from her window on saints' days and a guarantee that the rent on her house (which was owned by the procurators of San Marco) would never be raised. Both of her requests were granted. It is not clear when the rent on the house was raised (for it eventually was), but there are documents that testify that as late as 1468 the rate still had not changed. Today, a white marble tablet marks the spot where the mortar hit the Tiepolos' standard bearer. Another interesting personal result of the conspiracy's defeat was the fate of the informer Donato. He was ennobled and admitted to the Grand Council. His descendants, better known by Donà, the Venetian version of the family name, became an illustrious patrician clan.

The botched coup attempt reveals some interesting things about fourteenth-century Venice. On a broad level, as historian D. S. Chambers put it, the defeat of the Querini-Tiepolo conspiracy 'illustrates the practical difficulty of . . . coordinating a rebellion in a water-bound maze of a city without gates, walls, escape routes or central rallying points'. It also shows that the commoners, and even the bulk of the nobility, were not so discontented with their lot, even when ruled by a Doge like Pietro Gradenigo who was, as John Julius Norwich asserts, probably the most hated man in Venice at the time. Besides marking a victory for the new political order, the conspiracy also led the newly empowered Great Council to establish an emergency body that was eventually to become a permanent, and much written about, fixture of the Venetian political structure: the Council of Ten.

THE COUNCIL OF TEN

Del mille tresento e diese
A mezzo el mese delle ceriese,
Bagiamonte passò el ponte
E per esso fo fatto il consegio di diese.

In one thousand three hundred and ten,

When the cherries were ripening again,
Old Bajamonte
Passed over the Ponte
And they founded the Council of Ten.

As the lines of this old Venetian folk song (here in a version quoted by John Julius Norwich) make clear, one of the consequences of the failed Querini-Tiepolo conspiracy was the founding of one of the most famous, and feared, of all Venetian governmental institutions: the Council of Ten. The Ten eventually became so important in the overall Venetian political system that it is easy to forgot that this council was set up initially as a temporary, emergency measure.

After Bajamonte Tiepolo and many of his supporters were exiled, the Venetian government immediately faced the problem of making sure that the exiles behaved themselves. This was by no means to be taken for granted. Numerous exiles (among the most famous of whom was Dante) from Genoa, Florence, and other northern Italian cities engaged in plots and schemes to return to their homes, preferably in triumph. It was with this in mind that on 10 July 1310, the Great Council established the Council of Ten and gave it wide powers to keep track of the exiled Tiepolos and Querinis and to otherwise make sure that their rebellion had indeed been completely snuffed out. Initially, the Council of Ten was set up for a two-month period. After this time was up, however, the Great Council extended its mandate for another two months. The Ten proved to be so useful that their existence was prolonged for longer and longer periods until the Great Council finally voted to make the Council of Ten permanent in 1334.

The Ten were, first and foremost, responsible for the security of the Republic, that is to say, the security and maintenance of the complex, interlocking system of councils and committees that were controlled by the patrician families of Venice. Initially, in this regard, they focused on making sure that the exiled Querini-Tiepolo conspirators behaved themselves. In point of fact, Bajamonte Tiepolo and many of his followers escaped from their exile in Dalmatia soon after being expelled from Venice, settling in Padua, and began to plot their revenge. In an effort to thwart their plans, the Ten began to build up an army of spies, informers, and assassins that eventually operated, not only in Venice, but across the length and breadth of Europe. One by one, the exiled conspirators were eliminated, until 1329, when Bajamonte Tiepolo's name mysteriously disappears from any historical records.

Even though the threat from the exiles was therefore ended, the Great Council, as we have seen, decided to maintain the Council of the Ten. The conspiracy had come as a tremendous shock to the patricians, especially since it might have succeeded. The Ten were needed as a safeguard against any similar challenges in the future. But the Ten also proved useful for another reason, namely, they helped streamline the decision-making process in the government. The Great Council had already developed the habit of setting up temporary committees of 'sages' (*savii*) to handle specialized or urgent business. But the dithering over how to handle Pope Clement's threat of excommunication convinced many patricians that some permanent body had to be established that would be able to act quickly and decisively in an emergency. The Ten filled just such a role.

Even though subsequent legends have portrayed the Council of Ten as being somehow above the law, it was subject to the same complex system of checks and balances that characterized the rest of the Venetian political order. The members of the Council of Ten were elected by the Great Council for a term of one year, and they were not eligible for re-election until another year had gone by. This was to provide a period during which any alleged abuses by the former member could be investigated. As an added safeguard, no two members of a single family could serve on the council at the same time. To make sure that no single member of the Ten could exercise too much individual power, executive control of the council was exercised by three heads (*Capi dei Dieci*) who served only one month each. As a final check on their powers, the Ten always acted together with the Doge and his six councillors.

THE DEVELOPMENT OF THE VENETIAN CONSTITUTION

The establishment of the Ten marked, for all intents and purposes, the final development of what can be called the 'Venetian Constitution'. Like the constitution of another great European power, this was an unwritten, but nevertheless vigorous and respected, body of law that determined the workings of the Republic. Before 1310, there were two other key developments that built the basic machinery of the *Serenissima*.

The first of these two was the finalization of the procedures for the election of the Doge. We have already seen how the office of Doge had evolved to this point. From its origins as a Byzantine official appointment, to a sort of elected King, the office of Doge had, by the mid-thirteenth century, evolved into what we might describe as a chief magistrate. This constitutional evolution was certainly the result of the reaction by the patricians against the attempts of various families to establish ducal dynasties. But the patricians also by this time had become terrified of the possibility of one of their number setting himself up as a dictator. Thus, the entire Venetian constitution was shot through with checks and balances, committees and counter-committees, all established with the aim of preventing any single person monopolizing power.

The second of these developments was that the patricians became thoroughly embedded in the machinery of the state, as a kind of service nobility. This situation clearly had pluses and minuses. On the plus side, it meant that the Republic could rely on a body of patriotic civil servants whose material survival was predicated on a healthy and powerful state. On the other hand, it meant that the patricians needed to identify with the state. When they sought their fortunes in fields other than commerce, as happened during the eighteenth century, their willingness to work for the Republic declined.

At any rate, the procedure for election of the Doge, fixed in 1268, provides a wonderful example of the devilishly complex set of controls put in place by the patricians, lest one of their number try to rig an election and therefore take over control of the Republic.

As detailed by historian Frederic Lane, the procedure went like this:

> From the Great Council there was chosen by lot 30;
> the 30 were reduced by lot to 9;
> the 9 named 40;
> the 40 were reduced by lot to 12;

the 12 named 25;
the 25 were reduced by lot to 9;
the 9 named 45;
the 45 were reduced by lot to 11;
the 11 named 41;
the 41 nominated the doge, for approval by the Assembly

Officially, the voting was supposed to last three days, but it sometimes lasted months. All the procedures were carried out in the Ducal Palace in the Room of the Four Doors, the Collegio, the Antecollegio, and the Pregadi Room. None of the electors were supposed to leave the palace or have any contact with the outside world while the balloting was in process.

The complex series of elections of the electors eventually drew to a close when, finally, the last ballot was to be drawn. The electors deposited their ballots into a box, called a 'hat' (*cappello*) probably because originally it had indeed been a hat. One of the patricians present was chosen by lot to leave the Palace and approach the first boy he saw. This boy, subsequently known as the *ballottino* then was invited into the Palace to draw the winning ballot. The *ballottino* subsequently became an important part of the new Doge's entourage. One can see, in a fragment of a mosaic in the museum of St Mark's Basilica, the *ballottino* clearly indicated in a ducal procession.

Nobles and Citizens

The changes in the Venetian constitution meant that by the end of the fourteenth century, society had become more stratified than ever before and that mobility between the classes also became more difficult. With minor changes, the situation would remain unchanged until the end of the Republic.

At the top of this socio-economic and political pyramid were, of course, the nobles, comprising about two hundred families. The adult male members of these families, close to two thousand strong, made up the Great Council. This council monopolized all government committees, the judiciary, and naval commands. Of these families, about twenty or thirty were fabulously well-to-do and had a tradition of prestigious political and military service to the Republic. Most nobles, however, were not especially wealthy and worked as merchants, like many well-off commoners. Indeed, while most of the patrician families were wealthy, by no means all of the wealthy families of Venice were patricians. Historian Frederic Lane calculated, based on records from 1379, that about one-eighth of the heads-of-households (a total of 2,128 people) were considered 'wealthy' according to the officially recognized meanings of that term (i.e., individuals with property valued at three hundred gold ducats). To put this figure into some sort of perspective, a skilled craftsman could expect to earn no more than one hundred ducats a year. Of these 2,128 rich folk, 1,211 were nobles and 917 were commoners, a close ratio indeed.

THE *SCUOLE*

While the patrician families were consolidating their monopoly on the exercise of political power, other social forces (personified by the wealthy, but non-noble Polo family) began to exert political and social influence. The growing social strength and self-confidence of the *cittadini* of Venice (its merchants, tradesmen, and professionals) were manifested in the development of a peculiarly Venetian institution, the *Scuola*, during the second half of the thirteenth century. The first of these, the Scuola di Santa Maria della Carita, seems to have grown out of contacts between the lay brotherhoods of the city's Franciscans and Dominicans and the flagellant orders. By the middle of the sixteenth century, there were five large *scuole*, the *Scuole Grande*, and hundreds of smaller ones, the *Scuole Minore*. All the *scuole* had the same basic functions. They were confraternities that provided a place for communal worship and mutual aid. They also functioned as philanthropic organizations and provided support to the Venetian population in case of war, plague, or some natural disaster. The *scuole* are probably best known to the modern visitor to Venice, however, for their great patronage of the arts as they strove to outdo each other in the decoration of their headquarters.

Membership in the *scuole* were limited to citizens. That is, patricians could not be full members. Thus, while they had no legal political function, the *Scuole Grande* eventually came to be effective pressure groups. As in most other aspects of Venetian society, it is interesting to note that the *scuole* never sought to overturn the existing political order. Rather, they were organizations in which wealthy citizens sought a way to contribute to the strength and prosperity of Venice within an orderly and well-organized framework.

The Plague

During the first half of the fourteenth century the rivalry between Genoa and Venice grew steadily. Much tension arose out of the struggle for control of the important trading posts and towns of the Black Sea basin. The Genoese dominated this trade in furs, slaves, and silk, but the Venetians managed to maintain a precarious presence as well. This was particularly important in the two main trading towns in the Crimea, Caffa and Soldaia (the modern Sudak). These were controlled by the Genoese, who nevertheless allowed the Venetians some limited trading rights. But the maintenance of the situation was convenient to neither side, and war was on the horizon, when a series of unforeseen catastrophes postponed their hostilities for almost three years.

In 1344, the Tatars who controlled most of the Crimea and its adjacent territory, attacked the Genoese possessions there. The attack prompted the Genoese Duke (the mythologized hero of Verdi's eponymous opera) Simone Boccanegra, to take the unprecedented step of proposing a military alliance with the Venetians against the Tatars. But the Tatars were usually well-behaved trading partners, and both the Venetians and Genoese were more fearful of each other than they were of the Tatars, so the proposed anti-Tatar alliance went nowhere. In any event, in 1346, the Tatar Khan broke off his siege of Caffa and his armies dispersed. The old animosities between Genoa and Venice immediately became paramount, and war seemed to be imminent.

The two sides had to wait for their war, however. Unbeknownst to the Italians, the Tatars raised the siege of Caffa and retired from the field because they were not feeling terribly well. As the Venetians and Genoese picked through the remains of the besiegers' camp, little did they realize that they were coming into contact with *Ratus ratus*, the common black rat, a creature dubbed by John Julius Norwich 'the most fateful quadruped in history'. The first Venetian ships to return from this aborted siege arrived in Venice during early January 1348. By March the population of the *Serenissima* was under attack, not by Tatars, Turks, or Genoese, but by the horrible, mysterious armies of what has become known as the Black Death.

The introduction of the plague to Europe is itself an interesting example of the degree to which Venice (and Genoa) integrated Europe into a much grander world system. Plague was actually endemic to South-east Asia, only occasionally breaking out into other parts of the world. Its geographic limitations were largely the result of the biology of the plague bacillus itself: it is carried and spread by the fleas which infest rodent populations, which, in turn, thrive in close proximity to human settlements. The disease is extremely lethal to rodents, and to humans, usually killing the latter within a few days of infection. Thus, infected animals or people usually died before they were able to spread the disease very far.

The Mongols, however, were famous for the speed of their cavalry and post-riders. It was they who presumably brought the plague to China when returning from raids into Burma in 1331. From there, the fast-moving Mongols introduced it to Central Asia. The Central Asian steppe, like all similar grassland ecosystems, teems with rodents who provide perfect hosts for plague-carrying fleas. The speed and sophistication of the Mongols' communication system across the steppe meant that the plague-carrying fleas moved swiftly across Eurasia until they infected the Tatars of the Crimea by the mid-1340s. Once the disease was picked up by the Venetians, they likewise spread the black rats (famous as excellent swimmers and climbers, thus quite at home on ships) quickly back to Europe in their fast-moving galleys.

In the settlements of the lagoon, the plague found a hospitable environment. By the summer of 1348, it is estimated that six hundred people a day were dying of the Black Death. The doctors, ignorant of the disease and its cure, tried to protect themselves while attending to their patients by wearing grotesque masks with large beaks (seen in mask shops all over Venice today), which contained various herbs

The masks doctors used during the plague to protect themselves. The inside of the beak was filled with aromatic herbs and spices to prevent contagion

thought to have prophylactic qualities. In any case, most doctors soon died or fled the city. One notable exception was a health officer in Venice named Francesco of Rome, who refused to leave (and in fact survived the plague). When he was asked why he had not fled the city during the Black Death, he said that he would rather die in Venice than live elsewhere. For his loyalty, he received an annual pension of 25 gold ducats upon his retirement. Meanwhile, however, the plague raged on. When it finally abated, fifty patrician families had become extinct and the Republic had lost three-fifths of its total population.

FISCAL POLICY AND COINAGE.

The vast increase in Venetian political and commercial power led to some interesting reforms in the coinage of the Republic, which had hitherto followed Byzantine conventions. Enrico Dandolo (1192–1205) introduced a new silver coin, the *grosso*, to finance the Fourth

Crusade. The *grosso* or groat, of 2.18 grams (and a fineness of .965 silver) became the standard Venetian coin and circulated widely throughout the eastern Mediterranean. The government carried out its financial transactions in *lira di grossi*, an amount equal to 240 silver *grossi*. Another common silver coin was the penny or *piccolo*. It was smaller than the *grosso* and contained much less silver (only about 25 per cent). Labourers and craftsmen were often paid their wages in *soldi di piccoli*, an amount equal to 12 *piccoli*, or in *lira di piccoli*, equal to 240 *piccoli*.

In 1284, Doge Giovanni Dandolo (1280-1289) issued the first gold ducats, to compete with the gold coins being minted in Florence. The Venetian ducat was maintained at 3.5 grams of gold (at an impressive fineness of .997) until the end of the Republic in 1797. It thus rapidly became the most trusted gold coin in the eastern Mediterranean. Despite the success of the ducat, Venice remained on the silver standard, with one gold ducat equal to 24 silver *grossi*, and all debts continued to be reckoned in silver *grossi*. After 1326, however, the value of gold relative to silver began to fall, and the government shifted to a gold standard by the middle of the fourteenth century, fixing the value of the gold ducat at 24 silver *grossi*. This shift, coming at a time of continuing war with Genoa, greatly helped the government to pay its bondholders, whose debt had been, of course, calculated in silver *grossi*.

SHIPS, SHIPBUILDING, AND THE ARSENAL

The social, political, and economic developments in Venice were paralleled by extensive changes in ship design and in maritime merchant practices during the fourteenth century. One of the most important of these changes involved the adoption of larger ships: the great galleys and cogs (which did not rely on oars). Another key advance in ship design during this period was the stern rudder, greatly facilitating the manoeuvrability of the new, larger ships, and the compass, which had a tremendous impact on navigation. These advances were reflected in the development of the Arsenal into a true shipbuilding complex.

Although many private shipyards remained in operation, the Venetian government increased its construction of galleys at the Arsenal, and then auctioned off or leased their products to different

The gateway to the Arsenal built in 1460.
The statues in front are late seventeenth century

shippers. The Arsenal, when originally built during the early twelfth century, was used mainly as a warehouse and repair shop. Most ship-building was still carried out in small, privately owned yards. By the middle of the fourteenth century, while the Arsenal remained an important warehouse and repair facility, it grew into a massive industrial enterprise, probably the biggest in the world. This unprecedented massing of workers in one place, all busily labouring amidst tools, furnaces and, especially, boiling pitch, famously inspired Dante's vision of 'Malebolge', deep in the Eighth Circle of Hell:

> ...As is done
> In winter, when the sticky pitch is boiled
>   In the Venetian Arsenal to caulk
>   Their unsound vessels while no ship can be sailed,
>
> And so instead one uses the time to make
>   His ship anew, another one repairs
>   Much-voyaged ribs, and some with hammers strike

> The prow, and some the stern; and this one makes oars
> > While that one might twist rope, another patch
> > The jib and mainsail...
> (Canto XXI, lines 6–15. Robert Pinsky's translation)

Dante's description hints at the breadth of activity in this facility which became Venice's main shipbuilding centre. During Dante's lifetime, the Arsenal complex quadrupled in size, becoming large enough to construct and maintain the Republic's entire fleet of merchant galleys.

MARINO FALIER'S COUP ATTEMPT

In the midst of plague and military catastrophe, the Great Council elected as Doge in 1354, Marino Falier, a patrician with a long history of exemplary service to the Republic. Despite the considerable good will that accompanied his election, he was to go down in history as the 'traitor Doge'.

Falier's strange coup attempt is the subject of numerous conflicting interpretations. A traditional, and perhaps romantic, explanation is that a young, dashing nobleman named Michele Steno had eyes for Falier's wife, a beauty named Alucia Gradenigo. Some rather unseemly drawings and notes, aimed ostensibly at Alucia but more probably at her elderly husband, were discovered in the Palace and attributed to Michele. Falier was allegedly so furious at this young upstart that he began to plot means to weaken the power of the patrician families and establish himself as a dictator.

Whatever the importance of the frisky Michele Steno in this whole story, it is nevertheless quite clear that Doge Falier indeed began preparations for a kind of *coup d'état*. He apparently tried to interest members of the *cittadini* in his scheme. For this reason, some historians have described his conspiracy as a kind of botched class war. He also was very likely influenced by what he saw as the rise of powerful princes elsewhere in Italy.

As things turned out, communications between the conspirators were poor and the plot was easily discovered by the Ten, which ironically, had included Falier as one of its members many years earlier. Falier was beheaded publicly in 1355 on the balcony of the Ducal

Palace (between the two red pillars) and received an unceremonious burial the next day. Falier is the only Doge not to be pictured in the grand frieze in the Hall of the Great Council in the Ducal Palace. Instead of a portrait, he is represented by a black shroud upon which is written: 'This is the space reserved for Marin Falier, beheaded for his crimes'. Byron called this the most moving monument in Venice. At the very least, it is an unmistakable symbol of the seriousness with which the patrician oligarchs were determined to guard the newly established political order.

The War of Chioggia

The fourteenth century, and this chapter, began with Marco Polo's capture by the Genoese at the Battle of Curzola, during the Third Genoese War. Indeed, as we have seen, the entire century was taken up with Venetian-Genoese wars. The long duel between the two powers was to end, as will this chapter, with the last of those conflicts.

Tensions between Genoa and Venice began to rise again in the early 1370s. In 1372, an argument between the Venetian and Genoese delegates at an official banquet on Cyprus led to a food-fight between the two parties at the dinner table. If this situation were not bad enough, the Genoese guests, in a gross breach of fourteenth-century dinner table etiquette, had concealed swords and daggers under their coats. The food-fight thus escalated into an all-out brawl, and then into a riot, in which much of the Genoese quarter of Famagusta was destroyed. In revenge, the Genoese dispatched a fleet, which effectively took command of Cyprus the following year.

The Venetians, feeling the security of their eastern Mediterranean routes threatened, retaliated by securing the possession of the tiny island of Tenedos, strategically located at the entrance to the Dardanelles, from the poverty-stricken Byzantine Emperor. The Genoese, through their intrigues in Constantinople that can be called 'Byzantine' in more ways than one, also claimed the island. In 1377, the Venetians at Tenedos, led by Pietro Mocenigo, defended the island from an attacking Genoese-Byzantine squadron. The Fourth Genoese War, to become known as the War of Chioggia, and the last of the wars between Venice and Genoa, had begun.

This war was complicated (from the Venetian perspective) by the Hungarian control of most of Dalmatia. While the Hungarians played little active role in actual combat against the Venetians, their hostility, and command of most of the eastern shore of the Adriatic, put Venice in an extremely difficult strategic situation. It also embroiled Venetians in a food-fight of a much larger magnitude: a considerable part of Venice's food supply came from Dalmatia.

At the outset of the war, the Venetian government entrusted naval operations to two famous patricians: Vettore Pisani and Carlo Zeno. Both were courageous, flamboyant, and adored by their crews and the Venetian public alike. Pisani was assigned to protect the Adriatic, while Zeno was ordered to take a fleet out into the Mediterranean to prey on Genoese shipping and colonies. On 30 May 1378, Pisani's fleet encountered the Genoese off Anzio. Despite (or perhaps because of) stormy weather, Pisani scored a tremendous victory, including the capture of the Genoese commander (who, the records tell us, was subsequently well looked after by the noble ladies of Venice). On his way back to the lagoon, Pisani's fleet captured the important Dalmatian towns of Cattaro (modern Kotor) and Sebenico (modern Sibenik). Denied permission by the government to return to Venice, Pisani reluctantly agreed to winter in Pola (now Pula). The next spring, while still sheltering from winter seas, the Venetians at Pola were surprised by a Genoese fleet about twice their strength. Much against his better judgment, Pisani bowed to the clamouring of his restless officers and crews and attacked the enemy. The Venetians were soundly defeated, and Pisani just barely managed to escape. Back in Venice, he was sentenced to six months in prison for his failure at the Battle of Pola.

With Pisani in prison, his fleet destroyed, and the Genoese in the northern Adriatic, the Venetians could do little but try to strengthen their defences and hope for the return of Zeno and his fleet. They fortified the Monastery of San Nicolò on the Lido and pulled up all of the stakes and markers which indicated the deep water canals and passages throughout the lagoon. Meanwhile, the Genoese, in August 1379, succeeded in taking the fortified city of Chioggia, at the southern point of the lagoon where the Lido islands meet the mainland.

The capture of Chioggia meant that the Genoese now commanded one of the deep water channels that opened into the lagoon itself.

The city of Venice now found itself in a situation not encountered since the invasion of Pepin in the ninth century. Moreover, the price of food had reached the point where the Venetian government ordered the wealthy to supply free meals to the poor. A forced loan, one of many in Venice's history, yielded over six million lire to help pay for mercenary forces on the mainland and for the rapid production of a new fleet, which workers somehow managed to churn out of the Arsenal. In recognition of the city's dire situation, the Senate bowed to the will of the *cittadini* and sailors of the city and released the still-adored Pisani from prison.

Restored to the command of the Republic's defences, Pisani at once devised a cunning plan. By sinking a large vessel in the Pelestrina and Brondolo channels that connected Chioggia to the lagoon, not only would the Genoese fleet be unable to attack Venice from Chioggia, but the Genoese would be cut off from any relief from the sea. On the night of 21 December 1379, Pisani and Doge Andrea Contarini led the attack. Despite meeting fierce resistance from the Genoese, they managed to sink three stone-filled ship hulls in the narrow channels. The besieging Genoese now found themselves besieged. Venetian spirits were further boosted by the long-awaited arrival of Zeno and his fleet on New Year's Day, 1380.

The war dragged on into the spring. The Venetians barely managed to fight off several Genoese relief expeditions and maintain the siege of Chioggia. By 24 June 1380, the remaining Genoese forces in Chioggia surrendered. A huge triumphal procession through Venice, pictured in Veronese's painting of the event in the Hall of the Great Council in the Ducal Palace, celebrated this important victory.

Yet the war continued between the old rivals despite the lifting of Chioggia's siege and the general exhaustion of both Venice and Genoa. In August, Pisani led a fleet into the Adriatic in search of the Genoese forces that had broken off from their support of Chioggia. He caught up with them near Apulia and was mortally wounded in the ensuing battle (in the course of which the Genoese made good their retreat). Pisani was buried in the Arsenal, but his body was eventually moved into its current resting place in the south-east apse of San Zanipolo.

Carlo Zeno now took over command of the Venetian naval forces. Some desultory fighting on land and sea continued until August 1381, when the two enemies signed the Peace of Turin, the terms of which did not grant Venice much. Indeed, the exhausted Republic gave up some territories (including Tenedos) and paid an indemnity to the King of Hungary. Yet, its institutions and remaining resources were strong and rich enough to ensure its gradual recovery. Genoa, on the other hand, though technically the war's victor, fell into a slow decline and was never again able to pose a serious threat to the security of Venice.

CHAPTER FIVE

The Imperial Age
1400–1571

Historian D. S. Chambers referred to the period between 1380 and 1580 as Venice's 'Imperial Age'. He did so, not because Venice became an empire, but that it became an Imperial power on mainland Italy and began to think of itself as the true successor to the Roman Empire. The preceding era, bracketed (somewhat arbitrarily) by the Byzantine reconquest of Constantinople in 1261 and the end of the War of Chioggia in 1380, was a time of cultural, economic, and political flux in Venice. The crippled neo-Byzantine state was, rather understandably, more inclined toward Genoese than Venetian merchants. In any case, the reconquest of 1261 squashed any pretensions the Venetian patricians might have had in succeeding Byzantium as a great Eastern, Christian empire. However, as the preceding chapter argued, the Venetian patricians and merchants continued to see their future as largely an eastern Mediterranean affair. It is true that the Venetians conquered Treviso, on the mainland, as early as 1339. They became involved in the affairs of northern Italy at this time, however, largely due to concerns that other forces there, particularly the Genoese and some of the families of Milan, were becoming threats to the Republic's security. In the case of the Genoese, these threats were conceived of largely in terms of Venice's Levantine trade.

By the end of the sixteenth century, however, this situation changed dramatically. Venice lost most of its Levantine empire and instead came to see its future tied to the maintenance and security of its land empire in northern Italy. The struggles with the other Italian states, and their complex connections to the French-Habsburg rivalry, now became important in the defence of the Venetian territorial empire in Italy, rather than part of Venice's attempts to guard the routes to its lucrative eastern colonies.

These changes had some interesting manifestations. Artistically, the fifteenth, and especially sixteenth, centuries witnessed a wholesale embrace of occidental forms in painting and architecture. Many churches previously constructed according to Greek plans were completely renovated according to the conventions of Renaissance architecture. The patriarchal church of San Pietro di Castello is one of the most dramatic examples of such a conversion. Venetian painters, such as Tintoretto and Carpaccio, were thoroughly immersed in the artistic movements from the rest of Italy.

In spite of its expanding mainland empire and Renaissance grandeur, most conventional histories of Venice of this period stress that omens of the Republic's eventual doom were already visible. The two most frequently mentioned signs are the Ottoman conquest of Constantinople in 1453 and Vasco da Gama's Indian expedition of 1492. With the benefit of historical hindsight we can see that these events were symbolic of forces that would eventually erode both Venice's Empire and its commercial might. Indeed, the news of da Gama's voyage was greeted with considerable anguish in Venice. As a matter of fact, however, neither the Portuguese expeditions to the Indian Ocean nor the rise of the Ottomans were terribly damaging to Venetian interests in the short run. Portuguese merchants (and soldiers) took several decades to consolidate their grip on the Indian Ocean trade, during which the actual volume of spices they transported to Lisbon was not great enough to damage Venetian trade in the same commodities. Additionally, the Portuguese crown levied high import tariffs on spices (as a revenue-generating measure) so that the actual wholesale price of oriental goods was not appreciably lower in Lisbon than in Venice. The volume and value of imports in Venice in 1520 was, in fact, greater than it had been in 1500, despite many years of Portuguese trade in the Indian Ocean.

Likewise, the Ottoman threat is easy to overstate. The Venetians fought several wars with the Ottomans during the fifteenth and sixteenth centuries but, as Gary Wills has pointed out, they were generally short, and the Venetians and Ottomans were in fact at peace during most of this period. Significantly for the shift of Venetian political attention to the West, the Republic did indeed lose some valuable and important chunks of real estate during these wars, but it held onto all of its Adriatic possessions and even some important Greek territory, such as Corfu and Crete. After each war, moreover, the Venetians secured the right to trade in Ottoman territory and to maintain their official representative, called the *bailo*, in Constantinople. Some historians have argued that what the Venetians lost in their Aegean empire they more than made up for in their extensive conquests on the Italian mainland. This expansion went together with an increased development of industry in Venice itself, especially in glass and textile production.

Rather than interpret the late fifteenth century as an era in which Venice began to decline, some historians have instead viewed it as the period in which Venice transformed from an eastern, maritime empire, into a powerful Italian city-state.

The Expansion on Terra Firma

As we have already seen, the Venetians conquered certain bits of real estate on the mainland as early as the fourteenth century. By 1420, it already had a sizeable territorial empire, including Friuli and Udine, which gave it control over most of the overland trade routes into Central Europe. At this point, the Venetian notables seem to have been divided about how to proceed. On the one hand, many continued to see the strength and vitality of the Republic as inextricably linked to the control of the sea routes and colonies of the eastern Mediterranean. On the other hand, the new mainland empire needed to be defended against the appetites of the other northern Italian powers. The expansion of Venetian power on *terra firma* had the potential to drag the Republic into the incessant struggles between different Italian city-states and dynasties.

On his deathbed in 1423, Doge Tomaso Mocenigo cautioned the members of his council against getting involved in further wars, especially on the mainland. He specifically warned them against the election of Francesco Foscari as the next Doge. Naturally, on 16 April 1423, Foscari was elected the new Doge, a post he would hold for

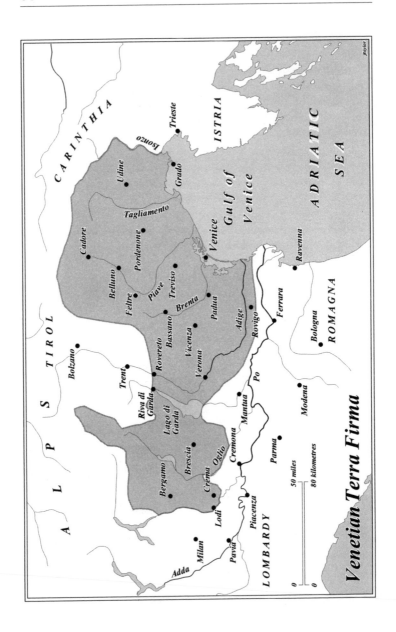

Venetian Terra Firma

thirty-four years until resigning in disgrace.

Foscari reflected the bold and bellicose sentiments of most of the nobility. It is also noteworthy that Foscari's election marked the final end of the power of the *aregno*, the ancient assembly of all adult male Venetians, which even after the *Serrata* of 1297, continued to exercise a ceremonial role at the time of a Doge's election. The people, moreover, did not seem to mind that the Doge took no notice of their political preferences as he scattered coins for them about the piazza. The oligarchs had indeed triumphed.

Barely three years after his election, just as Mocenigo had feared, Doge Foscari led Venice into a war against Milan. For most of the next nineteen years, Venice was embroiled in warfare against Milan and its allies. The Venetians were not used to extensive military campaigns on land, and so ended up relying on the services of some of fifteenth-century Italy's most famous (or infamous) mercenary captains, known as *condottieri*, including Erasmus of Narni (known as Gattamelata, or 'Honey Cat'), Bartolomeo Colleoni, and Francesco Bussone, better known as Carmagnola. The latter two are especially important, the former for his loyal service to the Republic, and the latter for his treachery.

Carmagnola was one of the most famous military commanders of his day and had long served the rulers of Milan. By 1425, however, his Milanese employers were beginning to worry about the loyalty of their military servant, and Carmagnola turned up in Venice to offer his services against his erstwhile paymasters. The Venetian government immediately and enthusiastically accepted his offer, granting him a monthly salary of one thousand gold ducats. His services over the next several years, however, were lacklustre. By the terms of a truce in 1428, Venice expanded its territories at Milan's expense, attaining in the process its greatest permanent borders in northern Italy. But these gains had little to do with Carmagnola's few (but important) victories. Indeed, this *condottiere* quickly demonstrated that, even though he was the commander in chief of Venice's land army, he had only his own interests in mind. Eventually he even began talking to his old Milanese employers again and it appeared that he might switch sides, taking his army with him. By 1431, it was obvious to all that Carmagnola

Doge, Francesco Foscari, 1423–57

intended to establish his own dynasty, most likely based in Milan. His increasing insubordination finally led to a decision by the Council of Ten that he would have to be disposed of.

In April 1432, the Ten summoned him to Venice, using every possible subterfuge to disguise their intentions. Upon his arrival, the unsuspecting *condottiere* was imprisoned and tried for treason. By early May, he was found guilty and publicly beheaded (after three blows) in the Molo. His fortune was confiscated, but the Venetian government buried him in the church of the Frari and gave his wife and two sons 20,000 ducats. As John Julius Norwich points out, 'in the circumstances, and considering where most of the wealth had come from, this was generous treatment indeed'. Carmagnola's current whereabouts, incidentally, are something of a mystery. His simple black tomb in the south aisle of the Frari was opened in 1874. The bones within it, however, bore no evidence that the head had been severed. Thus, whoever rests in Carmagnola's tomb, it cannot be him.

Carmagnola's ignominious (and rather mysterious) end stands in marked contrast to that of another great *condottiere* employed by the Venetians, Colleoni. He was born in Bergamo, and was thus a Venetian subject. For many years he fought in campaigns all over Italy, under both Carmagnola and Gattamelata. By 1455, however, he was hired by the Venetians as the new commander in chief of the land army, in which capacity he served loyally, even though he ended up having fought only one major campaign by the time he died in 1475. He is, in fact, famous not so much for his military genius and service to Venice as for Verrocchio's magnificent equestrian statue of him in front of the Scuola di San Marco (now the city hospital).

By the time of his death, Colleoni had amassed a huge fortune, most of which (216,000 ducats and at least double that amount in property and real estate) he willed to Venice. His only request was that the Republic build a statue in his honour in the Piazza San Marco. While the Venetian state was delighted to receive the money and property, there was considerable consternation at the thought of building a statue of the *condottiere* in front of the Basilica. After all, no one, not even the most illustrious of the city's Doges, had a statue in such a prominent place. After considerable discussion, the Venetian patricians in charge of the problem decided that they could honour the letter, if not the meaning of Colleoni's last request by commissioning a statue for the piazza of the Scuola di San Marco instead of the Basilica of San Marco. Gary Wills points out, however, that the Venetians debated many other sites for the statue, some not in any way associated with St Mark. Thus, he argues, they chose the site near the Scuola di San Marco on its own merits, and not as part of some legalistic sleight of hand. In any case, the resulting statue is an undeniable masterpiece.

In the meantime, Francesco Foscari's wars, as well as the expenses associated with the maintenance of the Empire in the Levant, bankrupted many of the nobility, drained the Republic's coffers, and closed several banks and merchant houses. Foscari's own father-in-law was forced into bankruptcy. Foscari was nevertheless a popular Doge, and even in the face of economic disaster, he had many supporters. But by the middle of the 1450s, he had also acquired many enemies. They were able to find a way to force him from office by using his only surviving son, Jacopo, as a scapegoat.

While deeply loved by his father, Jacopo seems to have possessed little of his father's mettle or integrity and was accused of accepting
bribes in exchange for various governmental favours. The Ten opened
an investigation in 1445, which yielded enough evidence to convict
him, sentencing him to exile in the Venetian colony of Modon. Jacopo
went to this colony in the Peloponnese, but failed to fulfill even the
most basic duties to which he had been assigned there. Nevertheless,
the Ten, in a remarkable show of clemency, pardoned him and allowed
him to move back to Venice in 1447, in light of his father's advanced
age and poor health. By 1450, Jacopo was again in trouble, this time
accused of murdering a senator. Although the evidence this time was
very weak, the Ten again sentenced him to exile, this time to Crete.
John Julius Norwich argues that the Ten might have by this time
become utterly fed up with Jacopo and so seized the murder as a pre-
text for getting rid of him. There were signs that the Ten might par-
don the Doge's son yet again when, in 1456, word reached Venice that
Jacopo had contacted the Turkish Sultan, asking to be rescued from his
exile. This was obviously the last straw. Jacopo was recalled to Venice
where he confessed to everything. Incredibly, the Ten once more
decided to show mercy. Instead of executing him, they returned
Jacopo to his Cretan exile. Already ill, he was allowed a final visit with
his distraught father. Six months later news reached the Doge that his
son was dead.

Francesco Foscari rapidly lost interest in affairs of state and, in
October 1457, a delegation led by the three *capi* of the Council of Ten
asked that the Doge resign. He at first resisted, but finally succumbed
to the pressure and resigned, retiring to the family palace, now part of
the University of Venice. A week later he was dead.

The patricians of Venice, most of them feeling horribly guilty about
the way they had treated the old man, gave him a tremendous funeral, after which he was buried in the famous Gothic/Renaissance tomb
in the Frari. But, as historian John Julius Norwich points out, a better
monument to his memory is the Porta della Carta, on the west front
of the Ducal Palace.

Most historians agree that Venice's impressive expansion on *terra firma* was closely connected in one way or another to the rising power of the Ottoman Turks. Some say that Foscari's concentration on building an Italian Empire led to the neglect and abandonment of the eastern Mediterranean colonies. Others argue that the Doge and his supporters might have reasoned that holding onto those remote territories was more trouble than replacing them with holdings closer to the lagoon. In any case, by 1503, the Venetians had lost almost their entire Levantine Empire to the Ottoman Turks.

The Rise of the Ottoman Empire and the Turkish Wars

The Ottoman Empire began to form around 1300 in western Asia Minor. Originally a fraternity of Muslim crusaders led by a charismatic warrior chief, Osman Ghazi (who gave his name to the dynasty), by 1350, the Ottomans were well on their way to building a centralized, bureaucratic empire. By around 1400, they had conquered much of the southern Balkans and western Asia Minor, leaving the Byzantine Empire as little more than the city of Constantinople. This expansion affected Venetian interests in the eastern Mediterranean, and the Venetians temporarily halted the Ottoman advance in the naval battle of Gallipoli in 1416.

By the mid-1400s, the Ottomans regained their strength and went on the offensive. Without a doubt, the most dramatic symbol of the Ottoman Empire's power was the conquest of the city of Constantinople in 1453, resulting in the fall of the Byzantine Empire. As the Ottomans prepared their siege that spring, the Christian powers of the West, including Venice, made numerous pledges of aid to the Byzantines. As early as 1438, John VIII Paleologos, who was to be the last Byzantine Emperor, stopped off in Venice on his way to a meeting in Ferrara with the leading temporal and spiritual leaders of Western Christendom. Incidentally, while in Venice, the Emperor stayed at the palace of the Marquis of Ferrara on the Grand Canal. Ironically, this palace was later converted into the hostel for Turkish merchants, the *Fondaco dei Turchi*. The meeting in Ferrara, and the subsequent guarantees and pledges made by the West, proved ultimately futile.

Nevertheless, the Venetian community in Constantinople, led by their *bailo* Minotto, fought bravely alongside the Constantinopolitans during the siege. Two Venetian shipmasters, Trevisiano and Diedo, happened to be in Constantinople when the siege began and offered to stay with their galleys and men. As the Ottomans stormed the city on 29 May 1453, some of the Venetians (such as Diedo) managed to escape, but Minotto was captured and subsequently executed.

The Ottoman conquest of Constantinople had tremendous consequences for Venice's Empire in the eastern Mediterranean. For two centuries, the Venetians had to contend only with other Italian city-states, especially the Genoese, or with the ramshackle neo-Byzantine Empire. After 1453, however, they confronted a Muslim power of great wealth and might that was clearly bent on conquering the entire Levant, and perhaps more. While the Venetians negotiated commercial treaties with the Ottomans, it was clear that the Republic's situation in the East had changed dramatically. The Ottomans were perfectly willing to trade with the Venetians, but on their own terms and without granting them any of the special privileges or monopolies to which the merchants of the *Serenissima* had long been accustomed. Moreover, and perhaps more importantly, the Ottomans clearly intended that the Venetians would be simply traders in the eastern Mediterranean, rather than masters of a territorial empire and important sea lanes.

The Ottomans wasted little time in consolidating control over the area. In 1479 they seized the important island of Negroponte (Euboea), a crucial Venetian base, as well as most of the Republic's other Aegean possessions. In 1499, the Ottomans struck again and conquered the southern Greek fortresses of Modon and Coron, the so-called 'Eyes of the Republic', which had belonged to Venice since 1204. Turkish raiding parties reached so far into Friuli that the rising smoke from the plundered villages could be seen from the campanile on the piazza.

In 1503, the Venetians sued for peace and surrendered their claims to all of the conquered territories and most of their remaining possessions in Greece and Albania. The Venetians maintained territories in Dalmatia as well as the important island of Crete. In the meantime, in a last effort at Levantine expansion, the Republic engineered a coup that led to the occupation of Cyprus.

CYPRUS AND CATHERINE CORNARO

One of the most distasteful episodes in the history of the Venetian Empire since the conquest of Constantinople was the acquisition of Cyprus. This strategically situated island had been important to the Venetians for centuries, and by the late fifteenth century, the Venetians had insinuated themselves into some important positions in the Cypriot administration. The master of Famagusta harbour, for example, was Marco Venier, a member of the powerful Venetian family.

By the 1460s, the King of Cyprus was James, a member of the old Lusignan family that had purchased Cyprus from the Knights Templar in 1192. He was known as a feckless playboy who had seized the throne from his sister. In light of these conditions it is no surprise that he faced opposition from his sister's supporters and seemed increasingly unable to defend his island kingdom from the growing power of the Ottomans. Venetian agents in Cyprus, sensing a golden opportunity, arranged a marriage between James and Catherine Cornaro, a pious and beautiful girl of fourteen. The Venetian government reckoned that her marriage to King James would help secure Venetian control of the island.

The Cornaro family, better known in the Venetian dialect as Corner, was an old patrician clan that owned several grand houses in the city. (Catherine's home, by the way, stood on the site of the current Palazzo Corner della Regina [built in 1724] on the right bank of the Grand Canal, near Ca'Pesaro. It is currently the headquarters of the Biennale). Catherine's betrothal was accompanied by a guarantee that, because of her young age, she would not have to consummate the marriage until she was sixteen. Nevertheless, the Venetian government, to say nothing of Venetian society, gave the *Serenissima's* first Queen a spectacular send-off in 1468 on her way to her new governmental and nuptial duties on Cyprus.

Despite this promising beginning, things rapidly deteriorated for the hapless Catherine. Her husband and the couple's infant son both died within two years of her arrival on the island. Even though her late husband had specifically named her as his successor, her situation became increasingly precarious as members of several different families and individuals (including Marco Venier), plotted her downfall, tried to marry her, or both. Furthermore, native Cypriot political factions schemed to seize power from the young, foreign-born Queen. Finally, in 1489, in the face of the growing danger of a coup by Cypriot nobles, and of the growing Ottoman threat, Queen Catherine gave in to relentless Venetian diplomatic pressure and turned over her Kingdom to the Republic.

As Gary Wills has pointed out, the Venetian Empire was ruled by male warrior-merchants who were not at all sure where a female ruler such as Catherine Cornaro, Queen of Cyprus, fitted into their conception of the political universe. She was nevertheless given a heroic welcome in Venice, by which the Venetians tried to disguise the fact that she was actually the victim of a Venetian coup. Her continued presence in the city, however, was deemed too dangerous and she was eventually granted a fief in Asolo, one of the Republic's *terra firma* possessions, where she maintained a rich, but ultimately tragic, court. Her activities were carefully watched by the Ten, who also prevented her from remarrying, lest she hatch plans for regaining her kingdom. She eventually returned to Venice, where she died in 1510, aged fifty-six. She was initially buried in the church of San Apostoli. Her body was eventually moved to a tomb in the church of San Salvador, where she continues to rest to this day beneath a plaque proclaiming her Queen of Cyprus.

The story of Catherine Cornaro is indicative of the ruthlessness of Venetian imperialism, yet, at the same time, it betrays a sort of 'guilty conscience'. The Venetian political establishment (meaning the patricians) went out of their way to portray Catherine's abdication and return to Venice as a voluntary, patriotic act. Catherine's story soon became conflated with the moving tale of St Ursula's martyrdom, commemorated in an awesome series of paintings by Carpaccio, currently in the Accademia.

THE LEAGUE OF CAMBRAI

At the same time as the Venetians' Empire expanded in the Levant at the expense of the hapless Queen Catherine, their power increased on the Italian mainland. By 1509, this seemingly relentless empire building on *terra firma* created so much consternation that Pope Julius II organized an alliance of virtually all the states in Christendom aimed at nothing less than the destruction of Venice as a great power. The Pope was joined by most of the other Italian states, as well as Spain, France, and the Holy Roman Empire in what was named the League of Cambrai.

The war initially went very badly for Venice and, by 1510, it had lost most of its possessions in northern Italy. So grave was the situation that the Republic seriously considered approaching their erstwhile arch-enemy, the Ottoman Sultan, for aid. As things turned out, Venice gradually recovered from its initial shocks and went on the offensive. In this the Venetians were actually aided by the large number of great powers arranged against them, since they were able to play one off against the other. By 1516, the member states of the League had signed separate peace treaties with Venice, restoring to her all of her lost territory. This great victory against staggering odds is commemorated by a famous allegorical painting by Palma Giovane in the Sala del Senato in the Ducal Palace. In it, the Doge Lorenzo Loredan, aided by the figure of Justice, and, naturally, a fearsome lion, confronts an armoured warrior riding the bull of Europa. The face of the enemy's shield is decorated with the coats-of-arms of the members of the League of Cambrai. In the distance, Padua, part of Venetian territory, stands defiantly against its long siege.

Despite this victory, the war changed Venice forever. Some scholars have even argued that it marked its end as a superpower. While victorious, Venice narrowly escaped a catastrophe, and its ruling classes knew it. Venice had been saved, once again, by its baffling geography, force of arms, and especially, skilful diplomacy. Would it be so lucky the next time? After the war of the League of Cambrai, Venice seldom acted independently, and rarely took the initiative in any great pursuits, whether commercial or martial. Over the next several decades, it gradually retreated from its Levantine Empire, its core and focus since at least the thirteenth century, and was transformed into another Italian state.

THE GHETTO

The War of the League of Cambrai had one very far reaching historic consequence: the establishment of the first Jewish ghetto in Christendom. Jews were allowed for many years to come to Venice by day and to participate in certain trades and professions. By the late fourteenth century, the Venetian government granted Jews the right to stay in Venice for fifteen consecutive days. They could only participate in certain trades, most importantly money-lending and dealing in second-hand goods, and had to wear special badges or markers to distinguish them as Jews.

During the War of the League of Cambrai, many hundreds of Jews on *terra firma* fled to Venice fearing persecution from the invading Imperial army and subsequently donated funds to aid in the defence of the city. After the end of the war, the Venetian government decided to 'reward' Venice's Jewish community by allowing Jews to settle permanently in Venice, provided they lived only in one particular area and under special rules and regulations. The site for this settlement was chosen carefully. It needed to be an island, so that Jews could be kept physically separate from the Christians, and also would ideally be on the outskirts of the main, settled areas of the city. The *Serenissima's* leaders eventually picked an area near a foundry, or *geto* in Venetian dialect, on the northern outskirts of Cannaregio. At the end of the war in 1516, the government decreed that the Jews would be allowed to settle on a small island called the Ghetto Nuovo where, as the name indicates, a new foundry had been planned but not completed. All Jews in the city were henceforth obliged to move into the cramped quarters of the ghetto. During the daytime they were allowed to travel or work in the rest of the city, but by nightfall they had to return to the ghetto. The gates to this island were then locked and guarded overnight by a Christian official, whose wages were paid by the Jews themselves. One can still see the remains of the iron hinges in the *sottoportego* in the Ghetto Nuovo. Furthermore, the buildings in the ghetto could not be more than one-third higher than the other buildings in the city. As the Jewish population grew in this cramped neighborhood, buildings' interiors were reconfigured and ceilings were made as low as possible to maximize the number of floors.

Despite these, and many other, restrictions on their liberties, Jews in Venice were relatively well treated in comparison with their brothers in the rest of Christendom. Indeed, the Jewish population of Venice increased steadily through the sixteenth century, swollen with refugees and migrants from Iberia, northern Italy, the Holy Roman Empire, and eventually, from parts of the eastern Mediterranean. By 1541, the community was allowed to expand into the area previously occupied by the old foundry, the Ghetto Vecchio. Thus, confusingly, the 'New' Ghetto is the older Jewish settlement.

The different Jewish communities established their own synagogues called *scole*. The oldest of these is the Scola Tedesca, built by Ashkenazi Jews in 1528, followed ten years later (according to a shaky oral tradition) by the Scola Levantina (for the Jews from the eastern Mediterranean) and, later in the century, the Scuola Spagnola for the Sephardim. The last of the major synagogues, the Scola Italiana, was built in 1575. Since Jews were forbidden to work either as architects or in the construction trades, the synagogues were designed and built by Christian craftsmen, sometimes resulting in lavish interiors reminiscent of churches, theatres, or palaces. A case in point is the sumptuous interior of the Scola Spagnola, designed by the famous architect Longhena.

A Sixteenth-Century Renovation

The city that we today know as Venice, that is, the concentrated urban settlement on the Rialtine islands, really began only in the ninth century. But the *look* of that city as it now exists dates from the sixteenth century. Many of the most famous landmarks, churches, and neighbourhoods of the city were all thoroughly renovated between around 1400 and 1600.

One of the earliest, and most famous, Venetian landmarks to undergo a massive renovation was the Palazzo Ducale. Between 1341 and 1425 several brilliant architects worked to create the massive structure that we know today. In 1508 the hostel of the German merchants, the Fondaco dei Tedeschi (now the Post Office) was rebuilt following a fire. Several years later, during the winter of 1514 in the midst of the darkest days of the War of the League of Cambrai, Venice suffered from yet another fire which completely destroyed the area around the Rialto. The winter was particularly harsh and the wells and even the canals were frozen. The fire thus burned unchecked for days. After the fire burned itself out and the damage was surveyed, there was serious discussion about moving the commercial centre of Venice to some other location. In the end, however, the merchants and statesmen decided to maintain the Rialto as Venice's economic heart. Making the best of a bad situation, the rulers of the Republic commissioned some of the finest architects and planners (including Sansovino) to redesign and rebuild the area. The rebuilt Rialto is much the same as we see it today. The Fabbriche Vecchie (the long arcade of shops along the Ruga degli Orefici), and Sansovino's Fabbriche Nuove, facing the Grand Canal, are still there, as are the public fish and vegetable markets. The old wooden drawbridge over the Grand Canal (the one pictured in Carpaccio's *Miracles of the Relic of the True Cross*) was also replaced, in 1591, with the stone bridge which one can see today.

Another important, though less noticeable development during the mid-sixteenth century was the alteration of the main shipping routes from the Adriatic into the lagoon. From very early in its history, the channel through the *lidi* running past San Nicolò di Lido was the main entrance to the lagoon and was called the Port of Venice. By the sixteenth century, however, the channel that connected the *Bacino* and entrance to the Grand Canal to San Nicolò had silted up. A report from 1558 notes that at low tide the water at San Nicolò was only 11 and a half feet deep. Since about 1525, most large ships headed for the *Bacino* or the Grand Canal had, in fact, been using a channel that cut through the *lidi* further south, called the Port of Malamocco. While this channel was further away from the urban area of Venice, it was much wider than the one at San Nicolò. This meant that the tidal flow through this break in the islands was much greater which, in turn, helped to scour the channel of silt. The Port of Malamocco remained the main entrance to the lagoon well into the nineteenth century.

The Venetians were actively working on various hydraulic engineering problems on the mainland as well. As early as the fourteenth century the Venetians realized that the rivers flowing into the lagoon would eventually cause it to silt up and turn into a marsh. Indeed, as early as the seventh century, the community on Torcello had begun to decline because silt and fresh water brought into its part of the lagoon by the Sile River had turned the surrounding area into a mosquito-infested swamp. By the fourteenth century the Venetians were busily diverting and otherwise tinkering with the rivers and streams that fed into the lagoon.

One of the most massive engineering projects of the sixteenth century involved the Piave River, into which many other streams (and the Sile River) had been previously diverted. In 1534 Venetian engineers (and armies of shovel-wielding workers) completed an immense structure called St Mark's Dike. It ran along the southern bank of the Piave from near the town of Oderzo all the way to the lagoon. It was meant to act as a wall to protect the mainland settlements (and the lagoon itself) from the Piave in the event of a flood.

THE RENAISSANCE REACHES VENICE

The competition for plans for the new Rialto Bridge drew quite a number of distinguished contestants, among them Michelangelo, Palladio, Sansovino, Vignola, and Scamozzi. The fact that the Rialto Bridge project was finally awarded to a less well known (but artfully named) Antonio da Ponte, should not obscure the fact that some of the greatest architects and sculptors of the time entered the competition. The Renaissance had reached Venice, and its phenomenal energy more than made up for its late arrival.

Renaissance attitudes toward painting (especially the centrality of the individual and the use of mathematical formulae) began to filter into the Venetian art world during the late fifteenth and early sixteenth centuries. Three of the most important painters of this early period were the brothers Gentile (c.1429-1507) and Giovanni (c.1430-1516) Bellini, and Vittore Carpaccio. One of the greatest painters of the High Renaissance, Titian (1485-1576), was born and lived in Venice, but his paintings are surprisingly scarce there today. Many of them were carted off by Napoleon. His long life and tremendously productive career make him one of the central figures of Renaissance painting. It is interesting to contrast the brilliant optimism and exuberance (which stunned the Venetian public) of Titian's 1518 *Assumption of the Virgin Mary* (in the Church of the Frari) with the dark anguish of his *Pietà* (now in the Accademia) painted shortly before his death. Some have seen in the harsh brush strokes and dark colours a grim foreboding of Venice's own decline. Venice's other great, native born, artist of the High Renaissance was Jacopo Robusto, better known as Tintoretto (1519-1594). Unlike Titian, Tintoretto's work is well represented in Venice, especially in the Scuola di San Rocco. Tintoretto's paintings are characterized especially by their turbulent emotions and energy, highlighted by his frequently startling use of light and shadow. Unlike many other artists before and since, Tintoretto shunned publicity even after he became famous. He raised a family and continued to live in his old neighbourhood near the Campo dei Mori.

The Loss of Cyprus

Even as the city recovered from various disasters and maintained its power in northern Italy, the Venetians suffered further losses in the East. These defeats were part of the overall trend, during the sixteenth century, of a Venetian transformation from a Levantine to an Italianate power. This development was itself widely debated by the Venetian nobility at the time. Many deplored the neglect of the few remaining colonies in the eastern Mediterranean, while others noted that Venice could not afford to abandon her (by now extensive) holdings on *terra firma*. The Venetians were, in fact, in a terrible position. While Christendom was supposedly united to confront the threat of the Turk, Venice found that she could not count on the unqualified support of her fellow Christian powers. Throughout the sixteenth century, the Spanish and Austrian Habsburgs posed at least as great a threat to the Republic's continued sovereignty as did the Ottomans. The War of the League of Cambrai reminded the rulers of the *Serenissima*, if any reminder was indeed necessary, that the Republic's continued survival lay in steering an almost impossible course between the dangerous shoals of Spanish and Ottoman expansionism. Fortunately, the Venetians had a history of navigating dangerous waters.

During the second half of the sixteenth century, the foreign policy, if one can call it that, of the Republic tilted sharply toward attending to northern Italy at the expense of affairs in the East. The year after the victory over the European powers of the League of Cambrai, the Ottomans seized the Levant and Egypt. The lucrative, though increasingly capricious, trade with the Mamluk Sultans was thus ended, and with it the various monopolies and privileges the Venetians had enjoyed in the region. A few years later, in 1522, the Ottomans took the island of Rhodes, which had been used by the Knights of St John as their headquarters. Much to the surprise of the Knights, the Ottomans allowed them to leave Rhodes more or less unmolested and they took up residence on the Habsburg possession of Malta.

The Venetian-Ottoman wars resumed in 1538. The different Christian powers united (at least in theory) and launched a major offensive. The Venetians reluctantly put their naval contribution under the command of Andrea Doria of Spain. Unbeknownst to them, however, he was under orders from the Empire only to confront the enemy if victory was certain. The Habsburg Emperor Charles V did not want to do anything to strengthen Venice too much. Thus, at the Battle of Preveza in 1538, Andrea Doria ordered the Imperial ships in the fleet to disengage from battle, leaving the Venetians outnumbered and disorganized. They lost seven galleys.

But much worse was yet to come. By the end of the sixteenth century, Crete and Cyprus held out as the last important Venetian colonies in the eastern Mediterranean. As early as the 1540s, some critics in Venice argued that the Republic was not spending enough on fortifications and ships to prepare for the defence of these islands. When the Ottomans issued an ultimatum in 1570 demanding the surrender of Cyprus, the Venetian position was probably strategically doomed. Nevertheless, the Republic put up a spirited and vigorous resistance.

The Ottomans invaded the island in July 1570, and by September, Venetian power was reduced to the city of Famagusta (Turkish Gazimaghusa). Marcantonio Bragadin, the Venetian commander, eventually realized that his situation was hopeless and negotiated a surrender with the Ottoman commander, Mustafa Pasha. What happened after the surrender is somewhat confusing, but ultimately horrible. Initially, the Ottomans allowed much of the population to depart peacefully and treated Bragadin and his lieutenants honourably. At some point, for unknown reasons, the Ottoman commander seems to have changed his mind and ordered Bragadin seized. Horrible tortures, culminating in his being publicly skinned alive, resulted. Mustafa Pasha brought Bragadin's head and skin with him as trophies when he returned to Constantinople in September 1571. The head was eventually lost, but the skin reappeared nine years later. A survivor of the siege of Famagusta, Girolamo Polidoro, managed to steal the skin from Constantinople and returned it to Bragadin's family. Finally, in 1596, the skin, in a lead casket, was deposited in a niche behind the urn of Bragadin's memorial in the Church of San Zanipolo. The hideous demise of Bragadin became an aspect of a kind of cult in Venice, closely connected with San Bartolomeo, who was martyred by being flayed, and the satyr Marsys, who met a similar end at the hands of Apollo.

The Battle of Lepanto

The loss of Cyprus and the news of Bragadin's horrifying fate reached Venice just before news of a more triumphant sort, namely, the victory over the Ottomans at Lepanto off the Greek coast. The Battle of Lepanto indeed became a defining moment in the history of Venice (and the subject of numerous paintings) paired, as it was, with the martyrdom of Bragadin. The specifics of the battle itself are well known. The Venetian fleet was the largest component of the allies of the Holy League, commanded by Don John of Austria. In the paintings one sees in Venice, however, the hero of the day is Sebastiano Venier of Venice. The battle itself commenced when the fleet of the Holy League encountered the Ottomans under Ali Pasha on 7 October 1571, St Justina's Day. In the course of the battle, the Christians had twelve galleys sunk and one captured (out of a combined fleet of 208 vessels), with no more than 15,000 dead. Among the many wounded was Miguel de Cervantes, serving on the ship *Marquesa*. He was shot three times, the last injury permanently maiming his left hand.

While the Christian loss of life was significant, the Ottoman forces were devastated, with 113 ships sunk and 117 captured. In addition, they lost at least 30,000 men with another 8,000 taken prisoner. Additionally, the victorious forces of the Holy League freed 15,000 galley slaves, most of them Christians, from the Ottoman fleet.

Some historians have seen Lepanto as the first modern sea battle because of the use of ship-mounted artillery by both sides. It might be better, however, to think of Lepanto as the last sea battle of antiquity. The primitive cannons used by the Ottomans and Venetians were inaccurate, dangerous to their users, and, in any case, difficult to mount and use effectively on oared galleys. Rather, the tactics and strategy of the battle, relying on ramming and boarding, had much more in common with the Battle of Salamis of 480 BCE than with the Battle of Trafalgar just two hundred years in the future.

Other historians have commented that, in terms of the overall balance of power in the Mediterranean, the Battle of Lepanto was not really that significant. Cyprus had, after all, been taken by the Ottomans, who, moreover, quickly rebuilt their fleet. On the other hand, the psychological effects on the mood in Christendom can hardly be overestimated. Before Lepanto, the Ottomans had been practically unstoppable. The battle showed the Christians that the Ottomans were not, in fact, invincible.

CHANGES IN SHIPBUILDING

The Battle of Lepanto was important in many other ways. It showcased a new sort of vessel upon which the Venetians came increasingly to rely, the *galleazze*. The history of this craft reveals much about the changed fortunes of Venetian commerce during the sixteenth century.

During the late fifteenth century, Venetian shipwrights developed a merchant galley, or great galley. It was significantly larger than a war galley, but still employed both sails and oarsmen. It was a *trireme*, that is, it was rowed by banks of men, three to a bench, each pulling a single oar. Since at this time Venetian oarsmen were all paid sailors (i.e., not slaves or convicts), these vessels were expensive to operate. On the other hand, they were swift, and not at the mercy of the unpredictable winds of the eastern Mediterranean. Venetian merchants also managed to secure a favourable relationship with the Mamluk Sultans of Egypt, resulting in a virtual monopoly on the Alexandrian spice trade for the

Venetians in their fast galleys. The increasingly extortionate duties and fees charged by the cash-poor military dictatorship of Mamluk Egypt did not seem to have a detrimental effect on this trade. It was in the interests of both the Venetians and the Mamluk officials that the Venetian merchants enter and leave Alexandria as quickly as possible. For this sort of fast, low-volume, high-value trade, the merchant galley was the ideal craft.

It was easy to find oarsmen for such voyages as well. By this time, almost all ships were being built according to government specifications in the Arsenal. Merchants would pool their resources to buy one of these ships, and then contract them out to commanders who would actually carry out the voyage and hire the crew. The wages of the oarsmen, sailors, carpenters, and other crew members were fixed by the Senate, but shipmasters frequently had to pay extra to secure a crew. Service on a merchant galley, despite its hazards, was greatly sought after because each crewman could carry an amount of goods, duty free, to be bought or sold during the voyage. Such trade was not insignificant. One pilgrim recalls a merchant galley's arrival in Alexandria harbour. Even before the ship's official cargo was allowed to unload by the Mamluk harbourmaster, swarms of local traders rowed up alongside the galley and boarded it to trade with the crew.

During the first decade of the sixteenth century, however, this situation was already changing. The Mamluk Sultans and generals, desperate for cash, charged increasingly extortionate duties and fees from the Venetians which cut into the expensive overhead to operate the galleys. Even worse, from the Venetian perspective, was the conquest of Egypt by the Ottomans in 1517. The Ottomans were perfectly happy to allow Venetian merchants to trade in Ottoman territory (during times of peace, of course), but they were certainly not going to grant the Venetians any special privileges or trading monopolies. Practically at a stroke, therefore, the merchant galley became an expensive and outmoded means of transport. The Venetians were suddenly in possession of a large number of commercial vessels for which there was no further use. These ships were quickly sent back to the Arsenal, retrofitted as warships, and renamed *galeazze* or galleasses. As it turned out, these large, heavy vessels were much better suited for (the increasingly popular) naval artillery than were the lighter war galleys.

But the Ottoman conquest had changed much else besides. The trading voyages to the Levant were not as profitable as they were once. Opportunities for the crews of merchant or warships to trade or loot dwindled in the face of the powerful Ottomans. It became, therefore, increasingly difficult for shipmasters to hire a crew. Thus, the Venetians slowly began to make use of convicts, and occasionally, a shipmaster's own slaves, for use as oarsmen. At the Battle of Lepanto, sixteen of the fifty-four galleys based in Venice were rowed by convicts. By 1580, the Venetian galley fleet in charge of patrolling the northern Adriatic was rowed almost exclusively by convicts chained to their benches.

The design and building of the great galleys created additional

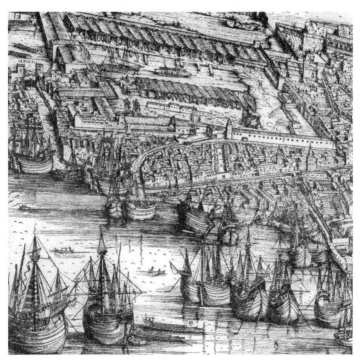

The Arsenal in 1500. In the foreground are freight-carrying round ships

engineering challenges for the workers of the Arsenal. Even more important, however, was the threat represented by the unprecedented sizes of the Ottoman and Spanish fleets that menaced the Venetian Empire. These pressures led to a reorganization of the Venetian ship-building industry during the late fifteenth and early sixteenth centuries centred, of course, on the Arsenal.

The Arsenal was already an impressive industrial establishment when it terrified Dante during the early fourteenth century. By the late fifteenth century, the overall size of the Arsenal complex had doubled with the construction of yet another massive building, the Newest Arsenal. Besides the merchant galleys that the Arsenal had traditionally produced, the state now reorganized the Arsenal for the production of the Republic's warships. It was during this period that the Arsenal perfected the rapid assembly line construction of the galley, the principal ship in the Venetian fleet. By the sixteenth century, the standard Venetian galley was 50 metres (c.164 feet) long and 13 metres (c.43 feet) wide and armed with 30 guns. It had a total crew of 700, of which 343 were oarsmen. By 1540, the Venetian government determined that the Arsenal should at all times maintain a reserve fleet of 100 light war galleys (in addition to 34 other assorted warships), 75 of which were supposed to be stored under cover in the Arsenal's sheds. Until 1633 (when the galley reserve was lowered to 50), the maintenance of this 100 ship reserve was the main activity of the Arsenal.

By the second half of the sixteenth century, the Arsenal was probably the largest single industrial plant in the world. Its different buildings and basins covered 24 hectares (60 acres) and employed, on average, about two thousand workers. To prepare for the Venetian defence of Cyprus in 1570, the *arsenalotti* produced one hundred battle-ready galleys in two months.

The impressive abilities of the *arsenalotti* were due largely to their organization, a sort of combination of medieval craft guild production and assembly-line procedure. This guild-organized means of production operated within the broader framework of the Arsenal. The ships themselves were constructed by tradesmen (e.g., caulkers, sawyers, carpenters, etc.) who belonged to craft guilds and were, thus, subject to the rules, standards, and discipline of the guild. Different guild masters worked with the overall manager of the Arsenal, called the Admiral of the Arsenal, to organize the ship production process. This admiral, was not a nobleman, but was usually a well-respected and experienced seaman. Assisted by about a dozen clerks, he was responsible for procuring and accounting for the raw materials needed by the Arsenal assembly crews and also for all of the provisioning and outfitting of the finished crafts.

Over the centuries, the different buildings in the Arsenal complex acquired different, specialized functions, so that by the sixteenth century a sort of assembly-line process had developed. One of the most remarkable of these buildings (though not technically part of the Arsenal itself) was the 316-metre-long (1,037 ft) Corderia, or Tana, built in 1579 to wind the hemp cables needed by the ships (it is now used as an exhibition space by the Biennale). Within the Arsenal complex proper, the New Arsenal or Newest Arsenal buildings were used for the construction of ships' hulls, which were then towed to the Old Arsenal wherein they were moved past a series of stations or windows. At each station they received the particular items necessary for their missions: rope, weapons, oars, and, finally, barrels of ship biscuits.

This quasi-assembly-line style of production, along with the ever increasing demand for warships during the sixteenth century, encouraged the standardization of parts and equipment. The Arsenal foremen and admirals came to the conclusion that such standardization would be simpler if as many parts and fittings as possible could be made directly in the Arsenal itself, rather than subcontracted out to private workshops. Thus, the Arsenal eventually produced not only the ships themselves, but all of their planks, pulleys, oars, benches, and ironwork as well. The quest for standardization reached such heights that the guild masters in charge of the different *arsenalotti* crews went in person to the forests to select the logs that they wanted not only for the production of masts, planks, spars, etc., but even for such mundane items as oars and pikes.

PERSONAL AND PUBLIC FINANCES

Despite the loss of most of its Levantine Empire by the end of the sixteenth century, the overall fiscal situation of the Republic and its inhabitants improved markedly over the course of the century. Annual revenues, calculated by Frederic Lane, at about one million gold ducats in the late 1400s, grew to two million by 1570. These increases in revenue meant more government jobs, which meant, in turn, more jobs for the nobility. Not only that, but the wages paid for these jobs seem to have increased. This prosperity led to an increase in the numbers of nobles. According to Lane, before the plague year 1575, the city's population reached a peak of about 190,000 people, the highest level, incidentally, in the entire history of Venice. Of those, there were approximately 3,000 noblemen over twenty-one years of age. In comparison, there were about 4,000 adult male *cittadini*.

Despite the Cyprus War, during which the government borrowed six million ducats, there was practically no public debt at all by the early seventeenth century. This favourable fiscal situation was the result of the Republic's clever monetary policy. Since 1350 Venice had been officially on a Gold Standard since gold was more plentiful (and hence cheaper) than silver. Silver continued to circulate, although the old *grosso* had long since disappeared, but was denominated in gold ducats. To stabilize the situation, in 1455 the government fixed an exchange rate of 124 *soldi di piccoli* to one gold ducat.

By the early sixteenth century, however, when silver from the Americas began to flood into the European market, the value of silver relative to gold plummeted, and the government switched to a Silver Standard. The public debt, calculated in gold ducats, could therefore be paid off using (the now cheaper) silver, still officially reckoned at 124 *soldi di piccoli* to one gold ducat. The word 'ducat' itself gradually came to refer simply to an accounting unit, instead of to the coin itself. The mint continued to produce gold coins at the old standard of 3.5 grams of pure gold, but this coin was called a *zecchino* (from which we gain the English word sequin). In 1562, the mint produced a silver coin called a 'ducat', stamped with the number 124, showing its official value in *soldi di piccoli*.

CONCLUSION

Venice (and its allies) had scored an impressive victory over the seemingly invincible 'Turk' at Lepanto. Some scholars have pointed out, correctly, that the Ottomans quickly rebuilt their navy and went on to conquer more territory in Central and Eastern Europe (and, incidentally, most of Venice's own remaining possessions in the Aegean). The battle is nevertheless important for the history of Europe, and especially Venice. It provided a crucial boost to the morale of Christendom and secured Venetian society in its view that the Republic had a special history and destiny. Indeed, the paintings of the sixteenth century reveal a clear preoccupation with the theme of the Israelites, an earlier 'chosen people'. God had obviously chosen the Venetians as his own specially protected people, entrusted with an awesome destiny. This attitude perfectly fitted the Venetians in their Imperial Age.

The artistic and architectural images of wealth, power, and destiny that characterize the Venetian Renaissance and Baroque periods mask some crucial turning points in the history of the *Serenissima*. The gradual reorientation of Venetian attention to the West, especially to northern Italy, that occurred between about 1400 and 1600 was accompanied by the retreat of Venice from virtually its entire Levantine Empire. Some, like historian Frederic Lane, have argued that this reorientation was a result of the lack of will on the part of the Venetians to maintain naval supremacy in the face of the Ottoman and Spanish superpowers. This 'lack of will' was itself part of the 'westernization' of Venice. As more and more patricians made their money, and thus concentrated their attentions, on their estates or industrial ventures on *terra firma*, they not only lost interest in the increasingly risky maritime commerce of the East, but fewer and fewer of them learned to sail the Mediterranean's troubled waters. Beginning in the late sixteenth century, Venetian galleys were frequently commanded by patricians who had little naval experience. Thus, the old Venetian practice of appointing noblemen to command the fleets, which had worked very well during the earlier periods of Venetian history, was increasingly ill-suited to new realities. Indeed, the *Serenissima's* next hundred years proved to be a long, uneven period of military and economic decline.

CHAPTER SIX

A Glorious Decline
1571-1699

The question of decline in Venetian history, or indeed in the history of any society, is a complex one, strongly informed by the personal prejudices of the observer. Ruskin, for example, considered Venice as already hopelessly decadent by the end of the fifteenth century. On the other hand, others have argued that Venice was still an important regional power as late as the seventeenth century. Most historians would probably agree, at least, that the decline of Venice was more relative than absolute. In other words, since Venice had become so phenomenally wealthy and powerful by the end of the sixteenth century, its decline was a long process, characterized by many peaks and valleys. Nevertheless, the century marked by the Battle of Lepanto (1571) and the Peace of Karlowitz (1699) represents a transitional period in Venetian history, similar in some ways to the period between 1000 and 1261. If that earlier period can be thought of as marking a transition from a localized, mercantile power to a regional superpower, then the period between about 1571 and 1699 might be considered one in which Venice became progressively less 'Imperial'. During this period, it was increasingly unable to project its power, or to dominate the Adriatic and the eastern Mediterranean in the way it had earlier. Even its seventeenth-century victories, such as those over the papal interdict of 1605 or over the Ottomans in the form of the Peace of Karlowitz, were overshadowed by the uncomfortable feeling (on the part of the Venetians themselves) that they were somehow incomplete and unsatisfying.

The reasons for the slow weakening of Imperial Venice during this period are traceable to several broad historical forces. The single most important of these is the shift of the world focus of power from the

Mediterranean to the Atlantic that began as early as 1521 with the Spanish conquest of Mexico. This shift was coupled with the increasing aggressiveness of English and Dutch naval expansion in the East Indies. The Dutch, who displaced the Portuguese as the dominant Christian power in the East Indies by the late sixteenth century, were able to exploit that area's resources far more efficiently (or ruthlessly) than had the Portuguese. By the end of the seventeenth century, English and Dutch vessels were out-competing Venetian ones in the eastern Mediterranean itself. The economic decline was linked to the general European depression of 1620 that accompanied the horrors of the Thirty Years' War. But Venice's economic problems were also, at least partially, the fault of some of the Venetian government's own decisions.

Another cause of the decline in Venice's economic fortunes at this time was the stagnation in Venetian shipbuilding techniques and the size of the Venetian military and merchant marine fleets. The Battle of Lepanto, while a great victory for the Holy Alliance (and especially Venice), also revealed a great deal about the state of the Venetian military. Most of the Venetian galleys were armed with light cannons by the time of Lepanto, but artillery had not been fully integrated into the strategy and tactics of naval warfare. The ships' cannons were difficult to mount effectively in oared galleys, and were in any case inaccurate and awkward to use. This engagement bore no resemblance to the kind of naval warfare that was about to appear in the Atlantic basin, which involved manoeuvring ships under sail to deliver broadsides of artillery fire. Apparently, Venetian naval officers were unable, or unwilling, to adapt themselves very effectively to this kind of warfare and the Arsenal continued to turn out oared galleys until the end of the Republic.

THE END OF THE TURKISH WAR (1573)

After Lepanto, the Venetians were anxious to press on and attack Istanbul itself. In the fall of 1572, the Holy League's forces (led again by Don John) compelled the hastily rebuilt Ottoman navy to retreat to the fortified port of Modon (which the Venetians had surrendered to the Turks in 1500). To the surprise of the other members of the

League, however, Don John announced that he was breaking off the operation and returning to Spain. Dumbfounded, the Venetians begged him to reconsider, but he was obviously following King Philip's orders. Unable to deal with the Ottomans alone, the Venetians reluctantly returned home as well.

In fact, King Philip had stepped up his intrigues in France and, as a result, had lost interest in the war against the Ottomans. He probably reasoned that his efforts to take over Western Europe were more important than his struggle with the Turks. In any event, he had always hated Venice and calculated that there was no point in weakening the Ottoman Empire too much, when such a development could only strengthen the Venetians. So, in March 1573, the Venetians, abandoned by their allies, were forced to sign a peace treaty with the Ottoman Empire, in which (among other things) they acknowledged the loss of Cyprus and agreed to pay the Sultan an indemnity.

Although many Venetians were disappointed with this anti-climactic aftermath of the Battle of Lepanto, it did bring Venice some gains. For one thing, the end of the war meant that peaceful mercantile activity could resume. Venetian merchants were soon active once more in trade with the Levant, and even regained an important place on Cyprus itself. More importantly, perhaps, the Venetians and the Ottomans promised to behave as friends and allies and to help each other in the protection of the shipping lanes from pirates. These generally cordial relations are reflected in the establishment of a hostel for Turkish merchants, the Fondaco dei Turchi (now the Natural History Museum) in the old palace of the Marquis of Ferrara, in 1621.

The Ottoman Imperial government, in fact, made an effort in good faith to suppress the activities of the Muslim pirates of the north African and Albanian coasts, though with mixed results. Ottoman authorities even allowed Venetian galleys patrolling the Adriatic and eastern Mediterranean to harbour occasionally in Ottoman ports. This unprecedented Ottoman-Venetian alliance manifested itself in other ways as well. One of the most startling occurred during the so-called 'Valtelline War' of 1624, in which Venice supported France and Savoy against Spain in a war over the Swiss region of Valtelline. During this war, the Venetians asked for, and received, permission from Istanbul to recruit mercenaries in (Ottoman ruled) Bosnia and Albania for war in what the Ottoman records call 'Valtuniye in Frengistan'.

THE ECONOMIC DECLINE

The Venetians thus found themselves at peace for almost a century with their erstwhile Ottoman enemies. In the meantime, however, the world, and the Venetian place in it, had changed drastically. By the last quarter of the sixteenth century, the Portuguese share of the spice trade had greatly increased. Yet, a more serious development in the spice trade occurred between 1595 and 1641, when the Dutch seized control of most of the pepper and spice producing territories of South-east Asia. The Portuguese, ruthless as they were, had always operated largely from their bases in India, much as the Muslim merchants had done. There, they bought (or 'intercepted') spices and other precious cargoes coming from the East Indies. They also tried, with limited success, to prevent any Muslim ships from operating in the Indian Ocean, Red Sea, or Persian Gulf.

The Dutch adopted a much more daring, and in the end, more effective policy. Rather than try to control the trade in these commodities, as the Portuguese had attempted, the Dutch simply took over the sources of supply. After the Dutch had succeeded in defeating their Portuguese and East Indian enemies, they were able to monopolize the entire process of production, transportation, and marketing of spices. As a result, during the early 1600s, the ancient spice trade through the Persian Gulf and Red Sea declined precipitously. Small quantities of spices and other products of course got through, but Muslim (and indeed Venetian) merchants were now in much the same position as everyone else: they had to buy these products from Dutch wholesalers.

The Venetians were faced with the naval strength of the English and Dutch even in the familiar waters of the Adriatic and Mediterranean. After the English and Dutch made peace with Spain (in 1604 and 1609, respectively), they could sail in relative safety through the Straits of Gibraltar directly to ports in the Levant. Thus, by around 1630, English and Dutch merchants had established a bustling trade in cotton, silk, and dried fruit (among other commodities) based in the

Ottoman port of Izmir (Smyrna). By the early seventeenth century, even Venetian merchants relied on ships flying the flags of England or Holland rather than the Lion of San Marco.

There are several reasons for the decline of Venice as the pre-eminent commercial maritime force in the eastern Mediterranean, one of the most important being the conservativism of Venetian shipbuilding and design. This situation is all the more sobering when one recalls that the Arsenal was, before the industrial revolution, probably the biggest single industrial enterprise in all of Europe, maybe in all the world. More importantly, the *arsenalotti* developed the frame and plank method of shipbuilding that revolutionized the entire industry. But perhaps Venice was too fond of these techniques, and especially of the main product of the Arsenal: the galley. Indeed, the Venetians abandoned this ancient craft slowly and with great reluctance.

It should, in fairness, be noted that as early as the fifteenth century, Venetian merchants were ceasing to use the galley as a commercial vessel in favour of imported broad-beamed 'round ships'. These ships could hold more cargo and did not require rowers, thus making them better suited as merchant vessels. The Venetians stubbornly clung to the oared galley, however, as their preferred ship for warfare. It was only in 1667 that the Arsenal began to build modern galleons, using an imported English ship as a model. Still, as late as 1717, galleys made up half of the Venetian war fleet. Indeed, until 1695, the Captain General of the Sea was obliged by law to use a galley as his flagship.

The result of this conservative attitude was that the Dutch, English, and Spanish soon surpassed the Venetians in shipbuilding innovations. The new galleons developed in the sixteenth century employed complicated rigging that enabled them to sail against the wind. Perhaps even more important, these new ships were able to carry heavy cannon well below deck to aid in stability. They were thus faster and more defensible than either the old fashioned round ships or galleys still used by the Venetians. The lumbering Venetian round ships, easy prey for pirates, were forced to travel in (extremely expensive) convoys, sometimes under military protection. Dutch or English galleons, however, were well suited as merchant ships and were, moreover, perfectly capable of defending themselves against the endemic piracy of the

Mediterranean. Indeed, during the early sixteenth century, Venetian merchant shipping was under attack, both figuratively and literally, not only from English and Dutch merchants, but also from pirates from those countries. In 1603 alone, Venetian authorities calculated that the Republic had lost a dozen ships to English and Dutch pirates, on top of another dozen lost to Spanish corsairs.

The decline in the strength of Venice's shipping industry might have been reversed by opening Venice's ports as trans-shipment points for goods carried by other ships. As a matter of fact, English and Dutch merchants operating in the Levant, recognizing the many geographical and political advantages in such an opportunity, wanted to ship goods through Venice on their own ships. Some Venetians, such as Nicolo Donà (a wealthy merchant and brother of the former Doge Leonardo Donà), argued for lifting the old navigation laws that required all foreign merchant ships calling at Venice to carry only goods from their home countries and to sell them in Venice. Donà argued that a change in policy would reinvigorate Venetian commerce and would encourage the settlement and naturalization of Dutch and English seamen who would stimulate and replenish the dwindling ranks of native-born Venetian sailors. But the majority of the patricians who controlled the Venetian government, already sinking into a timid fear of changing anything about the political order, defeated the proposal. As a result, the foreign merchants turned increasingly to ports such as Ancona, Ragusa, or Leghorn to trans-ship their goods. Frederic Lane has estimated that between 1602 and 1612 the volume of trade moving through Venice declined by 40 per cent as a result of this short-sighted Venetian policy.

The Venetians dealt with the decline in the shipping industry as best they could. The dangers of piracy led to a renewed reliance on the old, heavy, merchant galleys, especially since many of these had been idle since the end of the Turkish Wars. A brisk trade using these galleys (with a quarter of their crews made up of soldiers) began operating between Venice and the port of Spalato (modern Split), which was becoming the main Adriatic terminus for Constantinople's overland trade. Relying on the speed and defensibility of these ships, as well as precise loading and unloading schedules, these galleys were able to make as many as six trips a year between Venice and Spalato between 1614 and 1619.

Manufacturing provided another alternative to the growing weakness of merchant shipping. In fact, during the second half of the sixteenth century, Venetian industrial output, especially in woollen textiles and glass, increased dramatically. Between 1550 and 1602, for example, the production of woollen textiles (using imported Spanish wool) tripled. Venetian merchants traded their high-quality woollen cloth and semi-luxury goods like glassware (from the island of Murano) in Aleppo and Izmir for cotton and silk. Revenues derived by the state from the increase in manufacturing were used to subsidize the lagging shipping industry.

By the 1630s, however, as we have already seen, the trade in the Levant was largely in the hands of the English and Dutch. Moreover, a serious financial crisis in the Ottoman Empire dampened demand for the expensive, high quality Venetian textiles (and glass), while increasing the demand for the cheaper woollen broadcloth carried on the English ships.

The reaction of the Venetian patricians to these developments was typically pragmatic. Trying to maintain what trade they could, they turned toward agriculture as a way of making money. And there was indeed money to be made. By 1600 many Venetian noble families had amassed significant estates on *terra firma*, and grain prices remained high during most of the seventeenth century, when many Venetian nobles abandoned mercantile pursuits and lived off rents and other revenues from their estates on the mainland.

The Visit of King Henry III of France

The end of the wars against the Ottoman Empire worsened the relations between Venice, on the one hand, and Spain, the Holy Roman Empire, and the Vatican, on the other. In such a difficult situation, the Venetian government directed its attention to its only possible ally: France. Similarly threatened by Spain, France was a natural ally of Venice, and, in the summer of 1574, the Venetians had an opportunity to promote a Franco-Venetian alliance with the sort of opulence and festivity for which they were justly famous.

As it happened, the King of France, Charles IX, unexpectedly died in May 1574. His younger brother, Henry, had been crowned King of Poland only three months earlier, but hearing of his brother's death, he quickly abandoned his new Kingdom (in disguise, and with a fortune in jewels filched from the Polish Crown) and headed for Paris to assume the crown of France. He stopped off in Venice on the way, and Doge Alvise Mocenigo I (1570–1577) and the rest of the city gave him a spectacular welcome, as pictured in Vicentino's painting in the Salla delle Quattro Porte in the Ducal Palace.

Henry stayed for a week as a guest in the Palazzo Foscari on the Grand Canal, during which time the authorities made sure that he enjoyed every possible pleasure and honour that the Republic could provide. He was made an honorary member of the Senate and had his portrait painted by Tintoretto, but he also spent (presumably pleasur-

The famous courtesan, Veronica Franco

able) time with Venice's most famous courtesan, Veronica Franco. According to some accounts, the Doge's council helped the young King make his choice of Venice's many 'attractions' by obligingly supplying him with a catalogue. It was also during this trip that the Arsenal put on its most famous show. Henry's hosts brought him to the Arsenal one morning to watch a ship's keel being built. That very night, after a day of entertainment and feasting, they returned to the Arsenal to see that the entire galley had been built and completely outfitted, right down to the armaments and provisions.

Toward the end of the King's visit, Doge Alvise broached the subject of politics and a possible alliance with France. Although Henry's response was vague and evasive, it soon became clear that the week had left a strong impression on the young King's mind. Venice's relationship with France, and as a result, its position regarding Spain, had been greatly strengthened.

Plagues and Fires

Venice was soon confronted with an enemy even more horrible than Spaniards or Turks: the plague. As it raged through 1575 and into the next year, most of the horrifying scenes of the Black Death repeated themselves. As the population dwindled many survivors fled to the mainland and shops and businesses closed. Doge Alvise and his cabinet continued to function, although the plague took its toll on the members of the government. By the autumn of 1576, the situation had become dire, and the state ordered all surviving Venetians quarantined to their homes for one week. Ignorant of the causes of the disease, the measures of course had no effect. By the winter of 1577, however, the plague was already showing signs of receding and on Sunday, 21 July 1577 the Venetian authorities proclaimed the plague to at last be over.

The plague wiped out a third of the city's population, including the painter Titian, who painted the horrifying *Pietà* in 1576 for his own tomb in the Frari. The Venetian population was around 175,000 in 1575, but two years later it had decreased to 124,000. The surviving Venetians were so relieved, and grateful at the plague's passing, that the

state commissioned Andrea Palladio to build a church to commemorate the deliverance of the city. The result, the church of the Redeemer
(*Redentore*) on Giudecca, has remained a place of devotion. The Doge
and his *Signoria* attended mass at the church on every third Sunday in
July to give thanks for the deliverance of the city from the plague, an
event commemorated ever since.

The city's population recovered quickly from the plague. The cen-
sus of 1581 recorded 134,871 inhabitants, and the number grew to
over 140,000 by 1624. Then, in 1630, just as the city had almost recovered, the plague struck again. The population of the city was reduced
to about 100,000 in a matter of months. Doge Nicolò Contarini himself became ill in January 1631, but continued to attend to his duties
until he succumbed in April. Before his illness, however, he convened
a special meeting of the Senate in October 1630 to deal with the
emergency. The Doge announced that he would lead the patricians of
the Senate in a solemn procession every Saturday for the next fifteen
Saturdays and would furthermore commission a church to the Virgin
Mary in order to beg for her help in ending the plague. He also
pledged that in every year to come, the Doge would lead a procession
of thanksgiving to the church, which would be called the Santa Maria
della Salute.

The plague ended soon thereafter and the commission for the
church was given to Baldassar Longhena. His baroque masterpiece, the
Salute, is now one of the most recognizable landmarks on the Grand
Canal. Every year on 21 November (The Feast of the Presentation of
the Virgin), a temporary bridge is built over the mouth of the Grand
Canal and a solemn procession of dignitaries and citizens crosses over
it, followed by a huge thanksgiving mass in the church.

Amidst the horrors of the plague, the Venetians had to contend with
other catastrophes as well. In 1574, a fire in the Ducal Palace destroyed
the rooms of the Collegio and the Senate. A much worse fire broke
out on 20 December 1577. The Hall of the Great Council and the Sala
dello Scrutino were both destroyed, along with paintings by Bellini,
Titian, Tintoretto, and Veronese. The damage to the building was so
great that some suggested that the entire building be razed and rebuilt
in Renaissance style complete with neo-classical flourishes such as

Doric, Ionic, and Corinthian columns. Contrary to the statements of Ruskin (that great hater of Renaissance style), the architect Palladio was not, in fact, among those who called for such a complete redesign of the building. He did, however, argue that its reconstruction should rely exclusively on masonry instead of timber. As it turned out, the Palace was rebuilt with its interiors rearranged and foundations strengthened, but its glorious Venetian Gothic façade largely unchanged. Another part of the reconstruction included the new prison, and with it the famous Bridge of Sighs, which were finished by 1614. Interestingly, most of the restoration work on the Palace relied heavily upon timber after all, expertly selected and crafted by master carpenters from the Arsenal. Modern-day visitors should certainly indulge in a tour of the Palace attics to view this one-of-a-kind engineering.

THE PAPAL INTERDICT OF 1605 AND PAOLO SARPI

While the seventeenth century is considered by most historians to have held the seeds of Venice's eventual decline, this era also shows many examples of its continued vigour. One such event occurred during its first decade that was also an important example of the way in which church-state relations and internal politics were evolving in the Republic.

Venice had always had a peculiar relationship with the Roman Catholic Church. The fact that Venice, unique in the Western Church, had its own Patriarch, has already been commented upon. The Patriarch of Venice had always been expected to be, first and foremost, a loyal servant of the Republic. By the first decade of the seventeenth century, this peculiar relationship was at the centre of a major political, ecclesiastical, and spiritual challenge to the people of the lagoon.

This crisis had two main sources. The first grew out of internal political developments in the Republic with the growth of a faction within the nobility sometimes called the 'Young'. The members of this group were not necessarily youthful (although many of them in fact were), but were instead described as 'Young' because they were, in general, interested in the scientific revolution and by the pre-Enlightenment ideas taking shape in the Low Countries, England, and

France. As it happened, in 1606, the Council had elected one of the 'Young', namely Leonardo Donà, as Doge. He was, by the way, seventy-two-years old. Donà was a keen-minded philosopher (and, incidentally, a close friend of Galileo) who had studied at the University of Padua. He was a devout and deeply moral man (and is pictured in the church of San Giovanni Elemanosario receiving holy water). Even a personal enemy of his was bound to admit (here quoted by Gary Wills) that the new Doge was 'incorrupt and restrained, applying his severity more to himself than to others, since he was approachable and human to all'.

The second cause for the Republic's early seventeenth-century crisis had, at least initially, very little to do with Venetian political developments. During Donà's first year as Doge, two friars committed serious crimes on the mainland territory of the Venetian Empire. One soiled the walls of a house belonging to a woman who had reportedly spurned his amorous advances. The other was accused of poisoning members of his own family. In the past, the Vatican had permitted the Venetian State (acting through the Council of Forty) to try certain narrowly circumscribed cases involving clergymen, but this time the Council of Ten arrested and tried the accused clerics. This situation drew the attention of Pope Paul V, a man described by Garry Wills as 'a stickler for canon law and papal prerogative' who had 'served on the Roman Inquisition' to boot. The Vatican had, in any case, long been irked by the *Serenissima's* insistence that the Church on Venetian territory should be subservient to the wishes of the State. The Pope was further incensed when the Venetian government restricted the property holdings of monasteries in its territories, and reduced the amount of rents and revenues they were allowed to send back to Rome. Pope Paul seems to have decided to use the trial of the friars as an opportunity to bring Venice to heel once and for all and demanded that the accused clerics be tried by an ecclesiastical court. Donà, for his part, immediately recognized the implications of this challenge to Venetian state power and could not resist defying the Holy See. The Vatican responded in 1606 with the most feared and terrible weapon at its disposal: the interdict. Theoretically, while the city was under interdiction, no clergy were allowed to administer any sacraments, thus, according to Catholic dogma, damning any Venetians who happened to die while the interdict was in force.

Doge Donà and the Venetian government were not to be cowed however, and adopted a two pronged counter-attack. Characteristically, the Doge simply ordered (through the Patriarch of Venice, of course) all clergy in Venetian territory to continue to minister to their flocks on pain of death. Significantly, almost all followed the orders of the Venetian State and the Patriarch of Venice. The story is told of one clergyman who protested that the Holy Ghost had ordered him to obey the terms of the papal interdict. The Council of Ten responded to this challenge by reporting that, strangely enough, this same member of the Trinitarian Godhead had ordered *them* to execute anyone who *obeyed* the interdict. The priest quickly realized that he must have been in error and resumed his duties. In fact, no one was executed for disobeying the Doge's orders, though some clergymen were imprisoned and some religious orders, notably the Capuchins and Jesuits, were expelled from Venice (although the Jesuits were allowed to come back in 1657). The major branch of the Franciscans (called the 'Conventuals'), as well as the Dominicans and Benedictines, defied Rome's orders and were thus allowed to remain in the city.

As the other part of the Doge's strategy to fight the interdict, he enlisted as his ally one of Venice's most famous and brilliant scholars, the Servite monk Father Paolo Sarpi. Father Sarpi was already famous for his work on theology, especially his discourses on the work of the Council of Trent, as well as for his scientific investigations, particularly in optics. He, like Donà, was a pious man who, nevertheless, was infected with the spirit of the times and could not resist the challenge of questioning the validity of the interdict.

Sarpi contended, in closely argued and persuasive writings, that the Pope, in fact, had no right in this case to place Venice under the interdict. His arguments, in conjunction with the very real pressures of the Venetian state, meant that few of the clergy in Venice actually observed the Pope's instructions on this matter. On the other hand, Donà, Sarpi, and their allies did not enjoy the outpouring of support they had expected. Among foreign governments, only King James I of far-off England (and his stridently Protestant ambassador in Venice, Sir Henry

Father Paoli Sarpi, one of Venice's most brilliant thinkers

Wotton, of whom more later) sided openly with Venice in the dispute. Other governments were, at best, neutral. Nor did the crisis lead to the calling of a council to discuss church reforms, as Sarpi apparently had hoped. French mediation ended the conflict after about a year and the interdict was lifted. Significantly, Venice was not obliged to admit any wrongdoing or to ask any forgiveness of the Pope. Some historians have observed that, coming during the Reformation, the episode of the Venetian interdict was another blow against the prestige and power of the Church.

Sarpi, though disappointed with the anti-climactic lifting of the interdict, became a kind of folk hero in Venice. Not everyone, however, thought of him fondly, and he survived an assassination attempt about six months after the end of the interdict. According to a famous story, after the attack he said: 'I recognize the style of the Holy See', making a pun on the stiletto (*stilo*, also the word for 'style') that had broken against his cheekbone. He died, of natural causes, many years later, on 15 January 1623. His remains were eventually buried in the church on the cemetery island of San Michele in 1828. Nowadays, a nineteenth-century monument to Sarpi can be found in front of the church of Santa Fosca.

The Wars against the Uskoks (1607–1617)

The Venetian difficulties with the Vatican were thus overcome. But the security of the Republic was soon threatened by the greatest Catholic dynasty in Europe, the Habsburgs. The Austrian branch of the family had long had designs on the northern Adriatic and relations with Venice were usually chilly. The situation was aggravated by the Habsburg sponsorship of a Christian people called the Uskoks who were based around the town of Segna (modern Senj) in northern Dalmatia. Composed mostly of refugees from the Ottoman Balkans, joined by political exiles and military adventurers, the Uskoks had been courted by the Austrian Habsburgs as frontier guards for use against the Ottomans. For the Uskoks, however, Venetian shipping and coastal settlements often provided more tempting targets for raids than did the impoverished villages along the Ottoman frontier. The Uskoks, in fact, preferred Venetian ships as targets since the crews (by this time salaried sailors who had no share or financial interests in the cargoes they were transporting) would rarely put up a fight in the hope that their fellow Christians would spare them. The Uskoks also posed a serious political problem for the Venetians. Since 1573, the Ottoman Empire and Venice had been at peace. But the depredations of the Uskoks on Ottoman territory in the north-western Balkans increased the chances that the Ottomans would decide to attack the northern Adriatic bases of these raiders, thus threatening the delicate alliance between Venice and Istanbul.

By 1615, the simmering hostility toward the Uskoks escalated into a war between Venice and the Habsburg Archduke Ferdinand, the Uskoks' main patron. A Venetian army (as usual, composed mainly of mercenaries) led by the future Doge Nicolò Contarini crossed the

Isonzo River and attacked Gradisca, in Habsburg territory, while Venice's navy raided the Uskok settlements around Segna. Although the Venetian military offensive quickly bogged down, Venetian diplomacy (accompanied, according to some reports, by the judicious use of bribery) ended what is known as the War of Gradisca on terms more-or-less favourable to Venice. While there were no territorial adjustments, their deal with Archduke Ferdinand provided for a resettlement of the Uskoks in the interior, where their disruptive actions could be minimized.

THE 'SPANISH CONSPIRACY' (1618)

While Venice had, for the time being, thus thwarted challenges from both the Papacy and the Austrian Habsburgs, it had still to contend with the machinations of the Spanish Habsburgs. Don Pedro, the Duke of Osuna, was the Spanish Habsburg ruler of Naples and a committed enemy of Venice. After the War of Gradisca, he organized a fleet, manned largely by Uskoks, to prey upon Venetian shipping. The Venetians succeeded in driving Osuna's ships out of the Adriatic by 1618, but only by relying on hired English and Dutch warships, whose sailors were quite willing to fight their Spanish enemies.

In that year, Venice found itself clogged with mercenaries fresh from the recent wars. Some, especially the English and Dutch, seem to have been motivated at least in part by their hatred of Catholics and Spaniards and so went on their way with the cessation of hostilities. Hundreds more, however, remained. These so-called *bravi* were simply hired killers, largely uninterested in religious or political ideologies. Many, indeed, had fought in Osuna's Adriatic fleet.

It was in this context that the Duke of Osuna hatched a wildly complex plan, to become known as the Spanish Conspiracy, in the spring of 1618. Working with the Spanish ambassador to the Republic, the Marquis of Bedmar, Spanish agents enlisted some of the *bravi* to mount a *coup d'état*, seize the Ducal Palace, and capture Venice. According to this plan, the mercenary cut-throats already in the city would be aided by a force of several hundred Spanish soldiers whom the Duke and the Marquis would somehow smuggle into Venice in disguise.

The conspiracy was so convoluted, and involved so many different people with diverse motivations and interests, that it could hardly be kept a secret. Indeed, the plot was revealed to the Ten by a French Protestant mercenary captain named Balthasar Juven who had no desire to assist Catholic Spain in such a plan. Word that the conspiracy had been discovered spread quickly among the foreign *bravi*, especially after they recognized some of their comrades hanging from the gallows in the Molo. The ringleaders were captured and executed, most after torture. All in all, about three hundred people were executed for their complicity in what turned out to have been a remarkably wide-ranging, though poorly organized, conspiracy. The Marquis of Bedmar and the Duke of Osuna were too powerful to be touched, of course, but Venice and its allies had certainly scored a fine propaganda victory over Spain by publicizing the details of the plot, which subsequently became the basis of Thomas Otway's 1682 play, *Venice Preserved.*

The Strange Story of Antonio Foscarini

The Spanish Conspiracy, though an improbable sort of plot from the start, left the Venetian authorities severely shaken. It also came on the heels of the interdict and the ongoing tensions with Rome. It was the bad luck of Senator Antonio Foscarini, a respected man from an old patrician family, to be implicated in yet another treasonous plot just as the dust was settling over the defeated Spanish Conspiracy.

Foscarini had been the Venetian ambassador to King Henry IV, King of France, and later to the court of James I, and had acquitted himself well in both posts. However, upon his return to Venice he was accused of various crimes, particularly selling state secrets, and was arrested by the Ten. By the summer of 1618 he was exonerated (after having spent the previous three years in prison), restored to his former position of privilege and government positions, and was even elected to the Senate.

In the meantime, an English noblewoman, Lady Arundel, had arrived in Venice in the company of her servants and two young sons. Establishing herself in the Palazzo Mocenigo-Nero, on the sharpest turn of the Grand Canal, she busied herself with collecting *objets d'art* (an occupation in which many of her future compatriots were to engage as well) and seeing that her two boys received a sound classical education. While she lived in Venice, Antonio Foscarini visited her occasionally. Future historians have debated the nature of their relationship. While some argue that the two were romantically involved, others contend that were not even particularly close friends.

Unfortunately, they both had powerful enemies. Lady Arundel, unlike most other English subjects, was a devout Catholic. The English ambassador to Venice, the famous English diplomat and poet Sir Henry Wotton (who had so admired Doge Donà and the rest of the 'Young') was, on the other hand, an equally devout Protestant and so regarded Lady Arundel with extreme suspicion. To further complicate

Sir Henry Wotton, the English ambassador to Venice who was both a diplomat and poet

matters, Sir Henry found his attempts at art collecting (on behalf of his patron the Duke of Buckingham) consistently foiled by Lady Arundel's highly refined taste and deep purse.

In 1622, the Ten received a tip that Foscarini had been plotting with Spaniards and various other arch-Catholics and that he had sold these nefarious parties state secrets. He was at once arrested. After a brief trial, he was convicted of treason and strangled. According to the rumours that instantly began to spread concerning the famous senator's demise, the Palazzo Mocenigo-Nero was at the centre of Foscarini's intrigues, and Lady Arundel was the sinister foreigner who co-ordinated the whole horrible business. Sir Henry quickly found out about Foscarini's fate, and its attendant rumours, and seems to have tried to use the situation to rid himself of the inconvenient Lady Arundel. He told her that she had been implicated in the plot and that she was about to be banished. He therefore advised her to quit Venice at once.

Much to the chagrin of Sir Henry, however, the plucky Lady Arundel decided to settle matters personally with the Doge himself. The very next day she arranged a meeting with Doge Antonio Priuli (1618-1623) during which she described Sir Henry's fears. The Doge assured her that, contrary to being considered in any way a threat to the Republic, she was highly regarded by one and all and was welcome to stay in Venice as long as she wished. The Ducal government, furthermore, readily acceded to her wishes that it publish a public letter clearing her of any wrong-doing or crimes. To underline the sincerity of his feelings, the Doge also arranged for her to attend the upcoming Marriage of the Sea celebrations as his personal guest. Six months later, when she headed back to England with her sons, the Venetian government allowed her to transport her considerable train of possessions, art, and other treasures (seventy bales of goods in all) duty free out of the Republic. Before she departed she made it a point to tell Sir Henry that she regarded the entire affair, which might have ended up quite badly, as entirely his fault. He was afraid that she might use her connections at court to relieve him of his position, but, apparently, she did not consider the matter, or possibly him, important enough and he continued his service as ambassador to the *Serenissima*.

As it turned out, he later became provost of Eton. A poet himself, he was good friends with John Donne and Izaak Walton. Among Wotton's many witty statements, he is perhaps best known for his quip that 'an ambassador is an honest man sent to lie abroad for the good of his country', an especially interesting remark given his conduct during the 'Arundel Affair'.

The surprises in this strange story did not end with Lady Arundel's departure, however. In August 1622, some information (it is not clear what it was or how it was discovered) was revealed that proved that the hapless Antonio Foscarini had actually been wrongly accused for a second time. The people who had framed him were themselves tried before the Three Inquisitors of State and subsequently executed. The members of the Council of Ten admitted they had made a tragic mistake, and posthumously acquitted Foscarini, who was given a funeral and reburied, at state expense, in the family chapel in the church of St Stae, where a plaque continues to declare his innocence to this day.

THE 'REFORMS' OF RANIERI ZEN AND THE TRIUMPH OF THE TEN

The fate of Antonio Foscarini symbolized, for many Venetians and especially members of the poorer nobility, what they considered the growing moral turpitude of their city, aggravated by the power and arrogance of the biggest and most powerful families. Coupled to this was the fear that the Council of Ten had become too powerful and was nothing but the tool of a dictatorial oligarchy. At the same time, the tensions between the 'Young' on the one hand, and the majority of the patricians, on the other, finally looked set to develop into some sort of party system.

These feelings and tensions contributed to an extraordinary episode in Venetian politics that, with the benefit of historical hindsight, marked the last serious attempt at reforming the Venetian constitutional and political order. The fact that the effort came to nothing says a great deal about the cautious and highly conservative attitudes of the majority of the Venetian nobility of the time.

The story began with the election of Giovanni Corner as Doge in 1625. The new Doge was, of course, from the old and wealthy family that had given Venice its first Queen, Catherine Corner (a.k.a. Cornaro), Queen of Cyprus. Doge Corner had never been especially interested in politics or business and his election came as something of a surprise. On the other hand, the Corner family had, over the years, done favours for a great many members of the Venetian nobility, as well as for the Papacy, and the Corners had every reason to expect some favours in return. Doge Corner was actually a moral and upright sort of person, who was greatly respected by the other old and wealthy families of the nobility. Unfortunately for him, however, his sons seem to have had much less concern about moral or legal niceties. For example, one of these sons, Frederico, Bishop of Bergamo, accepted a cardinal's hat from Pope Urban VIII. The other two were elected to a special committee (*zonta*) of the Senate in 1627 after some questionable balloting activities.

The Senate turned a blind eye to these elections and appointments, all of which were in stark violation of various existing laws and customs. They did not reckon, however, with a newly elected member of the Ten, a member of an old respected family, named Ranieri Zeno (or Zen in Venetian dialect). Zen already had a reputation as an eloquent, though somewhat arrogant and self-righteous, guardian of Venetian law and a champion of the poorer nobility against the richer. By 1627, he had become a sort of hero among many of the poorer nobility.

From the summer of 1627 through the autumn of 1628, Zen used the real or perceived abuses of power by Doge Corner and members of his family as a springboard for his demands that much of the machinery of the Venetian government, especially the Council of Ten, be thoroughly overhauled, and that the steady growth of the powers of the Ten be curtailed. His popularity among the poorer nobility and even among the commoners, was heightened after he survived an assassination attempt, on 30 December 1627, outside the Porta della Carta at the Palazzo. The Great Council finally formed a reform commission, headed by the old Nicolò Contarini, one of the 'Young', to work with Zen on a plan to reform the workings of the Council of Ten. Although initially supportive, Contarini gradually came to oppose, and perhaps fear, Zen. In particular, Contarini became increasingly uncomfortable with Zen's inflammatory language and his will-

ingness to stir up popular passions against the rich. These developments might have convinced Contarini that Zen had simply gone too
far. Indeed, Zen's self-righteous and increasingly shrill speeches even
began to frighten the members of the Great Council. In the autumn
of 1628, when that body reviewed the commission's plans for reining
in the powers of the Ten, it chose to change little. Even the poorer
patricians were apparently too frightened to contemplate any serious
reforms to the venerable structure of the Venetian political system.

After his defeat in the Great Council, Zen retired into his private
life where, in the words of John Julius Norwich, he enjoyed the
'respect of many but the friendship of none'. In any case, the energies
of the Venetians were soon absorbed in other matters.

The Cretan War (1644–1669)

After the end of the War of Gradisca (see above) in 1617, the threat of
Christian piracy slowly receded from the Adriatic and Mediterranean.
The destruction of the Spanish fleet by the Dutch in 1619, and the
gradual abandonment of piracy in favour of trade on the part of the
Dutch and English meant that Venetian merchant shipping, or what
was left of it, was considerably more secure by the 1630s than it had
been earlier in the century. The only real threat that remained was
posed by the Muslim pirates and corsairs of the Barbary Coast and the
eastern Mediterranean. By the terms of the Venetian–Ottoman peace
of 1573, the Ottoman authorities were supposed to suppress such piracy, and official Ottoman records and proclamations issued to the
regional governors and military commanders provide considerable
evidence that the Sultan's government made a good faith effort to
honour the terms of the peace. However, it seems that the relations
between the *Serenissima* and the Ottoman Empire were much better
at the official than at the local level. In fact, by the 1630s, many
Ottoman officials and governors along the coasts of Albania were in
open connivance with the Muslim corsairs. This situation led to an
increasing number of confrontations between the Venetians and the
forces under the control of the local Ottoman governors, culminating
in the 1638 Venetian attack on the Ottoman fortress town of Valona

(modern Vlorë), on the Albanian coast. These episodes severely strained the nominally peaceful Turco-Venetian relationship.

There were, of course, still Christian pirates operating in the Mediterranean who directed most of their raiding, theoretically at least, against Muslims. The most feared of these Christian corsairs by the mid-seventeenth century were the Knights of St John, operating from their bases on Malta. While continuing to cloak their activities in the language of the Crusades, they had really become nothing more than common pirates who, besides targeting Muslim ships, preyed on Christian vessels suspected of transporting goods belonging to Muslims or Jews. In consideration of their crusading mission, however, the Knights of St John, after having boarded a merchant ship, always were careful to torture the ship's captain until he 'confessed' that the cargo belonged to 'infidels' and thus could be seized by the Knights with their Christian consciences clear. While the Knights were a nuisance to Venetian merchants, their raids on Ottoman shipping and coastal towns in the Adriatic worsened the already strained Venetian-Ottoman relations. For just as the Ottomans were bound to control the Muslim corsairs in the Mediterranean, the Venetians were supposed to police the waters of the Adriatic.

Tensions continued to rise between the Venetians and Ottomans until 1644. In October of that year, a squadron of Knights captured an Ottoman ship carrying pilgrims on their way to Mecca via Alexandria. They were, however, no ordinary pilgrims; they were distinguished members of the Sultan's court, including thirty ladies of the Imperial harem. The vessel also carried a load of treasure and slaves. The Knights and their loot headed for Crete where the Venetian governor ordered them to move on, not wanting to be implicated in an act of piracy.

Nevertheless, when word of the raid reached Istanbul, the Sultan and many of his advisors were convinced that the Venetians were complicit in the incident. It is also likely that by this time relations with the Venetians had reached such a low level that the Ottomans reasoned that war was inevitable. In any case, the continued Venetian domination of Crete meant that the security of Ottoman shipping in the eastern Mediterranean would always be in jeopardy. In April 1645, an

Ottoman fleet of at least four hundred ships with fifty thousand men launched an attack on Crete.

The long war that followed revealed a great deal about the condition both of Venice and of its old enemy, the Ottoman Empire. Both of these great powers were in the midst of profound internal reorganizations and had just endured a number of crises. Neither could muster the sort of military resources they had been able to command just half a century earlier. Furthermore, the Venetians no longer relied as heavily on commerce with the Ottomans as they had in the previous century. In those earlier wars, as we have seen, it was in the interest of both belligerents to bring hostilities to a close as quickly as possible so that everyone could get back to the profitable trade in spices, textiles, and slaves. Thus, the Cretan War dragged on for decades with neither side able to administer a decisive defeat to the other. The Venetians were generally victorious in naval engagements, but were unable to prevent the Ottomans from reinforcing their positions on the island.

In an attempt to blockade the Ottoman navy, the Venetians tried to carry the war close to Istanbul itself. The most famous of such attempts was the Battle of Dardanelles (17-19 July 1657), considered by some historians as the greatest Ottoman naval defeat since Lepanto. The Venetian commander, Lazzaro Mocenigo, destroyed an Ottoman fleet several times larger than his own, and was poised to continue up the Straits to attack Istanbul. A direct hit from Ottoman coastal artillery, however, struck his flagship and blew up the powder magazine. Mocenigo was killed instantly by a falling mast, his dramatic end recorded in a painting now in the Naval Museum in Venice. Despite their defeat, the Ottomans reinforced their positions on Crete from naval bases elsewhere in the Aegean. Venetian control of Crete was finally reduced to the fortress of Candia which held out for twenty-two years and became a destination for all sorts of crusaders, adventurers, and bored young noblemen from throughout Christendom. It was, in fact, after one particularly dramatic (but utterly ineffectual) sortie out of the fortress led by some young French knights, that Francesco Morosini, the Venetian commander, determined that further resistance was futile. He negotiated a lenient truce with the Ottomans that allowed the Venetians to withdraw in good order (and with most of their belongings) and even maintained Venetian rule over some small Aegean islands. While some in Venice thought of Morosini as a traitor, most recognized that he had probably made the best of a bad situation.

FRANCESCO MOROSINI 'IL PELEPONNESIACO'

The Venetians did not have to wait long for their chance to avenge the loss of Crete. In 1683 the Ottomans besieged Vienna for the second time (the first siege was in 1526), and the city was saved only by the timely arrival of Polish troops under King Jan Sobieski. The Habsburgs then went on a counter-offensive led by the military genius, Prince Eugene of Savoy. A new Holy League was organized, which Venice joined in January 1684. The ensuing war was to mark the last episode of Venetian martial glory.

As it happened, the ducal throne was empty when Venice joined the Holy League against the Ottomans. The electors chose an elderly and pious bachelor, the scholar Marcantonio Giustinian, as the new Doge. Francesco Morosini, who had distinguished himself during the Cretan War, had wanted the ducal *corno* himself, but was instead picked to be captain general of the Republic's naval forces in this new war against the Turks. In July, Morosini's fleet of sixty-eight ships sailed off amidst considerable enthusiasm and excitement. The departure of the fleet, by the way, is pictured in a painting in Room XVII in the Museo Correr, along with numerous other paintings and artifacts from the life of 'il Peleponnesiaco'.

Over the next three years Morosini went from victory to victory, and Doge Giustinian was nicknamed the 'Te Deum Man' because of the numerous thanksgiving services over which he presided. The Republic hired a Swedish general, Count Otto Wilhelm von Konigsmarck (whose portrait hangs in Venice's Naval Museum) to command its land forces. With this help, the Venetians conquered almost the entire Morea, including some chunks of real estate which had been lost to the Ottomans over one hundred years earlier, such as Coron.

While the Venetians naturally celebrated their victories over the Ottomans, the war also included an event that (like the sack of

Constantinople during the ignominious Fourth Crusade) involved Venetian forces in an episode of breathtaking vandalism. By the fall of 1687, while Konigsmarck's men were consolidating control over the Morea, Morosini's fleet began its siege of Athens. On Monday, 26 September 1687, at around seven in the evening, a direct hit from one of Morosini's mortars almost destroyed the Parthenon, on the Acropolis of Athens, which the Ottomans had (rather unfortunately) decided to use as a gunpowder magazine. After his subsequent conquest of the city, Morosini further damaged the already weakened building by trying to remove the sculpture of Athena's horse-drawn chariot, which shattered on the ground. As consolation, he collected two lion sculptures, which ultimately ended up in front of the Arsenal building.

In the meantime, the much beloved Doge Giustinian died in 1688 and was laid to rest in the church of San Francesco della Vigna. The patricians straight away elected Francesco Morosini (*in absentia*) as his successor. Finally having achieved his lifelong aim, Morosini began preparations for his triumphal return to the lagoon, planning, on his way home, to capture Negroponte (the modern Euboea), a former Venetian colony that had been lost to the Ottomans back in 1470. His men, however, were tired, and some of the Imperial forces from Hanover mutinied. To make matters worse, an epidemic of some sort, possibly malaria, spread through the Venetian troops, killing a third of them within weeks. Konigsmarck himself died. Under these conditions, Morosini had to lift the siege of Negroponte and head for Venice. Along the way, he too fell ill, and it was in this condition that he returned to a hero's welcome.

Fighting against the Ottomans continued in the Aegean, without any major defeats but with no significant victories either. In the spring of 1693 the warrior Doge Morosini once again assumed personal command of the Republic's forces. But Francesco Morosini was by now an old man and had never fully recovered from the illness he had contracted off Negroponte. After achieving some important, but unspectacular, victories he died while wintering at Nauplion, in January 1694. He was buried in the church of Santo Stefano, where a bronze badge in the nave marks his tomb. He was also memorialized by the rather odd marble triumphal arch in the Sala dello Scrutino in the Ducal Palace, which also holds paintings representing his victories.

Under the next Doge, Silvestro Valier (1694–1700), the war against the Ottomans continued. Valier did not personally lead the Venetian forces, a situation stipulated by the patricians themselves. Many of the patricians, while admiring Morosini's exploits, were nevertheless uneasy with political and military power concentrated in one person. Accordingly, Venice's fleet was commanded by a series of captains general who, while scoring impressive victories, were unable to recapture Crete or Negroponte, and in fact, lost a major battle off the island of Chios.

By the winter of 1699, the Ottomans, though not totally defeated, were nevertheless exhausted and the warring parties met at Karlowitz (now Sremski Karlovci) to negotiate an end to the war. As far as Venice was concerned, the Peace of Karlowitz was a mixed victory. While the Venetians were able to hold onto their conquests in the Peloponnesus and Dalmatia, they were obliged by their allies in the Holy League to return to the Sultan territories in Attica, including Athens, as well as all the territory they had seized north of the Gulf of Corinth. Doge Valier reluctantly signed the treaty on 7 February 1699.

CONCLUSION

Thus, for the last time in its history, Venice once again had a land empire in the eastern Mediterranean and was once again able to imagine itself as a great power. In fact, Venice still had the appearance of a great and wealthy city. The recently completed (1681) church of Santa Maria della Salute was one indication of the Republic's artistic vigour. In the field of music, Claudio Monteverdi (1567–1643), probably the most important figure in early baroque music, was the musical director for St Mark's Basilica from 1613. While in Venice he composed a tremendous corpus of liturgical music, as well as his famous opera *L'incoronazione di Poppea* (1642). Less spectacularly, but perhaps more important in the day-to-day life of the people, the Merceria was finally paved in 1676.

Despite these accomplishments, the victories over the Ottoman Empire were to prove hollow. The fact that the Venetian delegates at

Karlowitz were unable to press successfully for their Republic's demands was indicative of the generally weakened state in which Venice found itself by the end of the seventeenth century. Both in foreign and domestic policy, Venice's strategy had evolved, by the end of the century, into one of timid neutrality. The end of the reform commission of Zen and Contarini had signalled the end of the possibility that either the poorer nobles, or the 'Young', or some combination of the two, would be able to build a party system to address some of the serious problems that had crept into Venice's (in many ways admirable) constitutional system. Instead, political life stagnated, and the Ten developed into something resembling what its critics had always accused it of being: a dictatorship of the oligarchy. In foreign affairs too, the patricians were unable, or unwilling, to contemplate the bold steps that would have been necessary to maintain Venice's military and commercial power. Instead, the Republic adopted a policy of unarmed neutrality, relying only on diplomacy to protect the interests of Venice and its citizens. As the events of the coming century would demonstrate, it was a fateful path.

Doge Silvestro Valier died on 7 July 1700 of a stroke after a ferocious argument with his wife. Perhaps contritely, she commissioned an immense tomb for her late husband (in which she was also eventually interred), which takes up a huge section of the south wall of San Zanipolo. As Norwich observed, 'It is somehow fitting that this, the last and perhaps most sumptuous of the great ducal tombs in all Venice, should have been reserved for the last doge of the seventeenth century'. Indeed. During the next century, the *Serenissima* was to enter a period of decadence and dotage, to end ultimately in its extinction almost exactly one hundred years after the death of Valier.

CHAPTER SEVEN

The Twilight of the Republic
1700-1797

The Treaty of Karlowitz allowed Venice to imagine itself a great Imperial power for one last time, and the victories of Morosini over the Ottomans, culminating in the conquest of the Morea, seemed to reconfirm this vision. Yet, these victories turned out to be hollow indeed. In fact, the rest of the eighteenth century would prove that the victories and conquests of the last few years of the seventeenth century were the last major triumphs that Venice would win. Instead, the Republic retreated into passivity and irrelevance until its independent existence was finally snuffed out a little over one thousand years after it had been born. The melancholy of this period was captured by many poets and artists, perhaps most famously Robert Browning, who wrote in *A Toccata of Galuppi's*:

> As for Venice and its people, merely born to bloom and drop
> Here on earth they bore their fruitage, mirth and folly were the crop:
> What of soul was left, I wonder, when the kissing had to stop?

Instead of the mighty capital of an empire, Venice in the eighteenth century became a prime tourist destination and the playground of Europe. And it is this Venice, the Venice of endless Carnival, courtesans, Casanovas, and Canalettos, that probably figures largest in the popular imagination of today. Contemporary Venetians and foreigners also had mixed feelings about what they saw around them. The paintings and frescoes of Gian Domenico Tiepolo (on view at the Ca' Rezzonico Museum) have an eerie sense of frivolity to them. They portray the blundering flirtations of clowns and dandies, or the pastimes of the

151

idle rich. Likewise, the scenes of aristocratic or bourgeois life painted by Pietro Longhi (1702-1785) give an idea of the pleasant, if unproductive, diversions that now occupied many of the Venetian moneyed classes.

On the other hand, it would be easy to argue that historians, and indeed many eighteenth-century observers of Venice, have been much too harsh in their judgments. It is true that Venice ceased to be a great Imperial power, winning military victories and dominating the seas. But, between 1718 and 1797, Venice managed, incredibly, to avoid the carnage of the wars that wracked most of Europe during this era. As John Julius Norwich suggested, it might be worth asking, especially in this day and age, if the maintenance of peace for eight decades, almost entirely through the use of diplomacy, is not in itself an impressive accomplishment.

Venice, in fact, remained an Imperial power right up until its end. From 1718 until 1797 the Venetian Empire, while reduced in size, held onto considerable real estate including much of the Albanian and Dalmatian coasts, including their many islands, the Ionian islands, Istria, and much of the Friuli and Veneto on the Italian mainland. While it did not gain any more territory, it was able to hang onto these possessions despite being almost completely surrounded by increasingly powerful and acquisitive neighbours. Likewise, contrary to common perceptions, the economic situation in Venice was quite strong, especially during the second half of the eighteenth century.

Yet the world had changed by this period and Venice's institutions had not evolved to meet the new challenges of the time. Indeed, as we saw in the last chapter, the patricians of the seventeenth century rejected any reform of their political system. The greater the threats that confronted Venice, the more determined the Venetian ruling classes were to maintain without alteration the venerable Venetian constitution.

The Peace of Passarowitz and the Loss of the Peloponnesus

An example of the military and diplomatic weakness of Venice presented itself early in the eighteenth century. The Venetians gained possession of the Peloponnesus by the terms of the Treaty of Karlowitz. Far from being a prize, the area, called the Morea by the Venetians, turned out to be poor and fractious. The Greek Orthodox inhabitants were only marginally more receptive to the rule of their fellow Christians than to their erstwhile Muslim masters. The Venetian administration of the territory, moreover, was hardly calculated to endear the inhabitants to Venice. The impressive fortifications constructed by Venetian engineers in the Peloponnesus were paid for by increased taxes on the local population, which also provided the conscript labour. The Venetians further aggravated local sensibilities by installing Catholic clergymen in the area, in the face of vociferous protests by the Orthodox Christian clerical establishment.

The return to the Ottomans of the northern shore of the Gulf of Corinth and the territory of Attica, provided for by the terms of the Treaty of Karlowitz, meant that the Venetians occupied a strategically untenable position in the Morea. The extent of this vulnerability was demonstrated in a very short time. In 1715, flushed with victory in a war with their Russian enemies, the Ottomans decided to go on the offensive against the Venetians in the Peloponnesus. Venice's forces were routed and the region completely re-occupied by the Ottomans in a matter of a few months. Venice's last remaining outposts on Crete, Suda and Spinalunga, were indefensible and also fell to the Ottomans. By 1716, only the Venetian fortress of Corfu held out. In August of that year, the Venetian forces under the command of the brilliant soldier-of-fortune Mathias Johann von der Schulenburg managed to break out of the siege and rout the Ottoman forces.

In the meantime, Venice's ally in the Holy League, the Habsburg Empire, came to the aid of the Republic. The military genius Prince Eugene of Savoy, commander of the Habsburg army, utterly defeated the Ottomans in the northern Balkans by 1718. The Ottomans now had to move troops north to face the new Habsburg threat and so suffered a number of defeats at the hands of the resurgent Venetians in the south. By May 1718 the Ottoman Empire decided to sue for peace. The resulting Peace of Passarowitz turned over several important slabs of Ottoman Balkan territory (including Belgrade) to the Habsburgs, but, significantly, the Ottomans were allowed to keep control of the Morea and their conquests of the remaining Venetian territory on Crete. The Venetian delegates at Passarowitz, led by the very able diplomat Carlo Ruzzini, were unable to convince their Habsburg allies to agree to a more generous settlement. For the Habsburgs, the Venetian demands did not need to be taken seriously.

An unintended consequence of the Venetian occupation of the Morea was the migration to the lagoon of an order of Armenian monks, the Mekhitarists. Founded by Mekhitar Bedrosian in Istanbul in 1700, the order was part of a broader intellectual revival among the Armenian population of the Middle East. The Mekhitarists were viewed by the established Armenian clergy as a serious threat, however, and sought refuge in Venetian-ruled Morea. When the Ottomans reconquered the area in 1715, Mekhitar and his order fled to Venice. In 1717, the Venetian authorities turned over the island of San Lazzaro, a former leper colony near the Lido, to Mekhitar and his small group of about twenty monks. The order rapidly developed the island into an important base of Armenian learning and became famous for their publishing activities.

ECONOMIC DECLINE?

The economic decline of Venice, like its decline in general, continues to be a hotly debated historical problem. As we have seen in the preceding chapter, most historians agree that signs of weakness were clearly evident as early as the seventeenth century. By the eighteenth these signs had become unmistakable. On the other hand, there are also indications that an economic revival was in progress.

The Venetian ship-building industry's decline during the seventeenth century contributed to the stagnation of Venice's maritime commerce, and consequently, to a decline in the Venetian state's revenues during the eighteenth century. Much of Venice's income had traditionally come from taxes and duties levied on ships transiting the Adriatic. Even vessels that did not stop in Venice had to pay a duty on certain items, especially salt. By the early eighteenth century, however, Dutch, English, and Spanish ships simply sailed past the outmoded Venetian galleys sent to intercept them.

The Venetian government belatedly acted to address these problems. In 1736, Doge Alvise Pisani (1735-1741) lifted the financially ruinous requirement that all ships had to travel in convoys. Instead, any ship of larger dimensions (at least 70 feet long, with a minimum crew of 40 and 24 guns) could sail unescorted. This immediately led to a ship-building boom as merchants rushed to purchase these larger ships. Perhaps more importantly, in the same year the government lifted many of its ancient protectionist policies. The effects were dramatic as merchandise and money poured into the Rialto. The historian Frederic Lane argued that the 'total tonnage moving through the port of Venice was larger in 1783...than ever before in the thousand years of the city's history'.

The Venetian government also finally moved to strengthen the lagoon's defences against the storms of the northern Adriatic. Unusually high seas in 1686 and 1691 had destroyed the ancient sea walls protecting the southern part of the lagoon at Pellestrina and Sottomarina. In 1744, under the reign of Doge Pietro Grimani (1741-1752) construction was finally begun on a new system of sea walls on the southern *lidi*. These walls, called the *Murazzi*, were huge structures, built of tremendous blocks of Istrian stone. In places the walls were fourteen metres (forty-six feet) wide, and four and one half metres (almost fifteen feet) high. This massive undertaking was not completed until 1783, during the time of Doge Paolo Renier (1779-1789). Other improvements to the urban landscape were carried out as well. In 1722, the brick paving in the Piazza was replaced with flagstones. The Campanile, which had been struck by lighting at least five times in the sixteenth century alone, was finally fitted with a lightning rod in 1776.

These economic developments and improvements to the infrastructure, while certainly dramatic, were also too little, too late. Significantly, even as Venetian shipping and commercial activity was reviving during the eighteenth century, industry declined. Venetian manufactured goods such as textiles (including lace), glass, and books continued to be produced and exported, but French competition had replaced Venice as the leading producer of luxury goods. In fact, Venetian industrial output declined, both relative to its earlier levels, as well as in relation to the growing productivity of other European industrial centres.

The eighteenth-century revival of merchant shipping, and the decline of industry, are both part of an interesting (and tragic) tale of the fate of Venetian nobility during this period. For by this time, the patricians had mostly lost interest in mercantile or industrial pursuits, both of which were handled increasingly by commoners, and even foreigners (especially Slavic immigrants from Dalmatia). Instead, the patricians came to regard agriculture as the only respectable way to make money, and relied on rents from their mainland estates to maintain their lavish lifestyles. The patricians had historically provided the backbone of the commercial, and thus political, structure of the Republic. Thus, this change within patrician culture had dire long-term consequences for the nobility as a class, as well as for the Republic in general.

THE DECLINE OF THE PATRICIANS

One of the side effects of Venice's social and economic transformation during the eighteenth century was the slow extinction of the patrician class. As commercial and industrial ventures proved increasingly less profitable (and more risky) many patrician families decided to abandon such pursuits and instead to live off rents from their mainland holdings, or from family fortunes. Some of the families who owned profitable estates on *terra firma* were able to make ends meet, but more and more patrician families slowly slid into poverty. This situation exacerbated a problem which had long plagued Venice's nobility: marriage. Since status and privilege passed through the male line, the son of a patrician family could marry a woman of *cittadini* rank and pass his privileges on to their children. Even in Venice's golden age, however, this seems rarely to have happened, and such 'mixed marriages' became virtually non-existent by the eighteenth century. The reason for this lack of intermarriage between classes was that, among the increasingly impoverished nobles, a bride's dowry became an important source of income for the newly married couple. As families fell on hard times, they frequently had enough money for only one daughter to marry. With fewer available mates, more patrician sons ended up as bachelors. Even during the sixteenth century about 50 per cent of the nobility never married, but that figure had soared to 66 per cent by the eighteenth century. A dramatic example of the situation is that, of the fourteen Doges in office between 1675 and 1775, only four had ever been married.

Thus, during the eighteenth century, many Venetian noble houses simply died out. In the middle of the sixteenth century, the Great Council included about 2,500 members. After some ups and downs, the number shrank to about 1,700 after the great plague of 1630. It never recovered. By 1775 it had fallen to 1,300 and in 1797 to only 1,090. Frederic Lane estimated that in 1520, 6.4 per cent of adult Venetian males were patricians. In 1797, the percentage was only 3.2.

The Great Council tried to increase its numbers by taking the unprecedented step of opening the Golden Book to anyone who could pay 100,000 ducats (a sum equal to over US$10 million in today's money) and could be personally recommended by a member of the Collegio. Between 1645 and 1718, 127 persons were thus ennobled. Even these drastic procedures were not enough to end the slow decline of the Venetian nobility.

Of even greater importance was the effect of the decline of the nobility on Venice's political institutions. The declining number of patricians meant that the numbers of candidates legally qualified to hold many government jobs (most of which had terms of only one year) were very low. For example, the post of *Savio Grande* was only open to a nobleman who had distinguished himself (not only by his intelligent diplomacy but also in his display of wealth) as ambassador to an important court, such as Paris or Rome. According to Frederic Lane, one late-seventeenth-century nobleman commented that there were only fourteen or fifteen patricians qualified to fill such a position. It is estimated that during the eighteenth century, there were only forty-two families who had the wealth, prestige, and qualifications necessary for government service.

Not only did the patricians decline as a group, but more and more individual nobles found themselves falling on hard economic times. These numbers were inflated by the throngs of suddenly impoverished nobles fleeing Crete after its fall to the Ottomans. They swelled the ranks of the poor nobles, called *Barnabotti*, since many lived in the neighbourhood of San Barnabo. Nobles were forbidden to learn a craft or to engage in manual labour, and the days of free-wheeling commerce in which an enterprising young nobleman could earn a fortune on galley journeys to the East were long gone. The Barnabotti thus became an embittered and restive sub-class within the nobility, reduced to selling their votes or trying to get government sinecures.

This peculiar auto-extinction of the patrician class contributed to the ever-growing number of unmarried (and unmarrigeable) young women. Again, this was an old problem in Venice, but it became acute during the eighteenth century. The traditional fate of these women was confinement to a convent, with which Venice was well supplied. Eventually, many (if not most) of the nuns in the city's religious orders were there not out of any personal religious conviction, or from a desire for a cloistered life style, but out of a sense of family duty and fatalistic resignation. As a result, many convents ended up hosting all manner of social events, especially literary discussions, as a way of passing the time. Perhaps inevitably, however, many also acquired a reputation for more intimate sorts of gatherings. Indeed, as early as 1497, one horrified Franciscan preacher described the convents of Venice as little more than brothels. In 1739, a French traveller in Venice alleged that the newly arrived Papal Nuncio had the choice of three mistresses, each supplied by a different Venetian convent.

The bachelorhood forced on many sons of the nobility and the enforced spinsterhood of their sisters created a strong demand for prostitutes. Even for a port city, the number of prostitutes in Venice was supposed to have been unusually high, and the ladies themselves were famous for their mastery of all sorts of exotic sexual positions and contortions.

EUROPE'S PLAYGROUND

The real or imagined delights offered by Venice's legions of prostitutes were but one reason that Venice developed into a prime tourist playground during the eighteenth century. Its breathtaking setting and magnificent architecture, not to mention its hoards of art, combined to make Venice an obligatory stop on the 'Grand Tour' of Europe that was considered a rite of passage for Europe's young educated gentlemen. Gambling also became a favourite pastime for visitors and locals. The Ridotto at San Moise became the most famous casino of them all, and indeed *ridotto* became the Venetian slang for a gambling hall. Another social institution that grew during the period, and which became at least as popular as the gambling halls, were coffee houses. There are a dozen ringing the Piazza alone, among the most famous being the Florian (opened in 1720) and the Quadri (1775).

The wealthy young gentlemen visiting Venice on the Grand Tour naturally wanted souvenirs, and what could be a better memento than a piece of art? Art collecting became so popular that the Council of Ten tried to inventory all of the art treasures in Venice's churches to prevent them from being spirited away by wealthy tourists. The demand for artworks also stimulated the development of a new genre in Venetian painting: urban landscapes. The masters of this new subject matter were certainly Giovanni Antonio Canal, better known as Canaletto (1679-1768), and Francesco Guardi (1712-1793). Both produced paintings of Venetian scenes aimed at the tourist market, but each developed a distinctive style. Canaletto became known for his sharply focused, crisply realistic views, while Guardi's style, sometimes called proto-impressionist, used bold, even messy, brush work to mimic the effects of light, reflection, and shadow.

Besides tales of prostitutes, gambling houses, and charming landscape paintings, the main symbol of eighteenth-century Venice is certainly the Carnival. Originally a two-month long period of feasting before the rigours of Lent, by the eighteenth century the Venetian Carnival season began in October and lasted five months. During this time of partying, people of all social classes mingled and cavorted, their identities hidden behind all manner of masks. By the end of the century, Carnival had become so important that the death of Doge Paolo Renier on 13 February 1789 was concealed from the public so as not to disturb the merrymaking.

Perhaps no figure symbolizes the mythology of eighteenth-century Venice better than Giovanni Giacomo Casanova (1725-1798). His name has, of course, become synonymous with passionate lovers and seducers, but Casanova's biography is illustrative of mid-eighteenth-

The notorious Giovanni Casanova (1725-98)

century Venice in a variety of other ways.

He was born into a family of actors and quickly became an accomplished musician. Casanova's musical abilities, not to mention his carefully cultivated charm, gave him access to Venetian high society and provided the material for many of his stories. His shenanigans finally brought him to the attention of the authorities, who accused him of practicing witchcraft and imprisoned him in the infamous *piombi*. His daring escape in 1755 was made possible largely because a servant in the Ducal Palace mistook him for a government functionary. After his escape, he made his way to Paris where he worked for a time as director of the state lottery and became acquainted with Louis XV, Madame de Pompadour, and Rousseau among others. By 1785, he had secured a comfortable position as the director of the library of a Bohemian nobleman, where he remained until his death. It was also during this time that he wrote his entertaining, but probably highly embellished, memoirs, published in twelve volumes after his death.

The titillating tales of courtesans, Carnival, and Casanova helped to create the enduring myth of a lascivious, morally decadent eighteenth-century Venice. Some historians have pointed out, however, that the populations of large eighteenth-century cities all over Europe were quite well acquainted with gambling, prostitution, adultery, and all the other vices for which Venice was famous. Frederic Lane has commented that what really made Venice such a desirable place for eighteenth-century partygoers was not 'the depths of its iniquity but the pervasiveness of its frivolity'.

The Arts

In the midst of the superficial gaiety of the Carnival, eighteenth-century Venice was also a place of impressive artistic accomplishments. During the second half of the seventeenth century, building on the work of Monteverdi, Venetian composers made Venice the leading operatic centre in Europe, with seventeen theatres by the end of the seventeenth century. Perhaps even more important than the music of these operas, however, were the breakthroughs of Venetian engineers and stage managers, who devised methods for the rapid change of stage sets and scenery. Venice also became famous for its organists, violinists, and girls' choirs.

The most famous of Venice's opera houses was (and remains) La Fenice ('The Phoenix'). When it was built in 1791-1792 it was the world's first public opera house. That is, it was not constructed by a government (or some individual nobleman) but rather by subscriptions from the city's wealthy patricians. These well-off opera fans purchased boxes in the opera house, which they passed down through the generations. Since the boxes were regarded by their holders as their personal property, many people would simply come to the theatre to socialize (instead of paying attention to the performance), a practice that later appalled Effie Ruskin. As she described the scene (here quoted by Mary Lutyens), one's box at the opera was '...a sort of tower of Babel...I complained of it...and they [the Venetian box-holders] were all against me; they said that the Theatre was public property and everybody had a right to call upon any body that they knew, and as most people went every night for an hour it was economical as it saved them lighting their rooms at home, and having a box at the opera was the cheapest way for all to see people and society.' Some of the box-holders eventually sold their boxes to others, and by the time World War I was over the responsibilities of owning a box became too oner-ous and the owners eventually sold them to the city of Venice, which now owns and operates the theatre.

La Fenice was small for an opera house (seating only about 900 peo-ple) but its interior acoustics were superb, due (some have speculated), at least in part to the large amounts of wood used in the interior con-struction. Unfortunately, this choice of building materials contributed to two terrific fires at the theatre. The first was in 1836, after which the theatre was quickly rebuilt, with a more opulent exterior than its spartan neo-classical original. The second fire, in 1996, which thor-oughly gutted the building, has been blamed on two electricians working on the building. Much to the locals' surprise, the reconstruc-tion work proceeded quickly and the theatre re-opened on schedule in December 2003. La Fenice, true to its name, has risen from the ashes yet again.

Probably Venice's most famous composer, Antonio Vivaldi (c.1675-1741), is best known today not for his operas (almost all of which are now lost) but for his numerous other works. Nicknamed *il prete rosso* (the red-haired priest), Vivaldi worked for most of his life as music director for the girls' orphanage Santa Maria della Pietà on the Riva Schiavoni. Besides his church music and operas, he also composed over four hundred concertos. Of these last, his string concertos made a pro-found impression on J. S. Bach. Although Vivaldi was probably born and lived most of his life in Venice, he left the city for Vienna shortly before his death in 1741.

Another of Venice's most famous composers, Baldassare Galuppi (1706-1762), worked for much of his professional life as the music director at the Ospedale dei Mendicanti. Born on the island of Burano (where his statue now stands), he overcame some initial disasters to become an internationally famous composer, especially of operas.

Much of Galuppi's work was in collaboration with one of the most important figures in the history of Italian theatre, the Venice-born

The composer Antonio Vivaldi (c. 1675–1741) nicknamed *il preto rosso* – the red priest

Carlo Goldoni (1707–1793) who is usually regarded as the creator of modern Italian theatrical comedy. He was compelled by his father to study law, which he in fact practised off and on during his life, but from a young age he was in love with the theatre. He ran away from home several times to join travelling theatrical groups, and it was during these sojourns that he became acquainted with the dominant Italian comedic style of the time, known as *commedia dell'arte*. This theatrical genre was characterized by improvisation on a basic story line using stock character types, usually identified by distinctive masks. The style thus highlighted the skill of the individual actors rather than plot or character development. Goldoni, initially building on some of the stock characters of the genre, wrote plays that substituted careful observation of everyday life, for the (frequently bawdy) and contrived improvisation of the *commedia dell'arte*. His best plays (some in Venetian dialect), written between 1748 and 1760, ironically, yet realistically portrayed the follies of Venetian middle and lower-class life. As noted above, he and Galuppi collaborated on a number of works. Galuppi wrote much of the music for Goldoni's plays, while Goldoni wrote many of the libretti for Galuppi's operas. Although Goldoni remained popular in Venice, he decided to leave in 1762 for Paris, where he became director of the Comédie Italienne. As a result of the French Revolution, however, he lost his position and fortune and died in poverty.

Although Goldoni's plays were popular and influential, they provoked a backlash led by Count Carol Gozzi (1720-1806) who accused him of abandoning Italian styles of comedy, and instead aping the French comedic style of Molière. Gozzi tried, with considerable success, to write plays that incorporated the traditional *commedia dell'arte* characters and themes, rather than the techniques and styles of foreign, especially French, theatre. He was also famous for his dramatization of classic fairy tales. One of his plays, *Re Turandot* (1762) eventually became the basis for Puccini's famous opera.

Any discussion of this rich artistic environment must include some mention of the famous sculptor Antonio Canova (1757-1822). From a family of stonemasons, the young Canova was deeply impressed with the classical sculptures he saw on a visit to Rome. He subsequently abandoned his earlier rococo style works and instead became the master of a neo-classical movement in sculpture. Although he deeply loved Venice, he (like Goldoni) ended up moving to Paris, where he became Napoleon's court sculptor. Today, much of his work (and a distinctive mausoleum containing his heart) can be seen in the Correr Museum in Venice.

The Fall of the Republic

Venice was not quite the economically bankrupt, and morally depraved place of popular mythology. Nor had its artistic energies been exhausted. Yet, the perception of Venetian weakness, both by outsiders and Venetians themselves, was a reflection of the inability of Venice's political and social institutions to adapt themselves to the world of late-eighteenth-century Europe. The fact is, Venice had by that time become largely irrelevant politically. The speed with which the Morea fell to the Ottomans (not, by the way, a particular power-ful military force themselves) in 1715 was one reflection of the sorry state of Venetian military strength, while their lack of diplomatic standing prevented any real gains from the Peace of Passarowitz.

There were, of course, some moves to try to ameliorate the situa-tion. One of the most important of these eighteenth-century reform-ers was the energetic and imaginative Admiral Angelo Emo (who died in 1792). Under his direction, the Venetians scored some notable vic-tories over the Barbary pirates (including a successful attack against Tunis in 1785), and the Arsenal began to produce up-to-date warships. However, as already noted, the patrician families (in which Emo, too, was rooted) had declined in wealth and numbers and had largely lost interest in affairs of state, to say nothing of warfare. A sober, even bleak, assessment of Venice's situation was offered by Doge Paolo Renier (1779-1789). Even as Admiral Emo was winning victories against the North African corsairs, Doge Renier said: 'If there is a state that is in need of concord it is ours. We have neither ground nor sea forces, nor even alliances, we who accept our fate as it comes and simply trust the caution of the Venetian Republic's government.'

As Doge Renier observed, Venice by 1789 was militarily weak, but had also decided not to seek strong allies as possible protectors. Any attempts to reform the political or military system had long since been stymied by the paralyzing 'caution' of the handful of powerful families that now ruled the Republic.

Renier's remarks were made in the context of one of the last gasps of the reformist spirit. The grievances voiced by Rainieri Zen in the mid-seventeenth century had been silenced, but they continued to fester among the poorer nobility who felt themselves, quite correctly, barred from any real political power. Two representatives of these dis-enfranchised and impoverished patricians, Giorgio Pisani and Carlo Contarini, managed to gain positions in the Venetian government and harangued the Great Council with accusations against the political establishment. But the handful of powerful families that actually ran Venice had no intention of listening to such upstarts and Pisani and Contarini were imprisoned.

Upon Renier's death in that fateful year of 1789, the Great Council met to elect what turned out to be Venice's last Doge. Their choice was Lodovico Manin, a member of a powerful family of Friulian origin that had only been admitted to the ranks of the nobility in 1651. Manin had a solid, if not terribly distinguished, record of service to the Republic, and was known for his personal honesty and an extremely shy personality. It is said that he was so agitated when he heard of his election to the office of Doge that he fainted. Nevertheless, the celebrations he staged as part of his coronation were among the grandest in living memory, and that put them up against some stiff competition.

Manin and the rest of the *Serenissima's* government were fully aware of the events in Paris beginning in the summer of 1789. As the years progressed, Venetian diplomats and agents in France reported, with growing alarm, the events of the Revolution. The Venetian ambassador grew so terrified that he simply fled Paris with his family in 1792 for the safety of London. While the members of Venice's small ruling elite were clearly shocked by the news coming out of France, the poorer patricians, still smarting over the treatment of their champions Pisani and Contarini, looked at these same events in a very different way. Indeed, growing numbers of Venetians became interested in the radical ideas of liberty, equality, and fraternity.

Meanwhile, the conservative governments of Europe were frantically making plans for the containment of the revolutionary energies which threatened at any moment to boil out of France. As early as 1791 the King of Sardinia proposed a defensive alliance of the Italian states, including Venice. A similar offer was made in 1792, and in 1793 the most powerful states in Europe, including Great Britain, Prussia, and Austria, had banded together for the war with France and invited Venice to join their coalition.

These overtures, coupled with the growing fear of a domestic revolution, again compelled some Venetian patricians to argue for drastic action and political reform. Yet, the frantic calls of the minority for an alliance with the anti-revolutionary forces and an immediate increase in military expenditures were silenced by the same majority of conservative great families. They argued that it was far too late for any sort of military reform, which would be, in any case, too expensive. The majority of the patricians argued that Venice's only course of action was in the maintenance of its neutrality.

Venice's neutral position proved more and more difficult to maintain as the wars between France and the conservative monarchies of Europe began; especially after 1795 when the wars moved onto Italian soil. By the summer of 1796, the French armies, now commanded by the young general Napoleon Bonaparte, controlled almost all of northern Italy except the Habsburg Duchy of Mantua. As the war continued, both Napoleon and the Austrians consistently violated Venice's neutrality, which it was, of course, much too weak to enforce. In the meantime, the Venetian government made some half-hearted efforts to arrange for the defence of the lagoon but the initial investigations into possible defensive strategies were discouraging. For example, out of the eleven warships available to defend the city, four were galleys, and all were obsolete.

During the autumn of 1796 relations between Venice and France worsened dramatically after the Senate rejected the unexpected offer of an alliance. The final blow to Franco-Venetian relations occurred during Easter 1797. Verona, a Venetian city occupied by the French, revolted against the French presence. With the bulk of the French army invading Austria, there were relatively few forces available to quell the uprising which lasted several days. Hardly had the French (or Venetians) had time to absorb the news of the abortive Verona revolt, than yet another incident occurred which sealed the fate of the Republic. Three French ships sailing in the northern Adriatic sought to enter the lagoon, unaware that the Council of Ten had issued an order banning all foreign warships from Venetian waters. The Venetian shore defences opened fire on the French. Two of the French vessels fled, but one, commanded by the squadron's leader, was unable to escape. Despite an offer of surrender, several of the French sailors, including their captain, were killed and their ship disabled.

The situation rapidly deteriorated. Napoleon, having arranged a truce with Austria, now moved to resolve the growing conflict with Venice. By 30 April 1797, the French occupied the lagoon's shoreline and positioned artillery well within range of the city itself. On 9 May the French issued an ultimatum. It amounted to a complete surrender of what remained of the Republic's territory. In particular, it called for the occupation of Venice by three thousand French soldiers and the establishment of a provisional government to take the place of the existing authorities.

On 12 May 1797, the Great Council met to discuss the ultimatum. So many patricians had already fled the city for their mainland estates that there were only 537 members present, sixty-three short of a quorum, but the meeting went on nevertheless. Doge Manin proposed accepting the ultimatum after which there was a hurried and panicked debate, and then the vote. As the votes were tallied, the patricians of the Great Council threw off their sumptuous robes of state and fled the chamber. The Great Council had voted itself, and the Most Serene Republic, out of existence, by 512 to twenty, with five abstentions. Doge Lodovico Manin, to his credit, did not run away, but calmly retired to his wing of the Palace. As he did so, he took off the distinctive ducal costume. Removing the small linen cap worn by the Doges, he handed it to his valet saying (here translated by John Julius Norwich), 'take it, I shall not be needing it again'. On 15 May 1797, for the first time in fifteen centuries, foreign troops entered the islands of the lagoon as the French occupied the territory of *La Serenissima*.

CONCLUSION

Thus ended the thousand-year history of the Duchy of Venice, the Most Serene Republic. The causes for its decline and fall have been hotly debated ever since. Ruskin, among others, believed that the Republic declined due to a loss of piety and discipline. As this chapter has argued, many eighteenth-century observers, and many Venetians themselves, believed that the state and society of the Republic were by then hopelessly decadent. Others, most recently Garry Wills, have pointed out that Venice declined not as a result of any inner decadence or depravity, but due to the force of 'outside influences (the growth of the Turkish Empire, the opening of the Adriatic, changes in the technology of war at sea). Venice simply had too small a base to maintain its empire for more than its five centuries of success. That is quite a record, and a testimony to the ethos of the ruling elite.'

Yet another sort of explanation for the fall of the Republic might be found in the growing conservativism among the patricians, especially after the mid-seventeenth century. Confronted with increasingly complex and dangerous 'outside influences' the reaction among the ruling class was to cling ever more tightly to the political and social institutions which had worked so well in the past. Perhaps the nobles were a bit too fond of their complex, even arcane, constitution, and too frightened for their own positions to attempt to modify it.

In any event, as Wills mentioned, it is worth remembering that Venice, despite its ignominious end, had an impressive record and the sadness felt by many over the events of 12 May 1797 were expressed well in William Wordsworth's famous poem 'On the Extinction of the Venetian Republic'.

> Once did She hold the gorgeous east in fee;
> And was the safeguard of the west: the worth
> Of Venice did not fall below her birth,
> Venice, the eldest Child of Liberty.
> She was a maiden City, bright and free;
> No guile seduced, no force could violate;
> And, when she took unto herself a Mate,
> She must espouse the everlasting Sea.
> And what if she had seen those glories fade,
> Those titles vanish, and that strength decay;
> Yet shall some tribute of regret be paid
> When her long life hath reached its final day:
> Men are we, and must grieve when even the Shade
> Of that which once was great, is passed away.

While the Republic indeed passed away in 1797, the history of Venice does not end there. Indeed, during the next hundred years, the people of Venice would demonstrate to the world that, despite the accusations of decadence and exhaustion levelled at their eighteenth-century ancestors, the Venetians still had energy, imagination, and the will to make their city prosperous again.

CHAPTER EIGHT

Venice and the Modern World
From 1797

The Most Serene Republic of Venice was one of the many casualties of the Napoleonic Wars. While many at the time lamented its passing (as Wordsworth's evocative poem suggested) the city of Venice recovered rather quickly from its loss of political independence and regained its position as an important port. Probably more important in the long run, however, was the development of Venice into Europe's premier tourist destination, a distinction it maintains to this day. While the history of modern Venice has certainly not been trouble free, the periodic announcements of the city's death have, thankfully, been greatly exaggerated.

Napoleon and the Treaty of Campoformio

Unbeknownst to its humiliated residents, Napoleon decided to conquer their Republic simply because he wanted to use Venice as a bargaining chip in peace negotiations with the Habsburgs. Although the French were poised to attack Vienna itself, for various tactical reasons (many of them having to do with his relations with personal rivals), Napoleon decided to make peace with Austria in the spring of 1797. In the Treaty of Campoformio, of October 1797, Venice (as well as other chunks of northern Italian territory and most of Venice's remaining Empire in Dalmatia) was turned over to the Habsburgs (as compensation for their loss of the Austrian Netherlands to France).

The last of the French troops evacuated the city on 18 January 1798 and were replaced on the same day by the Austrians. The French did not leave empty handed, however, and in the months between the signing of Campoformio and January 1798 they carried off almost

The sacking of Venice by Napoleonic troops

everything that was not nailed down and destroyed much that was. Most famously, the bronze horses were removed from St Mark's Basilica to begin a strange odyssey through Italy and France. Less well known, but perhaps more despicable, were the looting and subsequent melting down of much of the treasury of the Basilica, as well as the destruction of the last *Bucintoro*. The French allegedly wanted to salvage the gold leaf that encrusted its intricate sculptural decoration, but more probably it was burned as a potent symbol of the fall of the old regime.

The Austrian Interlude and the Second French Occupation

The Habsburg forces quickly moved to occupy their territories in Veneto and Lombardy. In Venice, the ex-Doge Manin led a delegation of patricians in swearing allegiance to the Habsburg Emperor. It was one of his last public acts. Shortly afterward he retired to the family villa on the mainland at Passariano where he lived out his remaining years, we are told, consumed with regret and suffering the insults of his former subjects. One wonders, however, given his options in the summer of 1797, what else he could have done. He died on 24 October 1802 and was buried in the church of the Scalzi. A simple inscription, '*Manini Cineres*' (Manin's Ashes), set into the floor, is his only memorial.

The Habsburg forces immediately began to set up their administration, but they were not in the city for long. In 1804, Napoleon declared himself 'Emperor of the French' and began a reorganization of his empire. His plans for an invasion of Great Britain led to what historians call the War of the Third Coalition (1805–1807). Within months, the French soundly defeated the Austrians, leading to the Peace of Pressburg on 26 December 1805. By the terms of the treaty Napoleon regained the northern Italian possessions he had so cavalierly pawned a few years previous, and in January 1806, French troops began their second occupation of Venice.

This second French occupation of the lagoon was to be longer lasting and left more of an indelible mark on the city than the first. Eugene de Beauharnais, Napoleon's stepson, was appointed 'Prince of Venice' and given the responsibility of running the place as part of Napoleon's Italian Kingdom. Eugene is chiefly remembered for radically changing the face of the Piazza by linking the two Procuratie buildings with a grand ballroom known as the Ala Napoleonica. The Ala Napoleonica, connected to the Procuratie Nuove building, together formed the Royal Palace.

A frieze running along the outside of the new wing contains statues of the Roman Emperors. The empty place in the centre of this display was, of course, reserved for a statue of Napoleon himself. As things turned out, it has remained empty. This is fitting in more ways than one. Not only did Napoleon's Empire have a much shorter shelf life than he had expected, but there is no evidence that Napoleon ever even set foot in Venice.

In the process of building the Imperial Palace (and thus enclosing the western side of the Piazza), Napoleon's architects destroyed the fine old Sansovino Church of San Geminiano. This was but one of the one hundred and sixty-five churches that were destroyed during the relatively short period during which Venice was part of Napoleon's Kingdom of Italy.

Several cases of this ecclesiastical demolition resulted in the construction of most of Venice's public parks. For example, the public gardens in the easternmost part of Venice were laid out on territory seized from the monasteries of San Domenico and San Antonio. Another plot of greenery, the Botanical Garden, was established in 1812, in the gardens and vineyards of the suppressed convent associated with the nearby church of San Giobbe. Prince Eugene established yet another famous Venetian garden, the Royal Gardens on the south side of the Procuratie Nuove (which, it will be recalled, he had converted into the Royal Palace). The planting of this garden required the destruction, not of a church this time, but of an old granary. At the edge of the garden, facing the water, is a charming little gazebo called the Casino da Caffè, built in 1812. It is now the city's main tourist office.

Besides the Ala Napoleonica, one of the most visible legacies of the Napoleonic period is the Gallerie dell'Accademia, established in 1807, much to the delight of future hordes of tourists and art lovers. Characteristically, Eugene housed this new collection primarily in a cluster of confiscated religious buildings; in this case, the church of Santa Maria della Carità, the Convento dei Canonici Lateranensi, and the Scuola della Carità. The gallery's collection is likewise made up largely of art treasures from other churches, scuole, convents, and monasteries that were closed (and then thoroughly looted) by the French authorities. While many of these paintings found their way into the Accademia, others were sent to France, and thousands of others were simply destroyed. One estimate is that Venice lost 25,000 paintings during the French occupation.

In the midst of the systematic looting of Venetian art treasures, the Venetian social and economic fabric became increasingly tattered. What remained of Venice's commercial vitality was further damaged when Napoleon instituted his 'Continental System', a kind of embargo on all British trade, on 21 November 1806.

THE END OF NAPOLEONIC ITALY AND AUSTRIAN OCCUPATION

In June 1812, Napoleon's Grand Army invaded Russia. After a number of pyrrhic victories, the French retreat began on 19 October 1812. By the summer of 1813, the War of the Fourth Coalition against Napoleon began. At the 'Battle of the Nations' at Leipzig (16-19 October 1813) Napoleon suffered a major defeat. The allies continued their advance and on 31 March 1813, they entered Paris. The French Bourbons were reinstated and Napoleon went off into exile on the island of Elba. In the meantime, the Austrians began a siege of Venice on 21 October 1813, and by the terms of the armistice of Schiarino Rizzino, finally reoccupied the city on 19 April 1814. The ensuing Congress of Vienna (September 1814-June 1815) confirmed these developments by awarding Venice and most of northern Italy to the Habsburgs who organized these territories into the Habsburg Kingdom of Lombardy-Venetia. On 3 May 1815, Venetian dignitaries swore allegiance to the Austrian Emperor in St Mark's Basilica. On the same day the four bronze horses returned to their place over the church's door, largely as a result of the tireless efforts of the famous Venetian sculptor, Antonio Canova. Milan and Venice were both established as seats of the Habsburg Viceroy, and the Austrians also set up Venice as the headquarters for the Imperial navy's high command. But the French occupation, and the long years of war had taken a terrible toll. A third of the city's population was considered officially indigent by the authorities and a quarter made their living by begging. The glass and textile industries, to say nothing of commerce and banking, were pale reflections of their former selves. To make ends meet, many of Venice's patrician families, and even some churches and religious orders, began to sell what paintings and other artworks they had managed to safeguard from the French, a process that went on throughout most of the nineteenth century. It has been estimated that only about 4 per cent of the *objets d'art* present in Venice in 1797 are still in the city today.

Gradually, however, the situation in Venice began to improve. Commercial life slowly revived, and eventually a new company, the Società Veneta Commerciale operated shipping lines in the Mediterranean and even the Atlantic. The moribund Arsenal also came back to life in its service to the Austrian Imperial navy. By the 1840s it employed 3,000 workers. But perhaps most important in the long run was the opening, on 15 January 1846, of a two-mile (three kilometre) long railway causeway across the lagoon connecting Venice to the mainland at Mestre.

The construction of the railway causeway was generally unpopular with Venetians. They saw it, quite rightly, as part of the Austrian occupiers' attempts to connect Venice more firmly to their other imperial possessions. To add insult to injury, the Austrians levied a tax on Venetians to pay for the project. The Venetians must have also been dismayed by the construction of the new railway station. Two palaces, a convent, a scuola, and two churches had to be destroyed to make way for the new station and the rail yards. One of these churches, Santa Lucia, gave its name to the train station. By the way, the relic of Santa Lucia herself (yet another part of the loot of 1204) was moved to the nearby church of San Geremia.

THE REVOLUTION OF 1848 AND THE 'REPUBLIC OF SAN MARCO'

Despite the 'improvements' wrought by the Austrians, or perhaps because of them, they were not all at popular with the majority of the Venetian population. Furthermore, the revolutionary ideas of liberalism and nationalism that grew throughout Europe during the first half of the nineteenth century had an affect on many of the city's intellectuals, although, in keeping with Venetian history, these ideas seem to have penetrated Venice later than in the rest of Italy. Thus, Venice played no part in the nationalist Carbonari rebellions of 1821-22. By the 1840s, however, the nationalist ideas of Mazzini's Young Italy movement began to influence the thinking of some Venetians. Among the most famous of these early nationalists were the Bandiera brothers, Emilio and Attilio. They were born in Venice at house number 3610 in the *campo* that currently bears their name: Campo Bandiera e Moro. Though officers in the Austrian navy, they joined Young Italy in 1842 and, for good measure, also founded a similar nationalist society, called *Esperia*, in Venice. After taking part in a failed insurrection against the Bourbon rulers of the Kingdom of the Two Sicilies, they were captured and executed by firing squad in the town of Cosenza (south of Naples) in 1844. They were eventually buried, along with their friend and fellow nationalist, Domenico Moro, in the north aisle of San Zanipolo.

As an alternative to armed insurrection, the lawyer Daniele Manin (no relation to the ill-fated last Doge) and Niccolo Tommaseo, a poet of Dalmatian origin, argued that their Austrian rulers needed to be confronted legally. They focused in particular on the problem of press censorship imposed by the conservative Austrian regime, as well as the Habsburgs' refusal to honour their 1815 promise to grant some sort of autonomy to Lombardy and Venetia. Even these sorts of challenges, however, were too much for the Habsburg authorities and both Manin and Tommaseo were jailed in January 1848. Luckily for them, however, Europe was about to be engulfed in a wave of liberal and nationalist revolutions. As revolution broke out in Vienna on 17 March 1848, Manin and Tommaseo were released from prison. On the 22nd,

A caricature of Daniele Manin, the revolutionary lawyer

Manin, leading a group of volunteers, took over the Arsenal and the Piazza and expelled the Austrian administration from the city (events subsequently commemorated in the name of the Calle Larga 22 Marzo). Manin's efforts to secure Austrian recognition for Venetian autonomy having failed, he declared the independent 'Republic of San Marco'. His failure to take bold measures to secure the support of other Italian nationalists, and in particular, the uncertain relationship between the Republic and the Kingdom of Piedmont (emerging as the leader in the struggle for Italian unification), led to a number of missed opportunities in the ensuing war against the Austrians. As it happened, the war did not go well for the Piedmontese and their allies among the Italian nationalists. They were defeated by the Austrians under Radetzky at the Battle of Custoza (in the Veneto) in July 1848, and again, this time decisively, at the Battle of Novara in March 1849. In the meantime, in the face of the collapse of the Piedmontese-sponsored war of Italian unification, Manin and the Venetian patriots refused to surrender and broke their ties with the defeated Piedmontese. On 2 April 1849, in a moving speech delivered from an upper floor window of the Procuratie Nuove, Manin declared to the crowds in the Piazza that Venice would 'resist at all costs'. Unable to take the city by storm, the Austrians began a siege from their bases on the mainland. Before evacuating their positions on *terra firma* and the outlying islands in May 1849, the Venetian forces took the precaution of mining the fortress of San Giuliano. The mines resulted in some Austrian casualties, but the fortress was nevertheless occupied. It, along with Campalto (on the mainland) were the principal Austrian strong points during the siege. The Austrians mounted their artillery on special decks at 45° angles so their shells were able to reach almost to the Piazza. The worst damage, naturally, was inflicted on closer Cannaregio. The increasingly frustrated Austrians also tried an aerial assault using twenty hot air balloons launched from ships anchored by the Lido. Most of the balloons, which were armed with bombs and grenades, exploded while drifting over the city, but some passed all the way across the lagoon, exploding over the Austrians' own positions on the island of S. Giuliano.

Within the besieged city the situation became increasingly precarious. To pay for the war, Manin's government had, as early as September 1848, raised a loan of three million lire from the wealthy citizens of Venice. This loan was used to back an issue of paper money called *moneta patriottica*. From December 1848 through June 1849, the government issued another series, guaranteed by loans and taxes, called *moneta del comune*. Through the siege, the Venetian population, rich and poor, contributed money to the revolutionary government. In the face of their desperate situation, the plucky Venetians apparently tried to make the best of the situation. Many built makeshift cupolas or platforms on the roofs of their houses so as to spend the long, hot, summer nights entertained by the pyrotechnic displays of the Austrian artillery bombardment. By the end of July, however, the situation in the besieged city worsened dramatically. Four hundred people died daily as cholera broke out and food supplies dwindled. The Austrians, exasperated at the continued resistance, rejected Manin's proposals to negotiate and instead intensified their artillery bombardment. After twenty days of nearly continuous shelling, Manin (using his by now dictatorial powers) surrendered Venice to the Austrians on 22 August 1849. On the 27th, Marshal Radetzky ordered Manin, his family, and forty of his allies exiled from the exhausted and demoralized city. Manin's wife died of cholera the next day.

Daniele Manin ended up in Paris where he eventually abandoned his republicanism in favour of the goal of a united Italian Kingdom under the House of Savoy (which ruled the Kingdom of Piedmont). He died in September 1857, aged fifty-three. A statue of him (dating from 1871) stands in the appropriately named Campo Manin, near his family home.

THE RE-ESTABLISHMENT OF AUSTRIAN RULE AND THE TOURIST INDUSTRY

The re-establishment of Austrian rule in Venice initially followed much the same patterns as elsewhere in the Habsburg Empire. While maintaining a strong, centralized state apparatus bolstered by armies of informers and police agents, the government also embarked on ambitious public works projects throughout the Empire, and the Italian provinces were no exception. By 1857 the railway line was completed to Milan, thus linking Venice to the general European rail network. Even as they were continuing work on the railway, the Austrian authorities did not overlook the importance of Venice as a port, though they relied increasingly on nearby Trieste. Among other improvements, the Austrians revived a plan, originally developed by French engineers during the Napoleonic occupation, for deepening the Port of Malamocco. This work was achieved by the construction of long, stone jetties along either side of the channel. The resulting narrow waterway was kept clear by the powerful tidal currents created by the jetties. Austrian engineers also completed an impressive water works, replacing the ancient *pozzi* with a system of public fountains supplied by water piped in from hundreds of miles away on the mainland. They also tried their hand at the restoration of the dilapidated *fondaco dei turchi*, with results that appalled Ruskin (and many since).

Despite (or perhaps because of) these various projects, the Austrians were cordially disliked by the bulk of the Venetian population. Nor did the Austrians win many friends with their position on Manin's paper currency. They announced that they would redeem the *moneta del commune* at half its face value (paid for by a special tax) but the revolutionary *moneta patriottica* was declared worthless, further impoverishing the already destitute population.

Anti–Austrian feelings grew in the city. For example, the two most famous (and oldest) cafés on the Piazza were self-segregating: the Austrians patronized the Quadri while the Venetians met at the Florian. The Fenice opera house became a centre of anti–Austrian protests. The Italian nationalist composer Giuseppe Verdi (whose *Rigoletto* and *La Traviata* both premiered in Venice) was especially popular, as his name was an acronym for 'Victor Emanuel, King of Italy' (*Vittorio Emanuele, Re d'Italia*). Thus, nationalist audiences could signal their coded defiance of the Austrian occupation (and support of the champion of Italian unification, the King of Piedmont) by shouting 'Viva Verdi' during performances.

In any event, the days of the Austrian presence were clearly numbered as the Italian wars of national unification, the *Risorgimento*, gathered force. In 1859 Piedmont, this time allied with France, again went to war with Austria. While Piedmont gained territory in Lombardy, the Austrians kept most of their other Italian possessions, including Venice. Over 4,000 Venetians, including many intellectuals and craftsmen, went into exile to protest the continuation of Austrian rule. Finally, during the third war with Austria in 1866, Italian troops entered Venice. After a plebiscite on 21 October 1866, Venice became part of the Kingdom of Italy.

The Growth of Tourism

The deterioration of Venice's economic and intellectual life under the Austrians was mirrored by an increase in its tourist trade. Venice had, of course, always attracted foreign travellers. During the Middle Ages and Renaissance they had come as crusaders and pilgrims on their way to the Holy Land, or as merchants or diplomats. During the eighteenth century, as we have seen, Venice became an obligatory stop on the 'Grand Tour' expected of all young European gentlemen.

By the early nineteenth century, however, Venice grew into a magnet for artists and intellectuals from all across Europe and the Americas. For these visitors, Venice was a beautiful, melancholy place for contemplation and romantic inspiration. Probably the most famous of these early visitors, indeed almost prototypical of them, was George Gordon, Sixth Baron Byron of Rochdale, a.k.a. Lord Byron. He arrived in Venice in November 1816 following a series a scandals in Great Britain, and lived there for the next six years. By 1819, he had settled in the Palazzo Mocenigo (the very one in which Lady Arundel had lived centuries before), along with a variable assortment of friends and visitors, as well as a small zoo. He had a number of love affairs, of course, the most important of which was with the seventeen-year-old Countess Theresa Guiciolli. In the midst of all these diversions he somehow managed to get quite a bit of writing done. Especially noteworthy was his completion of *Childe Harold's Pilgrimage*. More exotically, he spent several months helping the monks at the Armenian Monastery on San Lazzaro in their efforts to compile an Armenian-English dictionary.

Another famous foreign visitor to Venice during the time before mass tourism exploded was John Ruskin who, in the company of his long-suffering wife Effie, made two extended trips to Venice between 1849 and 1852. During most of that time, Ruskin collected information for his monumental three-volume *Stones of Venice*. As many critics and commentators have pointed out since then, despite its title, the book has relatively little to do with Venice and much more to say about Ruskin's views on architecture, religion, and beauty. For him, beauty and religion were tied together. In other words, true beauty was an expression of the attributes of God. Thus, he emerged as a fierce critic of the Renaissance and a champion of the Romanesque and Gothic. Likewise, he believed that the decline of Venice was tied to its (alleged) moral failure beginning during the Renaissance. His diatribes against the Venice of Palladio are in contrast to his careful and loving descriptions of the Cathedral of Torcello or the church of San Donato on Murano.

Byron and Ruskin bracketed a special period in the history of Venetian tourism. They were neither on the Grand Tour, but nor were they part of mass tourism. A convenient starting date for the latter phenomenon is 1867, the date of the first Thomas Cook tour to Venice. The numbers of tourists increased even more after the opening (in 1871) of the Mont Cenis tunnel through the Alps. By the 1880s even the Lido, much loved by Lord Byron for its rugged solitude, began to develop into a fashionable bathing spot, and by the end of the century was filled with restaurants, hotels, and summer villas. Mann imagined Aschenbach, the protagonist of *Death in Venice*, as wasting away on the Lido, in the sumptuous Hotel de Grands Bains. Thus, although many famous artists and intellectuals continued to flock to Venice (including such luminaries as Richard Wagner, Thomas Mann, Henry James, and Marcel Proust) they were joined by increasing numbers of middle-class tourists visiting Venice on package holidays.

VENICE IN THE KINGDOM OF ITALY

Although the importance of tourism grew steadily after Venice's unification with Italy, some of the older characteristically Venetian arts and crafts, especially lace-making and glass-blowing, experienced something of a renaissance. As early as 1859, during the Austrian peri-od, Antonio Salviati established a glass factory on Murano. Later, Abate Zanetti founded the glass museum on the island. During the 1920s, Paolo Venini tried to revive Murano glass-making by enlisting the help of modern designers. Similarly, Mariano Fortuny (1871-1949), an immigrant from Catalonia, established a factory on Giudecca for the production of his famous pleated frocks and fabrics. More traditional-ly, a school teaching the ancient Venetian art of lace-making (the Scuola dei Merletti) opened on Burano in 1872.

Venice also tried to revive its reputation as a centre of the art world in 1893 when the Venetian city council voted to organize a major artistic exposition to be called the *Esposizione Biennale Artistica Nazionale* (Biennial Exhibition of National Art), known ever since as 'the Biennale'. The council subsequently set up an organizing com-mittee, and agreed to allow foreign artists to participate as well. Thus, the first show, inaugurated in April 1895 was called the *Esposizione Internazionale d'Arte della Citta Venezia* (First International Art Exhibition of the City of Venice). The exhibition was an immediate success, with over 200,000 visitors, including the King and Queen of Italy. The city turned over part of the Giardini di Castello for use as exhibition space, and a large venue called the Palazzo dell'Esposizione was constructed in neo-classical style by Enrico Trevisanato and Marius De Maria. Several foreign countries soon built permanent exhibition pavilions as well, among them Belgium (1907), Germany and the United Kingdom (both in 1909), and France (1912). Eventually about forty countries built pavilions on the exhibition grounds (the USA opened its pavilion in 1930). In 1902, the Biennale committee acquired another space for displaying modern art when the Duchess Bevilacqua-La Masa turned over the Ca'Pesaro as the Modern Art Gallery, a function it continues to fulfill to this day.

By the early twentieth century, the Biennale was attracting members of the European artistic establishment, as well as the avant garde, and even artists from Africa. For example, the 1910 exhibition featured the works of Gustav Klimt, (which made a profound impression on the Venetian artist and designer Vittorio Zecchin). On the other hand, during the same exhibition, the Biennale secretariat ordered some of

Picasso's works removed.

Besides the renewed vigour in the production of glass, fine textiles, and art, Venice also became an important centre for flour milling thanks to the energy of Giovanni Stucky who built a milling empire on Giudecca. By the early twentieth century, Stucky had become one of the richest men in Venice by turning imported wheat into flour in his massive mill complex. The mill finally closed in 1954 and sat derelict until the 1990s when developers began to remodel the buildings as houses, offices, and a hotel, as well as a space for light industry. A fire in 2003 has put this project on hold.

Until World War I, Venice was still one of Italy's most important ports, and the Arsenal continued to build and repair warships for the Italian navy. The royal government, building on the infrastructure begun by the Austrians, also expanded the rail network. By 1890, it built a new industrial harbour in Venice, the *stazione marittima* (on the site of the old Austrian military parade grounds), where freighters could unload their cargo directly onto railroad cars. Another part of this industrial development was the reopening, after centuries, of the Port of Lido San Nicolò as the main port of Venice. Between 1882 and 1892, the authorities dredged out the channel from San Nicolò through the *bacino* and the Giudecca canal to the *stazione marittima* to allow large modern ships to pass. A system of jetties and breakwaters at the Port itself created an increased tidal flow that scoured the newly deepened channel.

The industrial development of the lagoon area continued through World War I and into the 1930s. But the nature of this development changed slightly. The Arsenal, for example, was abandoned by the Italian navy as a shipbuilding centre during World War I, due to its proximity to the border with the Austro-Hungarian enemy, and any large-scale shipbuilding activity quickly declined. During the 1920s, instead of maintaining Venice itself as a manufacturing centre, Italian economic planners decided to establish a new industrial zone on the mainland at Porto Marghera. Their idea was to preserve historic Venice as a tourist destination, while industry would move to the neighbouring mainland. The authorities also guessed that these industries would provide new jobs for Venice's (largely impoverished) citizens.

Mussolini's government was so concerned that the industrial zones on the mainland be provided with plentiful workers that in 1933 it supplemented the railway link to the mainland with a road for cars and buses. A serious result of this industrial expansion on the mainland was the increase in industrial pollution of the lagoon, as well as a gradual sinking of the land. In 1925, the Italian authorities allowed the refineries and factories at Porto Marghera to use ground water for their industrial processes. As John Keahey describes it, '…the subterranean water bubble that had undergirded the lagoon for millennia began to deflate'. The large amounts of industrial wastes dumped into the shallow lagoon also proved too much for the daily tides to wash out to the sea. Heavy metals, phosphates, and other modern chemicals built up in the lagoon's silty mud.

The Fascist government neglected the environmental safety of the lagoon in other ways as well. In particular, it ignored the maintenance of the *Murazzi*, the massive sea walls at the southern end of the lagoon, finished during the last years of the Republic. While under the Austrian occupation the walls were repaired and maintained with the annual importation of additional stone from Istria, such routine maintenance was neglected by the Fascist regime.

World War II

While the Fascists, in control of the Italian government since 1922, were busy altering Venice's economic landscape by the construction of their mainland industrial zones, they were also preparing the ground for a catastrophic alteration of the demography of Venice, and indeed of all of Italy.

Venetians were not immune to the siren-song of Fascism. Indeed, there is evidence that Venice was one of the first cities in Italy to have Fascist organizations (as early as 1919). Between 1936 and 1938, Mussolini stirred up anti-semitic factions within the Fascist movement, and in November 1938 issued the first anti-semitic legislation.

Italy, like all countries in Christian Europe, had a tradition of judeophobia or anti-semitism, but it was historically very weak. While Venice was (literally) home to the first Jewish ghetto, the treatment of

Jews in most of Italy, and Venice in particular, was quite good by European standards. During the nineteenth century, many Italian Jews assimilated into the political and economic life of the Kingdom with little or no difficulty. One particularly dramatic case was that of Luigi Luzzatti, scion of an important Venetian Jewish family. From 1891 to 1906 he held the position of Minister of Finance, on and off, and was appointed Prime Minister in 1910. It is worth noting (by way of comparison) that in 1902, practising Jews were forbidden to serve as commissioned officers in the German army, and that France did not have a Jewish Prime Minister until 1936. Italy's Jewish community was, in general, exceptionally patriotic. Some were even self-proclaimed Fascists.

If the anti-semitic laws passed by Mussolini's regime were aimed at the persecution and humiliation of Italy's Jews, they were only a prelude to the horror that awaited that community after the German occupation of much of Italy in September 1943. In the northern part of occupied Italy, the Nazis established an Italian Fascist puppet state, presided over by Mussolini, called the Italian Social Republic, but unofficially known as the Republic of Salò, after the Republic's 'capital'. In November 1943, the I.S.R. passed the infamous Police Order Number Five that provided for the arrest of all Jews in Italy and their internment in concentration camps on Italian territory. Several concentration camps were established, the most notorious of which were Fossoli and San Saba (also known as La Risiera) near Trieste. In February 1944, however, Nazi SS units in occupied Italy took over the operation of these camps and began to deport their inmates to Auschwitz.

Venice's Jewish community, which numbered 2,189 in 1938, was well integrated into the social, political, and economic life of the city. It was perhaps partially for this reason that the round-ups of Jews began only in December 1943. This interlude between the announcement of Police Order Number Five in November and the beginning of the abduction of the Jewish population of Venice might have given many Jews an opportunity to hide or flee. On 1 December 1943, the Italian police emptied a Jewish nursing home, the Casa Israelitica di Riposo, of its patients and then swept through the city arresting all the

Jews they could find. Some of the very old or sick were released (according to provisions in Police Order Five) but after several weeks of being held, under appalling conditions in Venice, the Italian Fascists sent 93 of the arrested Jews to Fossoli. They were all eventually deported to Auschwitz. As the months passed, and the Allies pushed into northern Italy, the Nazi SS grew increasingly impatient with the police and Fascist militias of the I.S.R. and in the spring of 1944, the SS began to arrest, and then deport, all the Jews they could find. Ignoring the exemptions observed (at least in some cases) by the Italian Fascists, the SS emptied Jewish nursing homes, hospitals, psychiatric sanatoria, and similar institutions of their patients and of their Jewish doctors and nurses, deporting them all directly to the death camps. In August 1944, SS units arrested thirteen people from a nursing home outside of Venice, and also seized those remaining in Venice from the time of the December 1943 raid. Altogether 35 people, including the Chief Rabbi of Venice, Adolfo Ottolenghi, were sent to the concentration camp at San Saba. None were ever heard from again.

These horrible accounts are tempered, somewhat, by the stories of courage and integrity demonstrated by many Italian gentiles. Of the approximately 2,000 Jews in Venice, 212 were deported. Of the rest, many escaped Venice between 1938 and 1945 and found refuge abroad, while some must have been able to hide or find shelter with non-Jewish friends or neighbours. Of those deported, only fifteen returned. There are about six hundred Jews in Venice today.

Tourism and Industry

Venice was liberated in April 1945. Although it had not suffered any physical damage during World War II, the effects of the war on the city, and the conditions of post war Italy, presented some profound challenges.

One of the most important developments in post-war Venice was its development into the most important tourist destination in Europe. As previous chapters in this book have pointed out, Venice has always been a mecca for foreign visitors, and as early as the eighteenth cen-

Venetian Administration

SANTA CROCE
60 Santa Lucia
61 Santa Croce
62 San Simeone Apostolo
63 San Simeone Profeta
64 San Giovanni Decollato
65 San Giacomo dell'Orio
66 San Stae
67 Santa Maria Mater Domini
68 San Cassiano

SAN POLO
51 San Tomà
52 San Stin
53 Sant'Agostino
54 San Boldo
55 San Polo
56 Sant'Aponal
57 San Silvestro
58 San Matteo
59 San Giovanni di Rialto

DORSODURO
40 San Gregorio
41 San Vio
42 Santa Agnese
43 San Trovaso
44 San Basilio
45 San Raffaele Arcangelo
46 San Nicolò dei Mendicoli
47 San Bàrnaba
48 Santa Margherita
49 San Pantaleone
50 Santa Eufemia

CANNAREGIO
28 San Geremia
29 San Leonardo
30 San Marcuola
31 Santa Maria Maddalena
32 Santa Fosca
33 San Marziale
34 San Felice
35 Santa Sofia
36 Santi Apostoli
37 San Giovanni Crisostomo
38 San Canciano
39 Santa Maria Nuova

SAN MARCO
12 San Marco
13 San Basso
14 San Giuliano
15 San Geminiano
16 San Moisè
17 San Santa Maria Zobenigo
18 San Maurizio
19 San Vitale
20 San Samuele
21 Sant'Angelo
22 San Benedetto
23 San Fantino
24 San Paterniano
25 San Luca
26 San Salvadore
27 San Bartolomeo

CASTELLO
1 San Pietro
2 San Biagio
3 San Martino
4 San Giovanni in Bragora
5 Santa Ternita
6 Santa Giustina
7 Sant'Antonin
8 San Giovanni Novo
9 Santa Maria Formosa
10 Santa Marina
11 San Lo

tury tourism has been an important source of income for the city. Yet, as late as World War I, Venice was still an important commercial port and manufacturing centre. Since the end of World War II, however, tourism has become the city's economic backbone.

The revival of post-war Venice as a great tourist destination, while welcome in many respects, also has created some serious problems. Around fifteen million tourists visit Venice annually. During high season, between 50,000 and 80,000 tourists arrive daily, most staying for less than twenty-four hours. The city's infrastructure has been seriously challenged by this influx. For example, on 3 May 1987 (known as 'Black Sunday'), something like 150,000 tourists came to Venice, overwhelming the city. This record was broken on 15 July 1989 when 200,000 people arrived in Venice to listen to Pink Floyd perform on a floating platform in the *bacino*. There is ongoing discussion about limiting the numbers of tourist visitors using a daily quota of some kind, but such suggestions inevitably run into problems given the tremendous importance of tourism for the local economy.

The growth of tourism coincided with the post-war revival of the Venetian art scene. The Biennale, closed since 1942, reappeared in 1948 (including a long overdue exhibition of work by Picasso). The cautious direction of the pre-war Biennale secretariat was replaced by a real dedication to the avant-garde, with contributions by such artists as Max Ernst, Hans Arp, Jackson Pollock, and Alexander Calder. The Venice Film Festival (inaugurated in 1932 as the Esposizione Internazionale d'Arte Cinematografica) was also revived, and the Leone di San Marco (subsequently renamed the Leone d'oro) was created as the prize for the best film at the festival. The first 'Leone' was awarded to Henri-George Clouzot's *Manon* in 1949, and the second, in 1951, to *Rashomon* by the relatively unknown (in the West) Akira Kurosawa.

The challenges posed by the explosion of tourism were mirrored by the relocation, and subsequent expansion, of industry from Venice to the mainland. The industrial growth on nearby *terra firma*, begun in the 1930s, continued after the end of the war, and by the 1970s the petroleum-based industries in the area around Mestre/Porto Marghera employed 40,000 people. The growth of the industrial zones was tied into the overall economic growth of post-war Italy. Additionally, the refineries at Porto Marghera were important for the same reasons that Venice had historically been such an important centre of trade and industry, namely, it was one of the best ports closest to the resources of the Middle East. But ships no longer unloaded spices – the new precious cargo of the East was petroleum. The growth of industry in these areas was also related to the deal making between various political and business interests inherent in any political environment (and certainly not unique to Italy).

The growth of these industries created a number of unforeseen problems. One was demographic. In the original plan for the industrial zones based on the village of Marghera and the nearby town of Mestre developed back in the 1920s, young workers from Venice would commute to these mainland jobs across the causeway, thus providing badly needed income for the native Venetians. What happened instead was that the young workers simply left Venice and moved their households to the mainland since housing on the mainland is cheaper and roomier than in Venice. The result is that the population of the city has declined steadily, from about 170,000 in 1945 to only around 70,000 in 1995. The population of Mestre, on the other hand, had grown to about 180,000 over that same period.

These demographic shifts combined with a new political arrangement to stymie easy solutions to the problems posed by the industrialization of the mainland. Since 1926, the political unit of 'Venice' has included not only the historical city, but also Mestre and Porto Marghera. The very different populations and needs of these areas contribute to all sorts of policy-making nightmares, since the interests of the island and mainland populations rarely coincide.

Probably the most noticeable impact of the industrialization of the Venetian mainland, or at least the one that gets the most attention in the media, is the connection between the industries in Mestre and Porto Marghera and the 'sinking of Venice'.

WATER, WATER, EVERYWHERE

As this book has shown, Venice has had through its long history a very ambivalent relationship with the lagoon. On the one hand, the very origins of the city and many of its unique institutions are at least in some way related to the unique environmental constraints posed by its watery setting. While the waters of the lagoon provided the early settlers with security from invaders and a source of food, they also posed the ever present threats of floods and, in places, malaria. As we have seen, floods have been a problem in Venice since its origins. The subsidence of the ground has likewise been ongoing. The undulating floors of ancient churches such as St Mark's Basilica or the church of San Donato on Murano (believed by Ruskin to be mimicking the waves of the sea) are one indication of the unstable ground beneath many of Venice's structures. Flexible terrazzo flooring was invented in Venice to adapt to this challenge. Likewise, many of the city's open squares, and the Piazza itself, have been raised and repaved many times to take account of the sinking ground level.

So, while flooding and soil subsidence are nothing terribly new in Venetian history, the relative frequency and speed of these phenomena over the last fifty years do seem unusual. The industrialization of

The flooded Piazza

Mestre and Marghera are at least partially to blame for both conditions. The industrial pumping of water that began in the area in 1925 seriously depleted the aquifers and led to a rapid sinking of the ground level. In 1973, the government finally banned the procedure, but by that time much damage had already been done. According to John Keahey, by the time the water pumping was stopped, the 'land...around Marghera had subsided more than 4.7 inches (twelve centimetres) and, around Venice, 3.1 inches (eight centimetres)'. Subsidence has been a historical process in the lagoon. Yet, it has been estimated that without the effects of industrialization, it would have taken until the year 2050 for the ground level to have reached the same point as it has reached today. Significantly, the first gauge for measuring tidal activity was not put in place until 1897, when one was built near the church of Santa Maria della Salute. Zero on the gauge marked sea level in 1897. Since then, due to the subsidence of the ground, sea level is twenty-three centimetres (about nine inches) above zero.

As the ground level has been sinking, albeit very slowly after the early 1970s, the water level has been rising. The rise in the sea level has many causes. For one thing, the Earth has been getting progressively warmer since the Ice Age ended about ten thousand years ago. At that time, so much of the planet's fresh water was tied up in glaciers and polar ice caps that the northern Adriatic was dry land. As the Earth warmed, the ice melted and the world's seas and oceans gradually took on the familiar contours they have today. Additionally, most climatologists believe that this natural warming of the planet's atmosphere has been accelerated due to the production of greenhouse gasses. Whatever the actual contribution of greenhouse gasses to global warming turns out to be, it is quite clear that sea levels have been rising. Over the past one hundred years, the sea level at the Venetian lagoon has risen at a yearly rate of 1.27 millimetres.

The subsidence of the ground level combined with rising sea levels have led to an increase in the incidence of flooding or, as it is known in Venice, *acqua alta*. The worst case in recent history was certainly the flood of 4 November 1966 when the water rose 1.94 metres (about six feet) above the zero mark on the tidal gauge at the Salute. Torrential rains swelled the rivers emptying into the canal, and a terrific storm in the northern Adriatic destroyed the *Murazzi* (which, it will be recalled, had not been well maintained since the time of the Austrian occupation). The flood waters rose above their previous record of 1.60 metres (reached in 1953) and climbed past the level of the city's electrical transformers at 1.90 metres, thus plunging the entire city into a blackout. To make matters worse, tanks of diesel fuel (then used extensively for home heating) ruptured turning the water black and oily. Residents remember the swollen canals filled with oil, refuse, and the carcasses of rats, cats, and dogs.

Serious floods like the one of 1966 are caused by the convergence of a whole host of factors (such as storms, high tides, etc.). Nevertheless, according to Keahey, between 1966 and 1995, there have been two hundred instances when the *acqua alta* was over one metre above sea level. Furthermore, he hastens to add, '...this measurement is compounded by the fact that the real zero on the tidal gauge at the Salute should be nine inches (twenty-three centimetres) above where the zero was locked into place more than one hundred years ago. So, when the measurement reads one metre above zero, in reality it is 1.23 metres above today's mean sea level'.

Since 1966, there have been numerous different plans and proposals on how best to deal with the increasing episodes of flooding. Some of these stress the importance of repairing the Venetian infrastructure. One of the main problems posed by the floods is that they expose the brick (of which most of Venice's buildings are constructed) to salt water, thus gradually eroding them. Some have suggested that, as in past centuries, the way to deal with the problem is to raise the foundations of buildings so that the water comes into contact with hard, Istrian stone instead of brick. Other projects advocate traditional solutions to the problem of rising sea levels, such as raising pavement levels.

Another set of solutions involves mechanical barriers to the sea itself. Many such projects, including the rebuilding and strengthening of the old *Murazzi* and the construction of new sea walls and jetties elsewhere, have already been completed or are underway. But without a doubt the boldest, and most controversial, of these plans is the MOSE (*Modulo Sperimentale Elettromeccanico* [Experimental

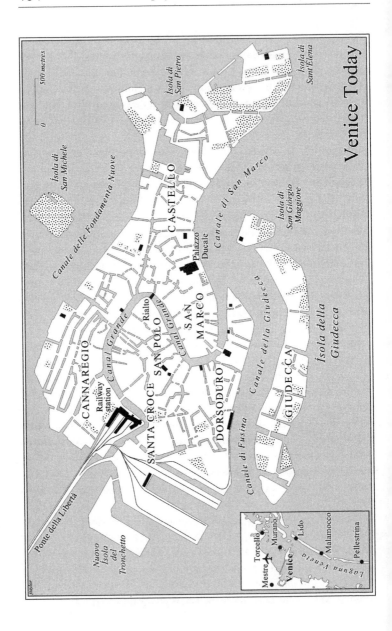

Venice Today

Electromechanical Module]) project of the Consorzio Venezia Nuova, a consortium of several major engineering companies. The project involves the construction of gates at the main entrances to the lagoon. These gates would be seventy-nine massive, hollow, steel flaps hinged to the floor of the lagoon. In calm weather, these gates would be filled with seawater and would lie flat on the lagoon's floor. When bad weather heightened the possibility of flooding, the flaps would be pumped full of air, swing up, and effectively close the water channel.

The project, quite predictably, has numerous fans, and equally large numbers of detractors. Its promoters argue that all climatological evidence points to an increase in the sorts of weather patterns that will cause severe flooding in the city. Without a way of mechanically shutting this weather out of the lagoon, the floods will eventually destroy Venice. Most of its critics base their arguments on the environmental harm that the project could cause to the lagoon's ecosystem. In particular, they fear that shutting out tidal activity for extended periods of time would eliminate the flushing action of the tides and further increase the pollution levels in the lagoon and in the city's canals. As things stand at this writing, however, the Consorzio has received a green light from the Italian government to go ahead with the project.

CONCLUSIONS

As so many people have observed through the centuries, Venice is a unique city. Its utterly unlikely setting certainly contributed to its evolution of a set of social and political institutions that were very different from those which evolved elsewhere in the area. The sense of being unique or exceptional was not lost on the Venetians themselves, and I am strongly inclined to agree with Garry Wills' argument that one can only really understand Venetian history by acknowledging the way in which the Venetians thought of themselves as exceptional. This 'exceptionalism' was very important in almost every aspect of Venetian history. In art it was reflected in the frequent portrayal of stories from the Old Testament, about the Israelites (another exceptional, chosen people). Institutionally, it manifested itself in a political and social system which stressed order and harmony. Naturally, these ideals were not always realized, but they nevertheless helped to maintain the Venetian notion of themselves as different from their neighbours. The belief the Venetians had of their own exceptionalism is certainly displayed in the origin myths they told about their city which always portrayed Venice as having been born in freedom and harmony. The myth surrounding St Mark became perhaps the most important of all. Venice, as the guardian of the Evangelist's relic, was a truly unique and powerful city, an equal, in fact, to Rome itself.

This exceptionalism continues to this day. While many of Venice's problems are shared by any other city, its relationship to the lagoon means that the question of its long-term survival is tied to a host of factors that seem unique to Venice. The problem of flood control is synonymous with the overall health of the lagoon, which, in turn, is connected to the fate of mainland industrial developments. All of this is, of course, connected to the importance of Venice as a place of countless architectural and artistic masterpieces. Since 1966, several important international organizations have been founded; among the best known are the UK's Venice in Peril and, the USA's Save Venice, dedicated to the restoration and preservation of the city's treasures.

Yet, as many have observed, there is no reason to try to save the city's churches and palaces if the city itself is doomed. And, as increasing numbers of people now argue, saving the city of Venice means encouraging more people to live and work in the city, which, in turn, probably means decreasing its over reliance on tourism, which now accounts for over 70 per cent of the city's economic activity. In any case, the growing realization that Venice faces many more problems than just the threat of *acqua alta*, and that these problems need to be addressed first and foremost by the people of Venice themselves, provides hope for the future. Groups such as the Spontaneous Committee for the Preservation of Venice, for example, made up mostly of Venetians, argue that, ultimately, lasting solutions to Venice's problems need to come from the people of Venice themselves. The Venetians have overcome challenges, many just as terrifying and seemingly intractable as those of today, for over a thousand years. There is no reason to think that they will not be able to overcome those of today.

Chronology of Major Events

421 AD	Legendary date of founding of Venice
476	Fall of the Western Roman Empire
493	Theodoric establishes Ostrogoth Kingdom in Ravenna
527	Justinian crowned Roman Emperor in Constantinople
537	Letter of Cassiodorous, of the Ostrogothic court, to the people of the lagoon
540	General Belisarius conquers Ravenna and much of Italy for Byzantine Empire
556	Death of Emperor Justinian
568-602	Lombards ravage Friuli, Padua, and Altino
638-639	Cittanova (Heraclea) founded in Venetian Lagoon
639	Dedication of Torcello cathedral
680	Byzantine-Lombard truce
697	Election of the first Doge, Paoluccio, according to the Chronicle of Diacono.
713-715	Election of Paoluccio, according to the *Cronicon Altinatae*
730	Election of Orso Ipato, first Doge of Venice
751	Lombards take Ravenna
756	King Astolfus of the Lombards cedes Ravenna to Pepin, King of the Franks
774	Charles, King of the Franks, destroys the Lombard Kingdom
800	Charlemagne is crowned Holy Roman Emperor
810	'Pax Nicophori' Peace treaty between Holy Roman Empire and the Byzantines. Constantinople's sovereignty over Venice is acknowledged. Duchy of Venice moved to Rialtine Islands
828	'Translation' of the relic of St Mark the Evangelist from Alexandria to Venice
883	Venice destroys Comacchio
992	Otto III, Holy Roman Emperor, visits Venice, confirms its privileges
1000	Victories over Dalmatian pirates by Doge Pietro Orseolo I. Origins of the 'Marriage to the Sea'

1071	End of Byzantine rule in southern Italy
1082	'Golden Bull' of Byzantine Emperor. Venetian merchants relieved of taxes and duties in Byzantine territories
1095	Pope Urban III preaches the First Crusade
1099	Venetians defeat Pisan fleet in Battle of Rhodes
1102	Major flooding in Venice
1104	Venetians victorious at Jaffa and Sidon
1124	Venetians destroy Egyptian fleet at Battle of Ascalon
1142–1144	Byzantine-Genoese alliance
1152	Friedrich Barbarossa becomes Holy Roman Emperor
1167	Venice and Papacy join anti-Imperial Lombard League
1172	Assassination of Doge Vitale Michiel II. Establishment of the Great Council
1177	Friedrich Barbarossa submits to Pope Alexander III in St Mark's Basilica
1204	Baldwin of Flanders is elected Latin Emperor in Constantinople
1207	Venetians conquer Corfu
1207–20	Establishment of the Council of Forty (Quarantia)
1209–10	Venetians conquer Crete
1222	Establishment of the Fondaco dei Tedeschi
1240	Major flooding in Venice
1253–68	First Genoese War
1261	Greek Paleologos dynasty established at Constantinople. End of the Latin Empire
c.1268	Venetian guild regulations instituted
1268	Major flooding in Venice. First reports of flood victims
1271	Marco Polo leaves for China with father and uncle
1284	First gold ducat minted
1291	Glass furnaces moved to Murano
1294–99	Second Genoese War
1297	*Serrata* of the Great Council
1298	Genoese defeat Venetians at Battle of Curzola (Korcula)
1302	Venetians negotiate trade agreements with Mamluk Egypt
1310	The failure of the Querini–Tiepolo Conspiracy. Establishment of the Council of Ten. The War of Ferrara
1323	Membership in the Great Council made hereditary
1324	Enlargement of the Arsenal
1339	Construction of the Venetian Mint (Zecca)
1351–55	Third Genoese War
1348	Black Death in Venice
1355	Execution of Doge Marin Falier
1373	Genoese occupy Famagusta, Cyprus

	Bragadin. Battle of Lepanto. Holy League destroys Ottoman fleet
1575–77	Plague in Venice
1605	Pope Paul V places Venice under the interdict
1615–17	War of Gradisca. Defeat of the Uskoks
1618	The defeat of the 'Spanish Conspiracy'
1630	Plague in Venice
1637	Opera house opens in Venice
1644–69	Cretan War. Ottomans conquer Crete
1684	Francesco Morosini 'il Peleponnasiaco' occupies the Morea. Parthenon damaged
1687	Consecration of Santa Maria della Salute
1699	Peace of Karlowitz (Sremski Karlovci). Venice gains Morea from Ottomans
1714–18	War with Ottomans ends with Peace of Passarowitz. Venice cedes Morea to Ottoman Empire
1762	Goldoni and Tiepolo both leave Venice, the former for France, the latter for Spain
1789	Completion of the Murazzi
1794	Major flooding in Venice
1796	Italian campaign of Napoleon Bonaparte
1797	15 May: Last Doge, Lodovico Manin, abdicates and French troops occupy Venice. 17 October: Treaty of Campoformio between France and Austria: Napoleon cedes Venice to Austria
1798	January. Last of French troops leave Venice, taking the horses of St Mark's Basilica. Re-occupation by Austria
1806–14	Second French occupation. Venice part of Napoleonic Kingdom of Italy
1814–66	Venice a province of Habsburg Kingdom of Lombardy-Venetia
1846	Railway causeway links Venice to mainland
1848	22 March: Daniele Manin proclaims independent Republic of Venice
1849	22 August: Austrians retake Venice after twenty days of bombardment
1866	Venice becomes part of Kingdom of Italy
1882–92	Port of the Lido re-opened to large shipping
1895	Inauguration of Venice Biennale. Prize for painting won by James Abbot McNeill Whistler
1917	Battleship production for Italian navy leaves Arsenal
1925	Industrial zone of Porto Marghera begins pumping of water from aquifer
1931	Harry's Bar opens

1933	Road bridge opens parallel to old railway causeway
1943–44	Deportation of 212 Venetian Jews, 15 return.
	April 1945: liberation of Venice
1948	Peggy Guggenheim (d.1979) moves into Palazzo Venier dei Leoni
1954	Closure of the Mulino Stucky on Giudecca
1966	Record-breaking flooding in Venice
1968	Biennale disrupted by student protests
1973	Use of groundwater by industries in mainland industrial zones banned
1987	3 May: 'Black Sunday.' 150,000 tourists visit Venice on this single day
1996	Fire destroys La Fenice
2003	Italian government approves Project MOSE for Venetian lagoon. La Fenice re-opened

List of Doges

Paoluccio Anafesto (mythical first Doge) *697-726*
Orso Ipato *726-737*
(Byzantine Interregnum) *737-742*
Teodato Ipato *742-755*
Galla Gaulo *755-756*
Domenico Monegario *756-764*
Maurizio Galbaio *764-775*
Giovanni Galbaio *775-804*
Obelario degli Antenori *804-811*
Agnello Participazio *811-827*
Giustiniano Participazio *827-829*
Giovanni Participazio I *829-836*
Pietro Tradonico *836-864*
Orso Participazio I *864-881*
Giovanni Participazio II *881-887*
Pietro Candiano I *887*
Pietro Tribuno *888-912*
Orso Participazio II *912-932*
Pietro Candiano II *932-939*
Pietro Participazio *939-942*
Pietro Candiano III *942-959*
Pietro Candiano IV *959-976*
Pietro Orseolo I *976-978*
Vitale Candiano *978-979*
Tribuno Memmo *979-991*
Pietro Orseolo II *991-1008*
Otto Orseolo *1008-1026*
Pietro Centranico *1026-1032*
Domenico Flabanico *1032-1043*
Domenico Contarini *1043-1071*
Domenico Selvo *1071-1084*
Vitale Falier *1084-1096*
Vitale Michiel I *1096-1102*

Ordelafo Falier *1102-1118*
Domenico Michiel *1118-1130*
Pietro Polani *1130-1148*
Domenico Morosini *1148-1156*
Vitale Michiel II *1156-1172*
Sebastiano Ziani *1172-1178*
Orio Mastropiero *1178-1192*
Enrico Dandolo *1192-1205*
Pietro Aiani *1205-1229*
Giacomo Tiepolo *1229-1249*
Marino Morosini *1249-1253*
Renier Zeno *1253-1268*
Lorenzo Tiepolo *1268-1275*
Jacopo Contarini *1275-1280*
Giovanni Dandolo *1280-1289*
Pietro Gradenigo *1289-1311*
Marino Zorzi *1311-1312*
Giovanni Soranzo *1312-1328*
Francesco Dandolo *1329-1339*
Bartolomeo Gradenigo *1339-1342*
Andrea Dandolo *1343-1354*
Marino Falier *1354-1355*
Giovanni Gradenigo *1355-1356*
Giovanni Dolfin *1356-1361*
Lorenzo Celsi *1361-1365*
Marco Corner *1365-1368*
Andrea Contarini *1368-1382*
Michele Morosini *1382*
Antonio Venier *1382-1400*
Michele Steno *1400-1413*
Tommaso Mocenigo *1414-1423*
Francesco Foscari *1423-1457*
Pasquale Malipiero *1457-1462*
Cristoforo Moro *1462-1471*
Niccolo Tron *1471-1473*
Niccolo Marcello *1473-1474*
Pietro Mocenigo *1474-1476*
Andrea Vendramin *1476-1478*
Giovanni Mocenigo *1478-1485*
Marco Barbarigo *1485-1486*
Agostino Barbarigo *1486-1501*
Leonardo Loredan *1501-1521*
Antonio Grimani *1521-1523*
Andrea Gritti *1523-1538*

Pietro Lando *1539-1545*
Francesco Donà *1545-1553*
Marcantonio Trevisan *1553-1554*
Francesco Venier *1554-1556*
Lorenzo Priuli *1556-1559*
Girolamo Priuli *1559-1567*
Pietro Loredan *1567-1570*
Alvise Mocenigo I *1570-1577*
Sebastiano Venier *1577-1578*
Nicolò da Ponte *1578-1585*
Pasquale Cicogna *1585-1595*
Marino Germani *1595-1605*
Leonardo Donà *1606-1612*
Marcantonio Memmo *1612-1615*
Giovanni Bembo *1615-1618*
Niccolò Donà *1618*
Antonio Priuli *1618-1623*
Francesco Contarini *1623-1624*
Giovanni Corner I *1625-1629*
Nicolò Contarini *1630-1631*
Francesco Erizzo *1631-1646*
Francesco Molin *1646-1655*
Carlo Contarini *1655-1656*
Francesco Corner *1656*
Bertucci Valier *1656-1658*
Giovanni Pesaro *1658-1659*
Domenico Contarini *1659-1675*
Nicolò Sagredo *1675-1676*
Alvise Contarini *1676-1684*
Marcantonio Giustinian *1684-1688*
Francesco Morosini *1688-1694*
Silvestro Valier *1694-1700*
Alvise Mocenigo II *1700-1709*
Giovanni Corner II *1709-1722*
Alvise Mocenigo III *1722-1732*
Carlo Ruzzini *1732-1735*
Alvise Pisani *1735-1741*
Pietro Grimani *1741-1752*
Francesco Loredan *1752-1762*
Marco Foscarini *1762-1763*
Alvise Mocenigo IV *1763-1778*
Paolo Renier *1779-1789*
Lodovico Manin *1789-1797*

Churches and Synagogues

Venice is full of churches and this brief overview can only note a few of the artistic and historical gems among them.

San Marco

Without a doubt the most famous church in Venice, and indeed one of the most famous in all of Christendom, is St Mark's Basilica. This is also one of the oldest churches in Venice. Several churches, all of them built to house the relics of St Mark the Evangelist, have stood on this site since the ninth century. Common to all of them is a Latin Cross design. Thus, the 'basilica' of St Mark is not, architecturally speaking, a basilica at all. Another crucial fact about the history of this building is that it was not built as the cathedral of Venice, but rather as the private chapel of the Doge. Thus, the centres of both spiritual and political power both came to be located in the Piazza.

The original church, probably modelled on the (now destroyed) Church of the Holy Apostles in Constantinople, was begun shortly after the arrival of St Mark's relic and was completed in 832. This church burned down during the uprising that overthrew (and killed) Doge Pietro Candiano IV in 976. A second church, probably a replica of the first, was built on the same site by 978. The third (and final) basilica was begun under the reign of Doge Domenico Contarini (1043-1070) and finally consecrated in 1094.

Work on the exterior decoration of the building, however, continued into the nineteenth century. The oldest surviving bit is the mosaic in the lunette over the Portal of San Alipio, the one farthest to the left as one faces the church. The portal itself probably dates from the second basilica (the one completed in 978) while the mosaic was completed around 1260. This mosaic is especially interesting because it includes a picture of the basilica itself, giving an idea as to its appearance before its numerous subsequent Gothic and Renaissance additions.

Some of the most extensive 'renovations' of the church were carried out in the 1870s. Although Ruskin described St Mark's as 'a lovely dream, a seaborne vase of alabaster,' and 'the most magical and most mysterious of churches' some of his Victorian contemporaries were not quite so admiring and instead saw only 'its ill-shaped domes; its walls of brick encrusted with marble' and 'its chaotic disregard of symmetry' (here quoted by Links). It was in an effort to 'rectify' these problems that the church renovations were begun. They were soon halted, largely through the efforts of William Morris and his Society for the Protection of Ancient Buildings, which still exists. Unfortunately, the north and south facades of the building were permanently altered with the replacement of the original marble with poorly fitting slabs of grey stone.

The exterior of the building is studded with all manner of sculptures and reliefs, but the most famous exterior decorations of the basilica are certainly the four horses. These wonderful sculptures were ancient even when the Venetians filched them from the hippodrome in Constantinople in 1204. They were probably cast in the second century BCE and were originally part of a bigger sculpture which would have included a chariot. Their first home was probably in Rome on Trajan's Arch whence they eventually made their way to Constantinople. After their removal from that city, their first station in Venice was in front of the Arsenal, but they were soon moved to their place above the main entrance to the basilica. They were removed during the French occupation of the city and spent eighteen years in Paris before their return in 1815. But their travels had not quite ended. During World War I they were removed again and brought to Rome for safekeeping ('stabled' appropriately enough, in the gardens of the Palazzo Venezia). Having survived for centuries, finally the threat posed by air pollution brought them into the safety of the museum in the basilica, while replicas continue to prance outside.

San Pietro di Castello

While San Marco, the Doge's chapel, 'reliquary' for the body of St Mark, and symbol of Venetian state power, was located in the very heart of Venice, the Republic's cathedral was located on the eastern outskirts of the city on the island of Olivolo. There was a church dedicated to Saints Sergius and Bacchus on the site of San Pietro di Castello as early as the seventh century. The first church on the site dedicated to St Peter was built in the ninth century. The church was the seat of the Bishop of Venice until 1451 when Pope Nicholas V merged the Bishop's see with that of the Patriarch of Grado to create the Patriarchate of Venice. One can still see the patriarchal insignia on the outside of the church. The façade and exterior of the church were radically remodelled (according to plans made by Palladio) between 1594 and 1596, while the interior was rebuilt in 1619 by Giangirolamo Grapiglia. Of particular interest inside the church is the so-called 'Throne of St Peter'. A gift to the Doge from the Byzantine Emperor Michael III in the mid-ninth century, the chair is obviously composed of at least two separate objects. The seat itself might indeed be part of an antique Bishop's throne, but the back is clearly a fragment of an Islamic bas-relief.

Santa Maria Gloriosa dei Frari

San Marco and San Pietro represented the power of the Venetian state and patriarch, respectively. Another two of the city's most famous churches were the seats of the two most popular religious orders in Venice: the Franciscans and the Dominicans. The church of the former was Santa Maria Gloriosa dei Frari, usually abbreviated to the Church of the Frari, or simply, the Frari. The Franciscans were present in Venice from 1222 and operated out of an abandoned Benedictine abbey on the site of the present church. Their activities were so popular that by 1280 they had constructed a new church. Their importance continued to grow to such an extent that by the mid-fourteenth century construction began on a much larger church in a grand Gothic style. Despite (or perhaps because of) the intense support of the project by some of Venice's leading families, construction proceeded very slowly and work was not completed until the late 1430s.

The interior is host to some of the finest works of art in Venice. Titian was especially devoted to the Franciscans and the church has some of his finest pieces, especially the justly famous *Assumption of the Virgin Mary*. Also noteworthy are the stunning, almost three-dimensional *Virgin and Child with Saints* by Giovanni Bellini. The interior also serves as the final resting place for many of Venice's most notable sons. Titian himself was buried here in accordance with his last wishes, but in violation of the custom that prohibited plague victims from being buried in a church. Among the Doges who are buried here, one of the most touching memorials is that of Doge Foscari.

San Giovanni e Paolo (Zanipolo)

Not to be outdone by the magnificent Gothic bulk of the Franciscans' church, the Dominicans built their own Gothic masterpiece for themselves, the Church of Saints John and Paul, 'Zanipolo' in the impenetrable Venetian patois. The church is not, by the way, named after St John the Revelator and St Paul the Evangelist, but after two obscure saints of the same names martyred in the fourth century.

A Dominican church was built here in the mid-thirteenth century, but the version we see today was built between 1333 and 1430. The interior of the church contains numerous tombs of Doges and members of the various Venetian noble families (the Mocenigos are particularly well represented). This is also the final resting place for Marcantonio Bragadin (or at least for his desiccated skin) after his awful execution following the fall of Famagusta.

A much less grisly, but no less unique, point of interest is the large, Gothic stained-glass window. Such windows (a visitor to Venice's churches soon realizes) are rare in this city of unstable ground and sinking, shifting foundations. This very window would probably itself be cracked by now were it not for the work of the Venice in Peril fund.

Santisimo Redentore

Two of Venice's most famous churches were built in an outpouring of relief at the end of two bouts of the plague. The earlier of these is the Church of the Redeemer on the Giudecca, built on order of the Senate to commemorate the end of the plague of 1575-1577. The commission was awarded to Palladio, and the church is usually regarded as one of his finest works. On the third Sunday of July, the Doge led a pilgrimage to the church to give thanks for the ending of the plague. The staircase that opens up toward the water to receive the pilgrims is beautifully integrated with the overall structure of the church.

Santa Maria della Salute

Venice was struck yet again with the plague in 1630, and again the government commissioned the construction of a pilgrimage church to commemorate the occasion of its end. This time, the commission went to the architect Baldassar Longhena who constructed the baroque masterpiece of Santa Maria della Salute across the Grand Canal, facing the Piazza. As such it is one of the most famous sights in Venice. Each year on 21 November a procession crosses the Grand Canal for a thanksgiving mass at the church.

The baroque masterpiece of Santa Maria della Salute

The Scuola Spagnola

By the late sixteenth century, Venice had a thriving Jewish community. Though still confined to the cramped quarters of the Ghetto, the Jews had established themselves as an important part of Venetian economic life and many had become quite wealthy. This wealth expressed itself in the refurbishment and remodelling of many of the Ghetto's synagogues during the seventeenth century. Since Jews were forbidden to practise architecture or any of the construction trades, Christians were hired to design and build the synagogues. Thus, the Spanish-speaking congregation commissioned Baldassar Longhena himself to redesign their synagogue, the Scuola Spagnola. The interior is a masterpiece of baroque architecture and influenced the remodelling of most of the Ghetto's other important synagogues.

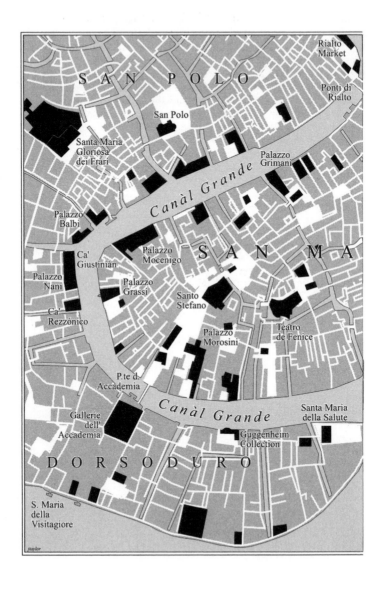

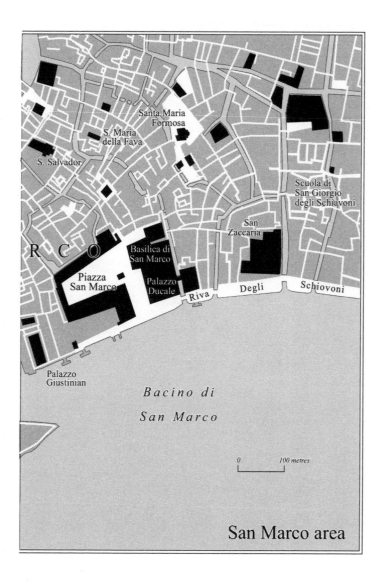

Santa Maria
Formosa

S. Maria
della Fava

S. Salvador

Scuola di
San Giorgio
degli Schiavoni

R C O

Basilica di
San Marco

San
Zaccaria

Piazza
San Marco

Palazzo
Ducale

Riva Degli Schiovoni

Palazzo
Giustinian

Bacino di

San Marco

0   100 metres

San Marco area

Historic Buildings & Museums

Doge's Palace

Called the 'Wedding Cake,' the 'Pink House,' or the 'Tablecloth,' besides St Mark's Basilica, this might be the most famous building in Venice, and rightly so. It is an excellent example of the uniquely Venetian blend of Islamic and Gothic architectural forms that appear so frequently in the city's palaces, and it one of the best examples of secular Gothic architecture anywhere in Europe. It is built on the same spot as the long-gone original palace. The building we see today dates largely from the fourteenth century.

Only part of the Palace was actually used by the Doge and his family as their private quarters. Most of the machinery of the *Serenissima* was in fact housed within these walls. The Great Council, the Council of Ten, the Senate, and other bodies, all held their meetings in this building. The other point about this building that must have amazed medieval and Renaissance visitors, is the absence of any pretence of defensibility. The supreme confidence of Venice's ruling classes that they were safe from external threats is demonstrated by the lack of the heavy walls and battlements characteristic of other medieval palaces in Italy, to say nothing of France and Germany.

La Accademia

While the Napoleonic occupation of Venice has been blamed (quite rightly) for the looting of artworks and the destruction of many fine old churches, La Accademia and its outstanding collection of Venetian Renaissance art is a considerably more ambivalent legacy of the Napoleonic period. It is nevertheless worth remembering that most of the art works currently housed in this museum were removed from churches and convents demolished by the French. The museum itself was originally supposed to supplement the Academy of Fine Arts, founded by Eugene Beauharnais, the Napoleonic 'Prince of Venice'. The school still exists, but has long since been overshadowed in the popular mind by its phenomenal collection of paintings.

While the museum has some excellent medieval paintings (look especially for Veneziano's *Madonna e Bambino con Due Votari*) the 'stars of the show' are the early Renaissance masters Bellini and Giorgione, and the High

Renaissance figures Tintoretto, Titian, and Veronese. The collection gives us an especially good opportunity to consider the career of Titian as we can contrast the bright optimism of his famous *Presentation of the Virgin*, with the dark and terrifying *Pietà*.

Museo Correr

For a great introduction to Venice's history, and as an escape from the crowds on the Piazza, this museum is a must. It is housed in the Ala Napoleonica and in part of the Procuratie Nuove. The core of the museum's collection is formed by the collection of the Venetian Teodoro Correr, who left his vast collection of artifacts to the city of Venice in 1830. It moved into its current home in 1922. Highlights include sculptures by Antonio Canova, an excellent collection of maps and artifacts from the life and times of Francesco Morosini '*il Peloponnessiaco.*'

Museum of Eighteenth Century Culture (Ca' Rezzonico)

Those parts of Correr's collection that related in some way to the eighteenth century eventually found their way to this museum, dedicated to an exploration of the artistic and material culture of this allegedly decadent period of Venetian history. The museum is housed in the magnificent palace of the Rezzonico family (designed by Longhena and Massari). It contains an excel-

The Palazzi Rezzonico, Guistiniani and Foscari along the Grand Canal

lent collection of eighteenth-century paintings, including those of Longhi, Guardi, and Canaletto, as well as pieces from the Tiepolo family. The museum also has displays of furniture, personal items, and clothing characteristic of a patrician family of the eighteenth century.

Museo del Vetro (Glass Museum)

This museum, housed in the Palazzo Giustiniani on Murano, gives the visitor some idea of the incredible diversity of objects produced by the area's artisans. The collection, spanning over a thousand years, has pieces ranging from the ridiculous to the sublime, with everything else in between.

Museo del Merletto (Lace Museum)

This museum, dedicated to the traditional Venetian art of lace-making, is housed in the Scuola di Merletti, founded in 1872 to help revive what was almost a lost art. The museum's collection contains many examples of the height of the craft from the sixteenth through the twentieth century. The museum also houses the school's archive. Sometimes local women, graduates of the school, are on hand to demonstrate their skill at this exacting art form.

International Gallery of Modern Art (Ca' Pesaro)

Housed in the recently (and painstakingly) restored Palazzo Pesaro on the Grand Canal, this museum's collection is made up largely of pieces purchased by the city of Venice at the Biennale. Included are samples of the work of Klimt, Chagall, Kandinsky, and many others, as well as a good selection of works by modern Italian artists.

Peggy Guggenheim Museum

While the Ca' Pesaro contains Venice's best *public* collection of modern art, the best *private* collection of modern art in Venice, or indeed much of the world, is the museum based on Peggy Guggenheim's personal gallery. During her life, Peggy Guggenheim (1898-1979) became one of the foremost promoters of modern artists and, almost single-handedly, introduced many of them to the American art world. She moved to Venice in 1948 and bought the Palazzo Venier dei Leoni, where she lived the rest of her life. During the 1950s and 60s, her home became a meeting place for most of the luminaries of modern art and music. The small, but absolutely first-rate collection, is now managed by the Guggenheim Foundation. Peggy's ashes are buried in the beautiful garden, touchingly surrounded by the graves of her many pet dogs.

The Palazzo Venier dei Leoni's vaguely modernist appearance is the result of the fact that only the ground floor was completed (giving it the nickname, the *Palazzo Nonfinito*). It was begun in 1759 by the famous Venier family, who intended it to be the biggest palace on the Grand Canal. There are two

stories explaining why they stopped work on the project. The first (and probably accurate) explanation is that they simply ran out of money. The second
(probably untrue but more interesting) version is that another venerable and
powerful patrician family, the Corners, had a palace across the canal and did
not want another (grander) palace within sight, blocking the view and the
sunlight.

Museo di Storia Naturale (Fondaco dei Turchi)

Another recently restored palace on the Grand Canal, this building for centuries was the hostel (*Fondaco*) for Turkish merchants in the city. By the early
nineteenth century it had fallen into ruin. Efforts by restorers horrified
Ruskin (and many others). The current collection includes various displays on
the flora and fauna of the lagoon as well as an important library.

Museo di Palazzo Mocenigo

This palace was one of the many owned by the powerful Mocenigo family. It
is now the headquarters of the Centre for the Study of the History of Textiles
and Costumes and houses the library of that organization. Much of the palace
is used to display a rich collection of eighteenth-century paintings and artifacts specializing, of course, in the costumes of the period.

Carlo Goldoni's House

The Palazzo Centani was the birthplace of the important eighteenth-century
Venetian playwright (and lawyer). It is important mainly because of its archive
and library which contain an extensive collection of original manuscripts. It
also has a small museum dedicated to the life and works of Goldoni and the
theatre of his time.

Bridges

It may come as a surprise to some that there are only three bridges over the Grand Canal. This shortage is hardly noticeable due to their strategic placement, as well as the profusion of those wonderfully utilitarian gondolas, the *traghetti*. There are, of course, hundreds of other, much smaller bridges in the different *sestiere*, some of which have interesting or amusing histories.

Ponte degli Scalzi

Starting from the northwest, the first of the bridges to cross the Grand Canal is the Ponte degli Scalzi, named after the nearby Church of the Scalzi. The original bridge here was built by the Austrians between 1858 and 1860, near the recently built train station of Santa Lucia. The original structure, built of iron, was replaced during the 1930s with the taller bridge we see today to accommodate the larger boats on the canal.

Ponte di Rialto

The next, and certainly most famous, of the bridges crossing the Grand Canal, is the Rialto Bridge. Until 1854 (with the opening of the Accademia Bridge, see below) this bridge was the only way to cross the Canal on foot. There were various wooden bridges here at least since the fourteenth century and one can see an interesting drawbridge in Carpaccio's *Miracle of the True Cross* (1494). The succession of wooden bridges were, however, notoriously unstable and the government finally made a decision to rebuild the bridge in stone shortly after the disastrous Rialto fire of 1514. The project was opened to competition and some of the best architects of the time (including Michaelangelo, Sansovino, and Palladio) were considered and rejected. The project was finally given to the appropriately named Antonio da Ponte.

Ponte dell'Accademia

This was the first of the iron bridges built by the Austrians over the Grand Canal (the second was the Ponte degli Scalzi). Opened in 1854, it proved too low for the increasing size of the boats plying the canal, and was replaced in

The Rialto

1932 with a taller temporary wooden bridge. This 'temporary' bridge, subsequently reinforced with steel, has remained in use until the present day.

Besides these important bridges over the Grand Canal, there are at least three others that are worthy of some mention. The first of these, because of its visibility, is the **The Bridge of Sighs**. Built in 1600 by Antonio Contino, it was meant to connect the Palace with the new block of prisons. Despite the romantic associations of its name, the new prison was intended mainly for petty criminals.

Another interesting, but far less famous, bridge is the **Ponte dei Pugni** (Bridge of Fists). For centuries this marked the spot for the ritualized brawls between two armies of young men, the Castellani and the Nicolotti, representing, more or less, the two main geographic divisions of the city. The two sides took up positions on either side of the Rio di San Barnaba, with their leaders' starting places on the bridge marked to this day by the inset marble footprints. The ensuing mêlées, though somewhat ritualized, were fierce and sometimes resulted in fatalities (the railings are a recent addition). Lethal weapons were banned in 1574 and the fights themselves were finally stopped in 1705. The famous regattas, now held at regular intervals in Venice, were devised as replacements for these pugilistic contests between the city's youths.

Finally, in the Sestieri San Polo, near the Palazzo Albrizzi, one finds the quaint little **Ponte delle Tette**. The name indicates that this bridge marked the edge of the Rialto's 'Red Light' district, where prostitutes 'advertised' their wares. Many of the old houses in the neighbourhood in fact have front and back doors to accommodate that oldest of businesses.

The Outer Islands

As we have seen, the collection of islands centred on the Rialto and the Piazza, which we now know as 'Venice', were not the first settlements in the lagoon. Indeed, the other islands maintained a semi-autonomous existence from the growing power of the Rialtine settlements for many years. Among the many islands which from one time or another were inhabited, four are especially noteworthy: Torcello, Murano, Burano, and the Lido.

Torcello

Ruskin called Torcello and Venice 'Mother and Daughter'. Indeed, one of the earliest settlements in the lagoon was on the island of Torcello and this island remained for several centuries the ecclesiastical heart of the lagoon settlements. Even after this importance declined, the diocese of Torcello remained independent and was not joined to that of Venice until 1805. Construction of the beautiful cathedral of Santa Maria dell'Assunta was begun in 639 and the charming church of Santa Fosca was built in the ninth century, and then rebuilt in 1008. The cathedral as we see it today was likewise constructed during the first decade of the eleventh century, though some elements are older. The interior is decorated with fabulous Byzantine mosaics, most notably the *Apotheosis of Christ* and the *Last Judgement*.

Unfortunately, the geographic situation of the island doomed its long-term viability as a place of significant settlement. The mouth of the River Sile, which emptied into the lagoon directly opposite from the island of Torcello, supplied the rich nutrients needed to maintain the fishing communities of the island. Unfortunately, the river also brought in silt and mud which eventually turned most of the environment around Torcello into a swampy breeding ground for malarial mosquitoes. By the fourteenth century the population had reached its highest point, at around 20,000 people, but then began to decline and about a century later it was virtually abandoned. Today, only about thirty people continue to live there year-round.

Murano

The history of the island of Murano is similar in some ways to that of Torcello, although it has managed to maintain a steadier existence. Like Torcello, Murano was home to some of the lagoon's earliest permanent settlements. And, again as on Torcello, a beautiful Venetian-Byzantine church (Santi Maria e Donato) provides evidence of the wealth and self-confidence of Murano's inhabitants. Like the Cathedral of Torcello, the Church of Santi Maria e Donato was first built during the seventh century, though the current building was substantially altered during the twelfth century. Also like the Torcello cathedral, the church is especially noteworthy because of its fabulous mosaics, and in particular its floor (completed in 1141). By the way, the undulating floor is not, contrary to Ruskin's romantic notions, meant to mimic the action of the sea, but instead is simply the result of centuries of soil subsidence.

Further into the lagoon than Torcello, Murano's climate is healthier and so the population did not face the same challenges from disease as the unfortunate inhabitants of Torcello. By 1291 when the lagoon's glass-making industry was relocated to Murano (to guard against fires in the more densely populated islands), the island's community was a prosperous one. It was home to a number of charming palaces used by the Republic's nobility as weekend or summer homes, and also had a certain degree of autonomy, including its own administration and judges.

The glass-making industry began a slow decline during the eighteenth century in the face of stiff competition from Bohemia and activity was further reduced during the Napoleonic and Austrian periods. It was only during the late nineteenth century that a revival of glass-blowing as a serious enterprise began.

Burano

Much less flashy than either Torcello or Murano is the little island of Burano, in the northeast corner of the lagoon. It was settled at around the same time as nearby Torcello, but, unlike Torcello, it has remained continuously inhabited. Historically, the island's people made their living as fishermen. The brightly painted houses that so delight modern visitors to the island are allegedly a legacy of this occupation, as fishermen would be able to identify their individual homes from afar as a result of their distinctive paint-jobs.

Today Burano is known for its lace-making. Although Burano has long been a centre of lace-making, this craft in fact had a tradition all over the lagoon and was engaged in by women of most classes, even the patricians. In a mirror-image of the fate of glass-blowing on Murano, lace-making declined during the eighteenth century. Its revival was due largely to the establishment of a school of lace-making in 1872 by Countess Andriana Marcello, at which time indigenous lace-making had all but died out. After enjoying a period of vibrancy during the first two decades of the twentieth century, the school gradually declined and, after a number of ups and downs, finally closed for good in 1972. The increased economic opportunities for the area's women, combined with the mind-boggling tedium of lace-making, probably doomed the long-term viability of the school. Today, the school is the Lace Museum. Elderly graduates of the school still give demonstrations of their craft, and others own some of the ubiquitous lace shops that currently fill the main streets of the island.

A twenty-minute boat ride from Burano takes one to the little island of San Francesco del Deserto (St Francis of the Desert). In 1220, St Francis of Assisi was shipwrecked here on a trip back from the East. Decades later, the island's owner turned it over to the Franciscans, who established the monastery which continues to function to this day. The chapel on the island, restored in 1962, was built in the fifteenth century on the site of St Francis' original church. Today, only a handful of friars live on the island.

San Michele

One of the most unusual of the outer islands is also the closest to Venice itself, the cemetery island of San Michele. Finding suitable ground for burials has been historically a constant problem for the Venetians. During the Napoleonic occupation, burials in the city of Venice were prohibited and the island was reorganized for use as a municipal cemetery.

The majority of the island is devoted to Venice's Catholic population. Traditionally, the deceased would be laid to rest in a coffin in one of the four-layered shelves. After twenty-five years, the remains would be disinterred and placed in a common ossuary. Recently, as cremation has become more popular, a deceased's ashes can be stored indefinitely in a small drawer in one of the tombs.

The island also has smaller areas where Orthodox Christians and Protestants rest in graves in the earth. Many famous people lie in each. Igor and Vera Stravinsky, and Joseph Brodsky, America's poet laureate, are buried in the Orthodox cemetery, while the Protestant cemetery is the final resting place for Ezra Pound.

The Lido

Among the largest of the outer islands is the Lido. The name means 'sandbar', and indeed the Lido is simply the longest of a string of narrow islets and sandbars that mark the edge of the lagoon, beyond which opens the Adriatic Sea. Its exposed geographic position meant that it was never a major population centre, except for its northern and southern 'ports', really channels through which shipping passed into or out of the lagoon. The northern Porto San Nicolò was, until the early sixteenth century the main passage for Venetian shipping, and the monastery of San Nicolò was built there to house the relic of Saint Nicholas. By the sixteenth century, however, the channel had become silted up and most traffic shifted instead to the southern 'port' of Malamocco.

Venice's rulers also designated a remote area in the northern half of the island as a cemetery for the Republic's Jewish subjects in 1386. To this day, the Jewish Cemetery on the Lido is poignant testimony to the long residence of Jews in the lagoon, and the tragic fate of the community in the 1940s.

As late as the 1810s, the Lido was still a rugged, sparsely inhabited place. All that began to change during the middle of the nineteenth century as mass tourism to Venice began. Very quickly the Lido was transformed into one of Europe's prime beach destinations and the shoreline became punctuated with magnificent hotels and villas. It is also home to Venice's summer casino (the winter casino is the Palazzo Vendramin-Calergi on the Grand Canal), built in 1938, which is an excellent example of Art Deco architecture.

Gondolas & Boats of the Lagoon

While the history of Venice is very much tied to different sorts of sea-going vessels, in the minds of most people the boat most associated with Venice is the gondola. Due to the sandbars and treacherous channels of the lagoon, the earliest Venetians developed various sorts of flat-bottomed boats which were often rowed or otherwise piloted standing up, in order to give the boatman a better view of his surroundings and thus avoid running aground. The gondola, perhaps the ultimate aquatic cliché of Venice, clearly evolved from these very early crafts.

While the word 'gundula' first appears in writing in 1094, the gondola we know today reached its present form only in the seventeenth century, although as early as the fifteenth century, gondolas had evolved into something very similar to those we see today. The first gondolas were much larger and propelled by twelve oars. After the fourteenth century, however, when the Venetian government banned horses within the city-limits, the nobility quickly turned to the gondola as their preferred means of transport and these boats began to take on their now-familiar characteristics.

In particular, by the late fifteenth century, two distinctive aspects of every gondola had developed: the *ferro*, the peculiar saw-toothed sabre-like metal projection in the prow of the craft, and the *forcola*, or specially carved oar-lock. The origins and meaning of the *ferro* are not known, but it might have evolved from a beak-like iron projection on the front of the earliest gondolas. Thus, some have speculated that it acts as a kind of bumper or that it serves as a counterweight to the gondolier in the bow. The odd shape of the *ferro* has also prompted numerous stories. Some say that it represents the ducal corno. Most people agree that the six 'teeth' of the *ferro* represent or symbolize the six *sestiere* of the city.

If the *ferro* is largely decorative, the *forcola*, together with the oar, function as the transmission and gearbox of the gondola. Each *forcola*, designed to provide pivots for the six different oar-positions necessary for the propulsion of a gondola, is custom made, usually out of cherry or walnut, for each gondolier. Two other aspects of these remarkable boats deserve mention.

Besides the evolution of the *ferro* and *forcola*, another important development in the history of the gondola occurred in 1562, when a law mandated

The gondola

that gondolas be painted black. During the preceding years, gondolas had become important status symbols, and members of the nobility tried to outdo one another in the ostentatious decorations and colours for their boats. As part of its ongoing programme of sumptuary legislation, the Venetian government decided that all gondolas should instead be painted black, the colour of all gondolas to this day.

Gondolas are traditionally constructed from eight types of wood (including cherry, elm, larch, lime, oak, pine, tannen, and walnut), in special shops called *squeri*. For example, oak is used for the bottom of the boat, elm for the ribs. Four *squeri* currently operate in Venice, the oldest of which is located near the church of San Trovaso. Its rather incongruous alpine-look is a reflection of the historical origin of many gondola builders, who came from the Dolomite Mountains. Today the *squeri* function mainly as repair shops, as a new gondola can take up to a year to construct.

The halves of a gondola are not symmetrical. This is necessary in order to keep the craft moving forward in a straight line, even though the gondolier's oar works on one side of the boat only. Despite its large size (all modern gondolas are 10.87 metres [a little over 35 feet] long and 1.42 metres [almost five feet] wide) it is said that the effort to row and steer a gondola loaded with four passengers is less than that needed to pedal a bicycle. Mark Twain, was full of admiration for the gondolas and the gondoliers. Here in a quote cited by Gary Wills, he describes the gondoliers' movements: 'Against that peg [the *forcola*] the gondolier takes a purchase with his oar, changing it at intervals to the other side of the peg or dropping it into another of the crooks, as the steering of the craft may demand – and how in the world he can back and fill, shoot straight ahead, or flirt [sic] suddenly around a corner, and make the oar stay in those insignificant notches is a problem to me and a never diminishing matter of interest. I am afraid I study the gondolier's marvelous skill more than I do the sculptured palaces we glide among....He makes all his calculations with the nicest precision, and goes darting in and out among a Broadway of confusion of busy craft with the easy confidence of the educated hackman.'

Nowadays, the five hundred or so gondolas in Venice mainly function as part of the tourist industry. Some, however, called *traghetti* still act as an important part of the Venice transportation system. Operating at eight crossing points on the Grand Canal, they are important trans-canal ferries, and can provide the visitor to Venice with the experience of a gondola ride while participating in the life of the city. Unlike the tourist gondolas, *traghetti* passengers usually remain standing during the short trip, a task which can be challenging for the more terrestrially inclined.

Another sort of gondola is important mainly for historical reasons, since it no longer exists. This was the *Bucintoro,* a unique craft used by the Venetian Doges on special occasions and state ceremonies. While there is general agreement that the first *Bucintoro* was built in 1277, the origins of the name are subject to debate. Some speculate that it has something to do with Alexander the Great's horse, Bucephalus, while most say it comes from *bucio* (an archaic word for a kind of boat) *d'oro* (thus, 'boat of gold'). In any case, these large gondolas (many scholars have preferred to describe them as barges) were indeed decorated with heavily gilded sculptures featuring real and mythical sea creatures. The last one, constructed in the Arsenal in 1728 was a magnificent vessel, rowed by 42 *arsenalotti*. It ended up as one of the casualties of the Napoleonic occupation. It was chopped to pieces and burned, allegedly to salvage the gold, some of which ended up as a ring for one of Napoleon's generals.

The last *bucintoro* thus passed into history, and the gondolas today are mainly tourist attractions (with the important exception of the *traghetti*). Yet, boats of various kinds are still crucial for the life of Venetians and visitors alike. The most common public water craft are called *vaporetti*. Although their name means 'little steamers' they have been for a long time powered by diesel engines (thus, incidentally, contributing to the pollution of the lagoon and the decay of its buildings). They are broad, slow-moving craft that ply the routes in and around Venice itself. The *vaporetto* route known to almost all tourists is the No.1. Although known as the *Accelerato*, it is among the slowest boats in Venice. It starts at the Piazzale Roma (one of Venice's parking lots) and proceeds down the Grand Canal, making every stop along the way, all the way to the Lido. It thus provides a charming, if sometimes excruciatingly slow, way to experience most of Venice's impressive architectural monuments the way they have been viewed for centuries: from the water.

Glimpses of Post-Modern Venice

Venice is a unique and beautiful place, but in many ways it is a modern city with modern problems. Like other modern cities, it has to find solutions to congestion and pollution, and it needs to work out a viable economic life for its citizens. There is, however, beside this real-world modern Venice, another 'mythic' Venice. This 'Post-Modern' Venice is filled with crystal clear canals, and all of Venice's icons: handsome singing gondoliers, the Rialto Bridge, the Campanile, the façade of the Ducal Palace, etc. This Post-Modern Venice is not simply a creation of the imagination visible only in the mind's eye, it really exists. It is called the Venetian Resort-Hotel-Casino in Las Vegas, Nevada, USA. The $1.5 billion dollar project opened in 1999 on the site of the old Sands Casino. One of the biggest hotels in the world, it has 3,036 suites, 16 restaurants, two Guggenheim museums, shops, as spa, and (of course) a 120,000 square-foot casino.

The first thing to strike the visitor to the Venetian is the utter improbability of the place. Even for Las Vegas, a town hardly known for its reserve, the idea of replicating a water-bound (occasionally water-logged) city in one of the most arid places in North America is almost breath-taking in its boldness. After overcoming this initial shock, the visitor to the Venetian (who is also familiar with Venice) notices the skilful use of space made by the resort's designers and architects, and their interesting choices about what to replicate and how. Two hundred and fifty craftsmen and artists, as well as two historians, worked in the design and building of the Venetian, and indeed, most of Venice's familiar landmarks are reproduced in full-scale, or nearly life-sized, replicas. There, for example, is the Campanile (although it is only for show; one cannot go up to the top for a look around). One also finds the Rialto Bridge and the Bridge of Sighs, the façades of the Ducal Palace and the Ca d'Oro, and the columns of the Molo, topped with San Teodoro and the Saint Mark's lion.

These Venetian architectural icons, while reproduced with considerable skill and taste, are not in the same spatial relationship to each other as their originals. At the Venetian, for example, the Rialto Bridge links the Ducal Palace with the Campanile. Similarly, the paintings which grace the ceilings of much of the hotel's interior are (very high quality) reproductions of those found in

231

many different settings and buildings throughout Venice. For example, by the concierge's desk one finds reproductions of works by Giambattista Tiepolo from the Palazzo Sandi in Venice. Yet, not far away is a monumental reproduction of Paolo Veronese's *Triumph of Venice*, the original of which is, of course, in the Ducal Palace.

Perhaps the most striking thing one eventually notices, however, is the absence of what, historically, was arguably the most important building in Venice: Saint Mark's Basilica. Thus, 'Venice' is recreated at the Venetian as a set of secular architectural landmarks and visual experiences, divorced from a historical setting. What is so compelling about this situation, is the degree to which the actual city of Venice is itself reduced, for the day-tripping tourist, to a similar set of visual images (most already familiar from books, magazines, or motion pictures), which are simply consumed without a deeper appreciation, or even awareness, of the complex historical and sociological realities which produced these artifacts. To a very real degree, then, the Post-Modern and Modern visions of Venice are converging on the same point: the presentation of a set of clichéd, though visually striking, images for the consumption of the casual tourist.

Further Reading

BARBARO, PAOLO, *Venice Revealed: An Intimate Portrait* (Steerforth Press, 2001)

BROWN, PATRICIA FORTINI, *Art and Life in Renaissance Venice* (Harry N. Abrams, 1997)

BROWN, PATRICIA FORTINI, *Venice and Antiquity* (Yale, 1996)

BROWN, PATRICIA FORTINI, *Venetian Narrative Painting in the Age of Carpaccio* (Yale, 1990)

BOUWSMA, WILLIAM J., *Venice and the Defense of Republican Liberty: Renaissance Values in the Age of the Counter Reformation* (Berkeley, 1968)

CHAMBERS, D.S., *The Imperial Age of Venice*, 1380-1580 (Thames and Hudson, 1970)

CROUZET-PAVAN, ELIZABETH, *Venice Triumphant* (Johns Hopkins, 2002)

FAROQUI, SURAIYA, *The Venetian Presence in the Ottoman Empire, 1600-1630* in HURI ISLAMOGLU-INAN, Ed *The Ottoman Empire and the World Economy* (Cambridge, 1987)

GEARY, PATRICK J., *Furta Sacra: Thefts of Relics in the Central Middle Ages* (Princeton, 1978)

GOY, RICHARD, *Venice: The City and its Architecture* (Phaidon, 1997)

HALE, J.R., *Renaissance Venice* (Faber, 1973)

HIBBERT, CHRSTOPHER, *Venice: The Biography of a City* (Harper Collins 1988)

HOWARD, DEBORAH, *The Architectural History of Venice* (London, 1980)

HOWARD, DEBORAH, *Venice and the East* (Yale, 2000)

HOWELLS, W.D, *Venetian Life* (Northwestern, 2001)

KEAHEY, JOHN, *Venice against the Sea* (St. Martins, 2002)

LANE, FREDERIC, *Venice and History* (Baltimore, 1966)

LANE, FREDERIC, *Venice, a Maritime Republic* (Baltimore, 1973)

LEVI, CARLO, *Christ Stopped at Eboli: The Story of a Year* (Noonday Press, 1995)

LINKS, J.G., *Venice for Pleasure* (Pallas, 2000)

LOGAN, OLIVER, *Culture and Society in Venice, 1470-1790* (London, 1972)

LONGWORTH, P., *The Rise and Fall of Venice* (London, 1974)

LORENZETTI, GIULIO., *Venice and its Lagoon* (Rome, 1961)

LUTYENS, MARY, *Effie in Venice* (Pallas, 1999)

MACKENNEY, RICHARD, *Tradesmen and Traders: The World of the Guilds in Venice and Europe, c.1250-1650* (Totowa, NJ, 1987)

MCCARTHY, MARY, *Venice Observed* (San Diego, 1963)

MCNEILL, W.H., *Venice, the Hinge of Europe, 1081-1797* (Chicago, 1974)

MORRIS, JAN, *The Venetian Empire: A Sea Voyage* (Harcourt Brace, 1980)

MORRIS, JAN, *The World of Venice* (Harcourt Brace, 1993)

MUIR, EDWARD, *Cultural Ritual in Renaissance Venice* (Princeton, 1981)

NICOL, D. M., *Byzantium and Venice* (Cambridge, 1988)

NICHOLS, TOM, *Tintoretto* (Reaktion Books, 1999)

NORWICH, JOHN JULIUS, *A History of Venice* (New York, 1982)

PEMBLE, JOHN, *Venice Rediscovered* (Oxford, 1995)

PULLAN, BRIAN, *The Jews of Europe and the Inquisition of Venice, 1550-1670* (Blackwell, 1983)

PULLAN, BRIAN, *Poverty and Charity: Europe, Italy, Venice: 1400-1700* (Brookfield, VT, 1994)

ROWDON, MAURICE, *The Fall of Venice* (Weidenfeld, 1970)

RUGGIERO, GUIDO, *The Boundaries of Eros: Sex Crime and Sexuality in Renaissance Venice* (New York, 1985)

STEER, JOHN, *A Concise History of Venetian Painting* (Thames and Hudson, 1985)

TENENTI, A., *Piracy and the Decline of Venice, 1580-1615* (London, 1967)

TUNG, ANTHONY, *Preserving the World's Great Cities: The Destruction and Renewal of the Historic Metropolis* (Clarkson Potter, 2001)

WILLS, GARY, *Venice: Lion City* (Washington Square Press, 2001)

ZORZI, ALVISE, *Venice: The Golden Age, 697-1797* (New York, 1980)

Index